how to live a **low-carbon life**

how to live a
low-carbon
life
the individual's guide to
tackling climate change

SECOND EDITION

Chris Goodall

publishing for a sustainable future

London • Washington, DC

Earthscan Ltd, Dunstan House, 14a St Cross Street, London EC1N 8XA, UK
Earthscan LLC, 1616 P Street, NW, Washington, DC 20036, USA

Earthscan publishes in association with the International Institute for Environment and Development

For more information on Earthscan publications, see www.earthscan.co.uk
or write to earthinfo@earthscan.co.uk

ISBN: 978-1-84407-909-4 hardback
      978-1-84407-910-0 paperback

Typeset by Domex e-Data, India
Cover design by Jonathan Chapman

A catalogue record for this book is available from the British Library

Library of Congress Cataloging-in-Publication Data
Goodall, Chris.
  How to live a low-carbon life : the individual's guide to tackling climate change / Chris Goodall. – 2nd ed.
      p. cm.
  Includes bibliographical references and index.
  ISBN 978-1-84407-909-4 (hardback) – ISBN 978-1-84407-910-0 (pbk.) 1. Atmospheric carbon dioxide–Climatic factors. 2. Atmospheric carbon dioxide–Environmental aspects.
3. Climatic changes–Social aspects. 4. Carbon dioxide–Environmental aspects. 5. Consumer education. I. Title.
  QC879.8.G62 2010
  363.738'7–dc22

                                          2010008541

At Earthscan we strive to minimize our environmental impacts and carbon footprint through reducing waste, recycling and offsetting our CO_2 emissions, including those created through publication of this book. For more details of our environmental policy, see www.earthscan.co.uk.

Printed and bound in the UK by TJ International, an ISO 14001 accredited company. The paper used is FSC certified and the inks are vegetable based.

Mixed Sources
Product group from well-managed
forests and other controlled sources
www.fsc.org Cert no. SGS-COC-2482
© 1996 Forest Stewardship Council
FSC

Contents

List of Figures, Tables and Boxes

FIGURES

TABLES

BOXES

Sources and Units of Measurement

I have standardized on kilowatt hours (kWh) as the unit of measurement. At various points in the book, conventional analysis might use 'million barrels of oil equivalent', kilocalories or petajoules. I hope it aids comprehensibility to use just one unit. When referring to large values I have sometimes made it clearer by referring to megawatt hours (MWh, equal to a thousand kWh) and gigawatt hours (GWh, equal to a thousand MWh or a million kWh). The huge numbers of noughts in many energy-related figures means that I am almost certain to have slipped up somewhere in making the hundreds of conversions I have calculated in this book. I apologize in advance for any errors.

The book uses information from many sources and I have often combined data from various places into a single table. Where I have merged or averaged multiple different sources, I have not credited any single author in order to avoid any misstating or misattribution. Where I just use data from one place, I credit this source beneath the table. When data is merged, the main sources are specified in endnotes.

Throughout the book, I have used the weight of carbon dioxide (CO_2) as the index of global warming effect. Much of the data in the field is actually expressed in terms of just carbon. To get from the weight of carbon to that of carbon dioxide, one multiplies by 3.6667. Thus, 1 tonne of carbon is equivalent to 3.6667 (three and two-thirds) tonnes of carbon dioxide. As explained in the text, other greenhouse gases, such as methane, are expressed in terms of the equivalent global warming effect of carbon dioxide. The weight of methane, for example, is multiplied by 21 to get to a carbon dioxide equivalent. Different international bodies use slightly different multipliers for the various gases, and I have used the official European figures.

When dealing with energy prices to households, I use round numbers for the costs in autumn 2009. I have assumed a figure of 3.5 pence per kilowatt hour for gas and 13 pence for electricity. Each kWh of gas produces about 0.19kg of carbon dioxide, but you will sometimes see a slightly higher figure. The figure for electricity depends crucially on the mix of fuels being used to generate power. I have taken a figure of 0.50kg per kWh, which is slightly lower than recent numbers but higher than the typical figures a few years ago. It has the huge advantage of being easy to use for calculations. Generally I have referred to UK pound sterling prices (denoted by £); if I use $ it means US dollars. By the time the book is published, some numbers will inevitably be wrong and in the event of substantial upward or downward movement readers may find that the figures need some adjustments. I am sorry for the inconvenience that this causes. I hope that most calculations will still be broadly correct.

Many of the numbers in this book have changed since the first edition in February 2007. The two most important are a reduction in the estimated warming effect of aircraft in flight and the inclusion of an estimate of the carbon footprint of the goods and services imported into the UK.

Chris Goodall
Oxford
March 2010

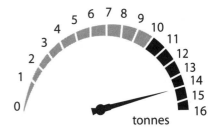

1

. . . .

getting from 14 tonnes to 2 tonnes of carbon dioxide per person

F ew people know the details of how the activities of our day-to-day lives generate emissions of carbon dioxide (CO_2) and other greenhouse gases. This book is intended to provide information and practical suggestions that will enable concerned individuals to do the best they can to reduce their personal responsibility for climate change. I have written it as a reference work to help people make decisions on how to reduce emissions. Individually, of course, we are powerless; but our actions influence those around us. Neighbours and colleagues are subtly influenced by determined and well-informed actions to reduce energy use. Your decisions will push companies to address the large market for low-carbon products, and governments will come to see that real action on climate change is not electorally disastrous.

Taking international air travel and the energy 'embedded' in imported goods into account, people in the UK are each responsible for about 14 tonnes of greenhouse gases a year.[1] This figure is approximately the same as the European Union (EU) average. It is somewhat lower than North American or Australian levels but about three or four times the average for China. To an extent that is perhaps still not recognized, individual decisions on what to buy or how to live determine an individual's greenhouse gas footprint. Increasingly, it is our day-to-day way of life that is causing the continued rise in carbon dioxide and other warming gases. We may like to put the responsibility onto faceless corporations or incompetent government but most of our personal share of the UK's carbon emissions is set by what we do and what we buy.

Today's level of 14 tonnes or so needs to fall to about 2 tonnes by 2050 if we are meet the UK government's targets for emissions. (The precise number depends on how one treats aviation and imported goods.) This an 80 or 90 per cent cut and it sounds an unattainable reduction, but the suggestions in this book show that quite small changes in lifestyle are able to take an individual a long way towards the target. In addition to individual actions, we will need the UK almost completely to stop using fossil fuel to generate electricity or to provide transport. 'Ten Technologies to Save the Planet', a book

I published in late 2008 as a complement to the first edition of this book, provides one assessment of the best ways to use technology to reduce national emissions.

WHY SHOULD INDIVIDUALS TAKE ANY ACTION?

Although global warming has been recognized as a serious issue by policy makers for at least 20 years, we have so far achieved only very limited reductions in emissions. In fact if we include international air travel and the growing volumes of imported goods, the UK's national output of greenhouse gases has gone up. Why is our record and that of other countries so bad? The reasons are simple. It is not in the interest of any single government to act to reduce carbon emissions if most of the rest of the world continues to pollute in growing volumes. If, for example, the UK were unilaterally to introduce higher taxes on gas use, and our competitors did not follow, gas-using industries would simply shift abroad. There is no electoral advantage in addressing climate change: applying real restraint on fossil fuel use would lose votes, at little benefit to the global atmosphere, unless every country acted similarly.

Corporations face a similar problem. Their senior executives do genuinely worry about the long-term impact of climate change on the world's peoples. I never cease to be impressed by the commitment of top businesspeople to doing what they can. However, in market economies, such as the UK, the role of business is no more and no less than to meet consumer requirements at the cheapest possible price. Companies will therefore use the least expensive source of energy, knowing that failure to do so will mean competitors are able to charge less. Furthermore, business will always be able to lobby successfully for the lowest possible energy prices in order that their prices remain internationally competitive.

Second, companies will always follow consumer tastes. If customers demand appliances with higher energy consumption – such as, for example, larger cars, big-screen TVs or American-style refrigerators – companies will supply the requirement. Any company that did not would consign itself to failure. In the modern economy, successful companies meet consumer demands rather than fight against them. Unfortunately, as this book will repeatedly illustrate, many consumers continue to prefer products and services that contain increasing amounts of fossil fuels.

The upshot is that neither government nor companies have much choice about climate change mitigation measures. They can talk a good story, advertise their green credentials and promise future virtue; but they will remain obdurately set in their ways. They will follow what the voters ask for or what purchasers require. We therefore cannot shift the responsibility for dealing with climate change onto others; the responsibility belongs to individual citizens of the world. In particular, it belongs to the educated members of prosperous societies. By our own actions as citizens and as consumers we can show governments and corporations that they should act now. We know enough – it is almost undeniable that climate change is going to devastate large areas of the world, particularly the rural South – and also that we have the capacity easily to reduce our own national impact.

A further point arises. It is not generally understood that it is the wealthiest members of wealthy countries who pollute the most. The heaviest responsibility for addressing the issues of climate change falls upon the economic elite. You may not think of yourself as a member of this club, but you probably are. If you travel abroad for holidays, run a reasonably sized saloon car and have a conventional middle-class lifestyle, your damage to the global environment may be double that of the UK national average. Responsible citizens need to change their habits to provide the signals to government and business that they genuinely want action on climate change. In their speeches and articles, government ministers are making it ever clearer that they want voters actively to support carbon reduction initiatives in order to give politicians more freedom to introduce stronger and stronger measures on climate change.

The year of 2009 has seen another burst of activity from citizen groups, such as the 10:10 campaign organization, spurring us into activity. But getting people to change their ways is rarely easy. We are all lazy and listen to siren voices that say that inertia is a perfectly satisfactory alternative or that responsibility lies elsewhere. Of course, the actions of single individuals, even multiplied a millionfold, are wholly insignificant. Nevertheless, the great movements in social improvement in Western society, such as the end of slavery, the universal franchise, control over child labour and universal primary education, all came after sustained and selfless action by small groups of committed individuals. Take one obvious example: although the Atlantic slave trade ceased because of parliamentary campaigning, this only happened after widespread public disquiet, symbolized by the West Indian sugar boycott. Hundreds of thousands of people – a substantial fraction of the UK population of the 1790s – gave their support to the anti-slavery message by refusing to buy sugar. Their actions gave politicians an important message. My thesis is that substantial action to address climate change can probably only happen in the same way.

This book contains detailed accounts of how today's lives generate carbon emissions. It tries to show how relatively small changes in lifestyles can cut personal greenhouse gas outputs in half.

THE ELEMENTARY SCIENCE

Almost 30 billion tonnes of carbon dioxide and other greenhouse gases enter the atmosphere as a result of human activities each year.[2] Carbon dioxide is one of the two main products of the combustion of hydrocarbons, such as coal and gas, which fuel the modern economy. This otherwise innocuous gas, the most important human contributor to global warming, still only constitutes about 385 parts per million of the world's atmosphere. The concentration is rising by 2 to 3 parts per million every year and, if current trends in emissions growth continue, looks set to exceed 500 parts per million (ppm) by 2050, or almost twice pre-industrial levels. Other greenhouse gases, such as methane and nitrous oxide, will push the concentrations to the equivalent of more than 550 ppm. Most climate scientists suggest that we need to set a 2050 target for all greenhouse gases at less than 450 ppm if we are to avoid a worrying possibility of substantial, dangerous and probably irreversible climate changes. Some very influential figures say the number should be 350 ppm, well below what it is at the moment. Of course, carbon emissions need to continue reducing after the 2050 target, ultimately aiming towards zero (or near zero) emissions per person.

Visible light from the sun warms the Earth's surface. Like a conventional room radiator, the surface eventually retransmits this energy outwards as heat in the form of infrared radiation and convection. Increasing levels of greenhouse gases render the atmosphere less transparent to the outgoing infrared radiation, and the heat is trapped. More carbon dioxide in the atmosphere will, all other things being equal, raise the temperature of the atmosphere at the Earth's surface.[3]

No one can be completely sure about the precise relationship between rising greenhouse gas concentrations and increasing temperatures. The consensus estimate is that a concentration of 550 parts per million is likely to increase temperatures by about 2 to 4 degrees Celsius (°C) above today's levels. The increase is likely to vary substantially between different parts of the world. The higher temperatures will have a variety of severe effects, ranging from drought in areas now reliant on the summer melting of rapidly disappearing glaciers to higher sea levels, making life impossible in the coastal areas that are home to a large fraction of the world's population. Some optimists claim we can cope with temperatures 4 degrees higher. In the temperate regions, this is possible. We can build higher sea walls, adjust our agriculture and acclimatize to higher temperatures. In countries living on the margin – stressed already by water shortages, coastal flooding, tropical hurricanes or temperatures too high for good agricultural productivity – this option is not available. In general, it is the poorest countries that are going to find it most difficult to adapt to rising temperatures and disruption of weather patterns. The carbon emissions of the rich world will ruin the lives of the poor.

The mid-point of the range of expected temperature rise by 2050 if we do nothing – 3 degrees – is about half the difference between the temperatures of the last ice age and the early modern period. It may not seem much; but this increase will totally alter the distribution of animal and insect life, often causing extinction as species fail to adapt in time. Even more worryingly, this increase may not be the maximum possible. The modest temperature increases already recorded are inducing changes likely to tip the world towards yet greater rises. These changes include the melting of northern tundras – causing the release of greenhouse gases that had been trapped in permafrost – and the reduction of permanent snow and ice cover, which will tend to reduce the reflection of solar energy back into space.

This story, put here in its simplest possible form, is now well understood and generally agreed by scientists, political policy makers and many concerned citizens around the world.

Newspapers devote pages to the problem. Politicians call it the most serious issue facing the globe. Pressure groups campaign ceaselessly to alert the public to particular implications of rising temperatures. There is still disagreement on many matters; but the single fact – universally acknowledged and the subject of no dispute – that carbon dioxide increases the atmosphere's opacity to infrared radiation from the Earth's surface – should be enough to convince us that greenhouse gas pollution is a serious problem that demands real action.

Carbon dioxide is not the only gas to act as a blanket in this way. Other greenhouse gases, such as methane and nitrous oxide, are produced in very much smaller volumes but have a much more virulent warming effect. In the UK, land-based sources of these other gases are tending to decline, except in the case of emissions from agriculture. Nitrous oxide emissions from aircraft engines are growing as the amount of air travel increases.

WITHOUT INDIVIDUAL ACTION EMISSIONS ARE BOUND TO GROW

Even after the price increases in the last few years, energy remains extremely cheap. Petrol may cost over a pound a litre in autumn 2009 and electricity may reach 13 pence a kilowatt hour (kWh) in some parts of the UK; but even at these prices fossil fuels are astonishingly good value for money. A strong human male, working at peak efficiency, can sustain an energy output of about 0.6kW for a few hours a day.[4] To employ this muscular individual as a labourer at the minimum wage costs something over £5 an hour. Even when working at his best, and without adding any ancillary costs, this man's work is 60 times as expensive as electricity and over 100 times the price of gas or petrol. This is the root of all our problems. Fossil fuel energy is so cheap and so convenient that its use permeates every aspect of our lives. And as more and more of the world's people move into the market economy, they will want to replace their labour with petrol or electricity.

The world's advance from subsistence agriculture to the modern post-industrial state is largely due to the use of huge quantities of fossil fuel to replace human labour. Where one man or woman ploughed the field, often but not always aided by a horse or other working animal, the farmer now employs a huge tractor. The tractor's parts took energy to make and each hectare of ploughing uses a few litres of diesel, which is taxed, incidentally, at a lower rate than when used in a passenger car. The world's industries use machines powered by gas or electricity, supervised by tiny numbers of operatives, whose only role is often to monitor the expensive technology that controls the processes. Walk round a modern steelworks and you will see a few employees dotted around in control rooms, their manual labour entirely replaced by expensive machinery and cheap energy. The increases in our standard of living have very largely come from reducing the hard physical work it used to take to make the goods and services we consume. Cheap energy has been a vital ingredient in this change.

Nothing demonstrates the fundamental cheapness of fossil fuels better than the rise of the low-price airline. Starting in the US, these nimble companies have captured a large fraction of Europe's air travel. In making air travel cheaper than any other form of transport, they have made foreign holidays available to most of the population. Last year, more than half of the UK's population made at least one flight.[5] The economics of flying make it easy to see why. EasyJet's routes average about 1100km in length and the average fuel cost per passenger carried is roughly £15, about the price of a new hardback book or a taxi ride across central London.[6] Because carbon fuels are so cheap in relation to the alternatives, the underlying demand is largely unresponsive to price changes. Between the first quarters of 2004 and 2006, the price of crude oil almost doubled, from just over $30 a barrel to about $60. In the same period, the total world demand for oil rose from 82.6 million to 85.1 million barrels a day, a rise of about 3 per cent.[7] The resilience in demand is tribute to the absolute reliance of the world economy upon freely available oil products, particularly petroleum. Of course, eventually the demand for oil may fall as the heaviest users begin to improve the efficiency of their energy-using processes. But for most customers, oil is still remarkably good value and weaning them off a reliance on fossil fuel energy is a demanding task.

The 2008/2009 recession dented oil demand far more than the huge rises in price. But as the world's economic forecasters began to cautiously predict an end to the downturn, early autumn 2009 saw a matching increase in the International Energy Agency's forecasts for the level of demand for oil. We certainly haven't found a way of continuing to grow our economies without using extra volumes of fossil fuel. The low prices for coal, gas and oil help deliver a high material standard of living to people in the developed world. For example, air freight and heated glasshouses can put food items on our plates that were previously unavailable for large portions of the year. However, producing 1kg of air-freighted winter salad takes about 200 times as much energy in heat and light as are contained in the vegetables. Across the rest of Western agriculture, this ratio is far less stark; but it still takes about nine units of energy to put one unit on the British plate. We'll show later in the book that the high energy density of agriculture is responsible for almost 20 per cent of all carbon emissions in the UK. The long-run downward trend in food prices in the UK is due, in large measure, to the replacement of expensive labour with cheap inputs of energy and with artificial fertilizer derived from natural gas.

The relative cheapness of energy affects our habits across daily life. Many of us leave computers on all the time. The energy use is not great enough to warrant avoiding the inconvenience of powering down the machines and then turning them on again. Our time is worth more to us than the savings we can possibly make by economizing on energy use. So in the circumstances when fossil fuel energy is a clear substitute for labour, the rational person almost always buys the electricity rather than do manual work. Tumble dryers cost about 25 pence to dry a full load. It might take half an hour to put this load on a washing line and take it in again at the end of the day, and therefore many people use dryers even on a windy dry day. The big problem with the successful modern economy is that economic growth makes climate change more and more difficult to fight. As society gets richer and its citizens better paid, it becomes more and more obvious that we should choose the tumble dryer rather than wasting our own time and energy. It certainly does not seem to be worth even turning off the lights in office blocks, whether used by private business or even government departments.

Another example is the recycling of soft drink cans. Making new aluminium is one of the most energy-intensive processes known to man. Each tonne of aluminium takes 15,000kWh to make, or four times the typical yearly electricity use of a UK home. This is one reason why aluminium smelters are often located close to sources of particularly cheap energy. If fossil fuel energy is used, each can of soft drink, weighing 18 grams (g) when empty, has contributed about 150g of carbon dioxide to the atmosphere, almost ten times as much. Recycling the can makes good sense in energy terms since it takes less than 10 per cent of the initial energy to recreate a new can. So, in some countries, such as Russia and Brazil, the soft drink industry operates a loop: the can is filled, collected and returned, melted down and refashioned, and then taken back to the factory for filling with another drink.[8] But this requires an army of poorer people for whom it is worth collecting cans for a penny or so. Does this system work in countries like the UK? No – there is nobody for whom a penny a can is enough to make it worth collecting the empties. Instead, we have to make or import large quantities of virgin aluminium and, across Europe, less than 50 per cent of new aluminium is reused. Increases in prosperity in developing countries – which none of us want to stop – will mean that the labour to collect cans will eventually dry up. It is true that in some rich countries – Sweden and Switzerland come to mind – strong social pressure can prompt high recycling rates; but these countries are still the exception.

Using fossil fuel energy is almost invariably the quickest, easiest and cheapest way of getting round life's problem, large and small. Whether it is getting the children to school, buying groceries, enjoying a good holiday or keeping warm in winter, the path of least resistance is usually to take the course that uses fossil fuel. The temptation to reach for the solution that uses energy is ever present in Western society and increasingly in other parts of the world, as well. Choosing to avoid carbon-based energy sources is often expensive, time consuming and inconvenient. The bus, for example, can be more expensive than a car, arrival times are unreliable and the journey takes longer. Society is increasingly designed around maximizing the labour and time-saving benefits of fossil fuel use.

We'll see throughout the book that the improving efficiency of fossil fuel use – getting more useful work out of a unit of coal, gas or oil – looks at first sight as if it reduces the need for fuels. However, this impact is almost invariably outweighed by increased levels of usage. This paradox – that energy efficiency improvements make it cheaper to use fuel fossils – is known as the 'rebound' hypothesis and helps explain why greenhouse gas emissions are intractably high. Make your house better insulated and you then tend to run the central heating at a higher temperature. Buy a fuel-efficient car and it gets used more because it is cheaper to drive. And, even more insidiously, even if you don't use as much petrol, the money you save tends to be spent on high-carbon goods and services such as foreign travel.

The richest 10 per cent of Britons spend over two and a half times as much as average people on foreign travel, twice as much fuelling their cars and, perhaps surprisingly, over three times as much on rail travel.[9] Rich people travel far more than the norm. People in the bottom 20 per cent of the income distribution in the UK travel less than 4000 miles (6400km) a year, compared to well over 10,000 miles (16,000km) for the top quintile.[10] And this travel tends to involve high expenditures of energy. Buses are relatively energy efficient. The wealthiest 20 per cent typically make 29 bus journeys a year, while people in the poorest quintile make 101. Where the average person takes one return flight a year, the rich family might take five. This fact alone probably means that their emissions are twice the national average. Cheap fossil fuels help make us prosperous and we use that prosperity to buy things that embed more fossil fuels. Energy efficiency gains of 1 per cent or so a year across a large range of activities – air travel, car transport, home appliances – will not by themselves ever reduce total energy demand.

Greater consumption is always a mark of the privileged. No society ever known has expected its rich to restrain their spending, and today's Western capitalist economy is no different. In fact, unconstrained display is a feature of many of the most successful societies. Continued growth is dependent upon it, as economists have pointed out for hundreds of years. Today, the maintenance of high status depends, as ever, on the purchase of bigger and better symbols of affluence. What prosperous person owns a ten-year-old car, a small house and takes his holiday in Skegness, or catches the bus to work? The dinner table is laden with foods flown in from Kenya or Thailand. The expensive halogen kitchen lighting is as bright as day. The children are shipped daily to a remote private school.

It's not simply that higher status requires spending on fossil fuel-intensive activities and goods, but also that failure to spend on these goods invites scorn from peers. Non-consumption can mean rejection by one's social group. Children are the worst; minor eccentricities, such as drying clothes on a line, rather than using the tumble dryer, become hugely embarrassing to them. The pressure to conform to high energy-using styles of life may be gradually diminishing, but is nevertheless an important reason for the stubborn buoyancy of electricity use in the home. The recession of 2009 did not dent domestic demand for electric power.

The list of the ways in which material progress drives up energy use is almost endless. We are buying larger TVs – entirely negating any benefits of energy efficiency from the switch to liquid crystal displays (LCDs) from old-fashioned cathode ray tubes. Our fridges are increasing in size, almost outweighing the very significant improvements in insulation in the last few years. Where our kitchens once had a couple of pale fluorescent tubes, we now have a galaxy of halogen spotlights. Our cars now have air-conditioning when we managed before with an open window.

As a general rule, we seem to take the gains we make in energy efficiency back in increased comfort, and appear to have an almost insatiable desire for an easier life, as insulated as possible from external climate or the need to engage in any form of manual work. As a result, of course, we are gaining weight. Perhaps surprisingly, we are actually not far from balance-of-food input versus energy output. I calculate that the typical middle-aged man gains about 400g (less than 1 pound) a year, and could walk this off in about 30 miles (48km) if he ate no more than before. Nevertheless, as a species we have an almost pathological laziness, and this almost universal human characteristic is reinforced by the ready availability of powered alternatives to human labour.

Power steering in cars, for example, reduces their fuel efficiency by approximately 5 per cent, although it is now absolutely standard on modern cars.[11] Few people will remember, but it used to take a real effort to turn a car at slow speed before cars were equipped with power steering. For people who drove around cities, this probably increased their own energy output by several per cent. Electric windows are another good example in cars. Reducing the amount of energy we burn off in our day-to-day activities has meant that populations of industrial societies have tended to gain weight. The response of the gradually thickening UK citizen has been to compensate by attendance at the local gym, where weight loss is attempted by using powered treadmills operating at over 1kW electric power. Compared to the typical 200W output of a middle-aged plodder trying to keep up with the running belt, this is a poor exchange. Even when trying to lose weight, we do so in energy-inefficient ways.

We all tend to use more energy as we get richer, and to substitute it for our own labour whenever we can. This is a continuing trend. The generations brought up in times when energy was much more expensive compared to manual labour are gradually disappearing. Their habits of turning off appliances or of walking rather than driving will die with them. Younger people may never have acquired these behaviours but, perhaps even more worryingly, also appear to be much less interested in environmental matters. Unlike earlier environmental movements of the 1960s and 1970s, interest in climate change appears to be lower in the young than among the old. Perhaps the footloose world travellers of today will become the environmental activists of tomorrow; but the signs are not auspicious.

The main forces in society all appear to point towards increasing fossil fuel use among individuals:

- greater prosperity means more temptation to replace manual effort with fossil fuels;
- the maintenance of personal status in the modern economy demands the purchase of bigger and more ostentatious consumer goods;
- social changes, such as the centralization of health services or places of employment, increase the need for travel and push people towards car ownership and use;
- the tradition of self-restraint and avoidance of 'waste' that characterizes the generations born before about 1960 has partly disappeared.

Will government or business change this? The next pages look at whether the central institutions of modern society have the incentive and the means to radically reduce carbon emissions or, whether they need to be pushed harder by carbon-conscious consumers.

THE ROLE OF GOVERNMENT

Democratic governments survive by following the demands of the electorate. Unpopular actions against the wishes of the voters will usually result in ejection at the next election. Unless a significant and vocal minority of the electorate lobby for action, governments seeking their own survival will never aggressively attack the problem of global warming. The inertia of governments across the world when faced with the evidence of climate change is a palpable demonstration of this truth. Governments will do what their electorates allow them: therefore, responsible individuals need to show by their individual actions that climate change measures are politically acceptable. We won't get governments to act unless the vanguard shows that it is willing to pay some price to reduce greenhouse gas emissions. At present, that willingness to accept substantial actions by our government to reduce carbon emissions is not clear to our leaders. One senior government adviser said to me in late 2008 that he believed that only one in twenty of the UK population would voluntarily accept a change in lifestyle as a response to the need to cut carbon dioxide emissions. So we need to make it absolutely obvious to politicians that we expect significant measures. Without this, governments will continue to engage in token schemes of no real benefit to the atmosphere. Even though trying to manage your own lifestyle to minimize CO_2 generation makes a negligible difference to overall emissions, it does help show our political leaders that an increasing number of people are prepared to support strong government action.

Not only do the leaders of the world face some scepticism and even hostility from their electorates, their administrations also face huge problems coordinating international action. One of the most obvious issues is that any single government has no chance of significantly affecting the total volume of world greenhouse gas output. The UK is responsible for about 2 per cent of global carbon dioxide output and it would make little difference to the global total if it ceased burning fossil fuels tomorrow. The growth rate in emissions from other countries is sufficient to replace the UK carbon within a year. It is difficult to envisage any individual country deciding to take unilateral action over emissions if the costs – either financial or in terms of material comfort – were substantial. No democratic country has ever engaged in significant self-denial for any sustained period of time without similar behaviour from other states. If international agreements are to work, they must impose equitable burdens on all parties. This is not easy: policy makers are searching for the means to develop what is, in effect, an international cartel that is both fair to developing countries and yet effective in reducing emissions. Mandatory reductions in outputs of carbon to the atmosphere will be painful to all the participating countries, with little or no benefit for decades or centuries to come. This makes any multilateral agreement extremely unstable. Countries will face temptations to renege on the agreement or to cheat on its obligations. Those states that do not join the contract will gain by their continued use of copious amounts of carbon-based fuels. So, any agreement can be undermined both by non-participants increasing their emissions in order to undercut the cartel members, and by participants cheating by using more fossil fuels.

The number of successful public cartels to reduce the global output of undesirable products is small. The 1987 Montreal Protocols were aimed at reducing the use of ozone-depleting chemicals and appear to have been reasonably effective, although it will take several decades for the dangerous hole over the Antarctic to be filled. Montreal worked, so why should we be pessimistic about a future greenhouse gas deal? First and foremost, the Montreal deal involved a small number of chemicals with an important but very limited role in the economy. It was easy to define what needed to be done, and although replacement chemicals were more expensive, they could be used by the existing manufacturers of refrigeration equipment and aerosols. There was no real economic dislocation. International agreement could be easily policed and enforced. Countries that agreed to cease production were able successfully to prohibit imports of goods using ozone-depleting chemicals.

The problems in organizing a successful agreement to restrict fossil fuel use are many orders of magnitude greater. Fossil fuel use is much more difficult to measure. One tonne of steel made by a country not adhering to the agreement will be chemically identical to one made in a participating country. Frankly, if the world cannot even control over-fishing of the oceans, its chances of making a dent in energy use or reducing deforestation are not great.

The existing structure of international treaties adds to the difficulties in arranging an agreement between states to restrict emissions. The most important treaties are probably those that underpin the world trade system, monitored by the World Trade Organization (WTO). The purpose of the various international agreements over the last generation has been to reduce the barriers to international trade. All trade is good, say the policy makers. Even though increasing international trade may well be having a deleterious effect on rates of greenhouse gas creation, the WTO pushes on with its prime objective. Attempts, for example, by one country to restrict imports of airlifted food because of the carbon cost of air travel would result in near-immediate legal action by the WTO. The agreements surrounding international aviation are even more powerful. A huge number of separate bilateral deals between sovereign states commit countries not to tax aviation fuel.[12] The UK and other states cannot increase the price of kerosene without overturning a huge number of signed protocols. And if action were taken across the whole of the European Union (EU), its effectiveness would be partly undermined by aircraft taking on more fuel in countries outside the EU that had chosen not to implement any tax. By 2012 the aviation industry will be placed inside the EU emissions trading scheme, but the looseness of the cap may mean that the growth of aviation will be barely constrained at all.

Attempts to restrict particular activities with severe impacts on carbon dioxide emissions run into similar problems. The manufacture of aluminium is one of the most energy-intensive industrial processes; but when the German government tried to restrict the use of metal drinks cans, it faced action from the European Commission.[13] The European court eventually ruled that trying to ban the use of cans that were freely available in other member states was a restriction on trade within the EU and was therefore illegal. Any action by an individual country within the EU that tried to weight consumers' choices towards less polluting alternatives would probably suffer a similar fate.

And it is not simply the strong bias in the world economic system towards free trade that makes action by individual countries difficult. Increasingly, we see that one environmental objective can sometimes get in the way of another. For example, reducing emissions of diesel particulates from buses gives the bus operator lower fuel economy.[14] Understandably, society also wants to give consideration to the impact on human health of poor air quality in city centres, so a trade-off is made between carbon dioxide emissions and the particulates from buses that may be causing increased levels of respiratory diseases such as asthma. Governments cannot give overwhelming priority to climate change mitigation without affecting its achievement of other targets.

Similarly, determined opposition from small groups of highly motivated protestors can delay or stop many initiatives to reduce emissions. The most obvious examples come from the experience of wind power developers. Wind farms take many years to get through planning processes and then face a further delay in the queue for connection to the national grid. Another illustration is the huge upgrade to the power lines in the north of Scotland to meet the increased need for the transmission of wind-generated electricity to consumers. Scotland's wind resources probably account for one-quarter of the total wind energy of the EU. Despite the active encouragement of wind farms by government, objectors worked assiduously to secure the refusal of planning permission for the pylons across beautiful countryside. Unless this decision is overturned, wind development in the region will be strictly curtailed. Without doubt the objectors have strong points – some of Scotland's best views would be affected by the new transmission line. Caught between those vociferously protecting something they hold dear, and the weaker and less organized forces arguing for measures to protect the global atmosphere, the protesters will always tend to carry more weight.

By deciding to take action to reduce your own emissions you are providing important background support for those who are working to remove the obstacles to the development of wind and other renewables. The unrestrained growth in air travel is perhaps the most intractable climate challenge facing governments. Although air travel is only responsible for less than 6 per cent of UK emissions at present, the amount of carbon dioxide pushed out by jet engines will probably double within 25 years.[15] And the side effects of airline emissions (dealt with in Chapter 9) make the position far worse. While we are struggling to generate the most modest of decreases in surface emissions of carbon dioxide, international air travel – untrammelled by controls imposed by Kyoto processes – races away and overwhelms any improvements we see in other fields. It is no good the government asking us to switch off our televisions when not in use (saving about 30kg of carbon dioxide a year) while waving us cheerfully away on our shopping trips to New York (over 2.5 tonnes of greenhouse gases per trip, or almost 100 times as much).

Statements by the government on air travel are invariably two sided. First, the administration gives a welcome to the impact of low fares, cheap carriers and better access to a huge range of destinations. If political success is measured by the volume of travellers leaving the UK during the holiday period, aviation is government's single greatest recent achievement. The 2003 White Paper said that the UK needed 'a balanced and measured approach to the future of air transport which ... reflects people's desire to travel further and more often by air, and to take advantage of the affordability of air travel and the opportunities this brings'.[16] These benefits should be balanced by ensuring that 'over time, aviation pays the external costs [that] its activities impose on society at large' (note the expression 'over time' – political code for 'when we think we can get away with it').

Nothing in UK government statements yet indicates any real intention to try to diminish the rate of growth in emissions from air travel. There has been support for participation in the carbon trading schemes, but nothing that suggests that politicians want to reduce the number of travellers or increase the price that they pay. The government's abdication of any form of direct responsibility for managing down airline emissions is particularly important because of the central role of the UK in handling international passengers. At any one moment, 20 per cent of international passengers are travelling to or from a UK airport.[17] Aviation is a UK success story and no politician will touch it without clear electoral backing. It is worth mentioning, perhaps, that if aircraft fuel were taxed at the same rate as petrol, the cost of a return flight across the Atlantic would be increased by £200.[18] It will probably be some time before there is widespread public support for such a charge.

What about an air travel emissions trading scheme? The 2012 EU scheme will allow airlines a certain volume of emissions above which they will have to buy more permits. The idea extends the current permit system that covers major industrial users and that has, so far, proved to be virtually no constraint on carbon use. Governments around Europe – and, indeed, the airline industry – are broadly welcoming the prospect of the scheme. Our suspicions should be aroused at this point: if the airlines are in favour, can it be good for the atmosphere? They'll have to pay for growth, but at current prices, the effect will be tiny. At the current permit price of €15 per tonne of emissions, the effect on the cost of flying from London to New York will be about £20. At €20 a tonne, the cost will be less than £30.[19]

Of equal importance to the airlines is the fact that they expect to get most of their initial allowances free, as the electricity generators did. If ticket prices rise, they might actually be able to increase their profits as a result of the introduction of the scheme. Certainly, there's widespread suspicion that the net effect of the current European permit scheme has been to hand the power generators windfall profits of billions of euros. The European Commission, in charge of designing the aviation scheme, is shameless when describing its likely effect. The first page of any early press release was full of quotations from European commissioners saying that the proposal would reduce emissions. But read on and the story gets a little cloudy. Later in the release the commission boasts that the impact on ticket prices is likely to be 'modest', with prices rising between €0 and €9 per return flight. 'With an increase of this level', it continues, 'aviation demand would simply grow at a slightly slower rate than otherwise.'[20] Emissions trading is going to do very little to protect the global atmosphere from the impact of rapid growth in passenger flights. The European Commission has caved in to the forces that seek to continue profiting from the ballooning growth in air travel.

Of course, this is unsurprising. Democratic societies are locked into competition with other open economies. Good, cheap aviation does not just deliver low-cost holidays in sunny Mediterranean resorts; it oils the wheels of the modern economy. Trying to restrict air travel will undoubtedly affect the ability of the UK economy to maintain relatively fast growth and a high share of investment from foreign countries. 'Britain's continuing success as a place in which to invest and do business depends crucially on the strength of our international transport links' says the UK's 2004 *Transport White Paper*.[21] So, the government must provide more capacity for aviation. Without a revolution in politics that allows the government to abandon its plans to add runways around the UK, the only way that aircraft emissions are going to be checked is by individuals deciding voluntarily that they are not going to fly.

Our governments could, of course, decide systematically to raise the price of fossil fuel energy. One sensible course of action might be to try to quadruple the cost over a period of, say, 15 years using the taxation system. The main problem would be the huge impact on the poorer members of society. The top 10 per cent of households spend less than 3 per cent of their income on gas and electricity. A major increase in prices would have little impact on these people. But the bottom decile has to spend over 10 per cent of its income on these things, and this figure will have risen considerably since the data was last collected. Quadrupled gas prices would mean that a large fraction of the UK population would be obliged to go cold in winter. This is simply not going to happen in a democracy. Governments' freedom to use the price mechanism to decrease the consumption of gas for heating or petrol for cars is extremely constrained.

It is fair to say that governments are continuing to search for painless ways to reduce carbon emissions. But the options open to it are depressingly few. A scheme of 'personal carbon allowances' is sometimes canvassed. Occasionally called carbon rationing, the suggestion is that each member of society is given a total allowance of carbon dioxide each year. It might currently be 5 tonnes, but would decrease year on year in order to reduce national emissions. The holder would be given a smart card containing the ration, with the balance reducing every time the holder made a purchase of fossil fuel-derived goods. Paying the electricity bill would result in a deduction from the balance, as would a top-up of fuel at the petrol station.

In some ways, this is a hugely attractive scheme. Rich people would have to buy more credits for their air travel from those who choose not to travel. Unlike using taxation, the scheme would not result in the price of home heating increasing for the poor. But carbon allowances are an administrative nightmare, impossibly complex to run, and could be circumvented in an almost infinite number of ways. Instead of driving my car, I could take a taxi. Whose allowance does that trip come from? Does the homeowner trying to keep warm in a draughty Victorian house get a larger ration? Will people off the mains gas network get larger allowances because of the greater carbon cost of heating by electricity? Tradable carbon allowances should continue to get serious investigation; but they are not a panacea within the next 15 years. In support of my scepticism, I need only point to the nearly unblemished record of total failure of most major government information technology projects in the UK over the last 20 years. Carbon rationing is an elegant and completely impractical solution.

Governments also have to wrestle with the implications of our preference for today's consumption over investments to protect our future. Generally, we assume that £1 today is worth more than £1 in a year's time. In fact, human beings often act as if £1 in a year's time has a very low value, indeed. We give the future very little weight in our thinking. This view, carried over to climate change, implies that the benefits of cheap energy today are worth having, even if the future costs are high. We'd rather have the good things now, even if our welfare is adversely affected in ten or twenty years' time. If you agree with this line of argument, it may well not be worth trying to avert climate change. It costs a lot now to reduce greenhouse gases, and we won't value the benefit very highly in the future. As a species, we do tend to eat the entire pudding for supper, rather than making it last several days. Climate change is a sort of borrowing from the future – we get a higher standard of living today in return for lower welfare in the future. Economists generally say that this sort of free choice is to be encouraged. But those who say that future generations can look after themselves (and, after all, they will probably have much greater material prosperity) need to acknowledge that the damage we are inflicting on the global atmosphere may well be irreparable.

Reducing the carbon dioxide emissions of a household can either be done by self-denial – cutting room temperatures, for example – or by installing technologies or devices that consume less energy. Many of these things cost several hundred UK pounds per tonne of carbon dioxide saved, although this book will show that many options are far cheaper than this. They do not seem financially attractive to the average householder, and perhaps they never will. To people borrowing money on a credit card at 25 per cent, the returns from installing solar panels – at perhaps 7 or 8 per cent a year – must look very unappealing. However, without huge investments in expensive energy-saving or carbon-reducing measures, we are very unlikely even to begin to get a grasp on carbon emissions. Unfortunately governments face very little pressure from voters to mandate these changes.

AREN'T COMPANIES DOING IT FOR US?

In a modern economy, in which economic competition is working actively, no company can choose to make decisions that raise its costs compared to its peers. It would only be a matter of months before its investors called for a change in strategy and began muttering about the need for a new management team. Indeed, most investors would say that companies have a duty to pursue profit, even at the expense of the wider environment, although they might not put it as crudely. Companies therefore tend to act as herd creatures, following trends as long as others are too, but never driving ahead into apparently unprofitable markets. While fossil fuel remains cheap – and it still is compared to the alternatives – we will not see sufficient innovation from large companies unless they see a prospective market from consumers actively seeking low-emissions products.

Companies generally require paybacks on their investments in less than five years, and often much less. Virtually no carbon-reducing technologies provide this sort of return. This is not to say that business is actually opposed to cuts in the level of greenhouse gas emissions. The corporate sector simply wants to ensure that no individual company is required to manage with a small allowance when its competitors are given more. Broadly speaking, as long as emissions reductions are equitably imposed, and right across Europe, business is in favour. Though no company, singly, can do much to reduce emissions, and doesn't want to on its own, business leaders press the government to introduce schemes that universally require reductions in energy use. For example, in early June 2006, a group of the most senior UK corporate heads, including people from companies as diverse as Shell and Vodafone, visited the prime minister to push for tighter, not looser, restrictions.[22] They argued for smaller allowances under the European Emissions Trading Scheme. They spoke in favour of steps to cut emissions from transport, such as congestion charging and road pricing. They even said that building regulations should be tighter in order to improve the energy losses from new buildings. Since 2006 these companies have continued to argue for greater action on climate change.

These proposals will tend to increase business costs. Companies very rarely press for measures that impose penalties on their activities. Why are senior executives asking national and international entities to tighten rules on emissions? I suspect that as individuals they feel uncomfortable leading companies that generate such large absolute amounts of greenhouse gases. As people – ordinary individuals with moral sensibility and a concern for the future of their race – they know that the arguments in favour of restraint are overwhelming. But as leaders paid to advance their company's wealth and size, they know that unilateral action is impossible. Shell UK is not going to stop drilling for gas just because its managers are nervous about the climate in 50 years' time. So these people want to pass the responsibility on to government, which will force them to be better behaved. We need to be clear: when business asks for lower carbon emissions, it does not intend to actually do anything unless forced by regulation. But as with many forms of regulation, equitably applied, most businesses would find greater restrictions on fossil fuel use perfectly possible to accommodate.

Those business leaders who think about the issue generally see the scale of the climate change problem. The employers' organization, the CBI, is one of the most active proponents of more urgent actions. Many businesses even think that initiatives to decelerate the pace of warming would have a beneficial effect on the European business sector by making it leaner and less energy-intensive. Many companies are now saying that they are using technology to reduce energy in their own operations. But the goods and services that they provide to householders – except a few token projects for public relations purposes – will only be fully re-engineered if consumers demand lower-carbon alternatives.

OTHER BLOCKS IN THE ROAD TO LOWER CARBON

There's an increasing literature on the non-tangible issues we need to address if carbon emissions are to be held down.[23] Fossil fuel consumption is largely invisible and unobtrusive. Awakening people to the effect of background activity, such as keeping the house warm with an inefficient boiler, is an extremely demanding communications task. This issue is magnified by the extraordinary pervasiveness of fossil fuel energy use. The typical consumer is unable to comprehend the multiple ways in which his or her lifestyle generates greenhouse gases. The ordinary house-owner might unconsciously take a decision to use fossil fuel several hundred times a day – boiling a kettle, flushing the toilet, buying a tin of beans, driving to the station, leaving the computer on at work – and cannot possibly be expected to weigh the carbon consequences of each action.

Many attempts to reduce carbon use are, regrettably, also the subject of potential derision from friends and colleagues. There is strong social pressure to conform to conventional behaviour. A simple decision not to use aeroplanes, the single most important statement a person can make that he or she regards climate change as an important issue, may pose problems for social relationships or prospects at work. Not going on a weekend party to Prague because of a principled refusal to fly is unlikely to endear one to one's friends. A willingness to drop everything and fly to the US is often a precondition of the most successful jobs. Who is going to abandon the hopes of a better paid and higher status job in order to defend a position that much air travel is unnecessary or even wrong?

Most importantly, the majority of people have no sense whatsoever of the scale of the fossil fuel consumption attached to each activity. Here's a comment from author Deborah Moggach, interviewed about a trip to the Galapagos Islands:

> *Like a lot of people, I'm a mass of contradictions. I recycle, compost and have hens that eat my leftovers and garden slugs. But I've got an old house that isn't really draft proofed and I never turn the TV off standby. I jump on planes, but I'm very good about cycling.*[24]

Deborah Moggach shouldn't be criticized for not realizing that an air trip to South America will have contributed 5 tonnes of carbon dioxide or more to the atmosphere, which will be 100 times more important than the impact of her recycling. No one except an expert could possibly hope to know even the approximate impacts of individual acts. The companies that market their goods to us are aware of this, and will try to sell their products as green, even when they fail to meet the most basic standards of energy efficiency.

Realizing that the ultimate responsibility rests on us, not on companies or political leaders, numerous individuals want to act on their own initiative. If the arguments in this book are correct, the only morally responsible position is to act on one's own because no institution or market mechanism has any prospect of effectively reducing fossil fuel use. It is up to individuals; we cannot rely on governments. And because our own personal actions are responsible for a larger and larger share of the total, our responsibility is increasing.

SELF-RESTRAINT, A MUCH UNDERRATED HUMAN VIRTUE

It sometimes seems that there is an immutable law of human nature that requires us to reach out for material possessions, even when we don't really need them. Offer people the chance for a higher material standard of living and they will take it. If we can have it, we want it, even at the cost of drought in Africa or flooding in Asia. This feature of human character makes dealing with climate change especially difficult. Democratic governments and profit-driven companies are simply agents that enable us to act out the pursuit of material gain. Battling climate change requires self-restraint, a trait that modern consumer society has almost, but not quite, obliterated.

If this pessimistic conclusion is right, then the battle against global warming was lost long ago. The huge success of modern dynamic capitalism at delivering material prosperity across the world, particularly in the last 15 years, makes the battle against greenhouse gases doubly difficult. First, it has, of course, required huge amounts of fossil fuel to make the goods and services on which we are now increasingly reliant. Second, it makes jumping off the economic escalator more difficult. This second point is a little complex to explain.

I will do so with reference to a particular example. By the late 1970s, the UK was widely regarded as an economic laggard, condemned to a slow relative decline. Over-powerful trade unions, sclerotic management, an ossified class structure, an ingrained anti-capitalist culture and an absurd romantic reverence for its rural past combined to depress the rate of the UK's economic growth.[25]

Margaret Thatcher, prime minister from 1979 to 1990, did more than anybody to change this. Her mission was to rid the UK of its abiding fatalism, its sense that relative decline was inevitable. She succeeded to an extent that now seems remarkable. The most important transformation in the underlying culture may have been a growing respect for material wealth and personal economic attainment. People had previously derived a substantial portion of their status from their job title, their family history or the name of their school, and relatively little from their income or material possessions.

By the end of the Thatcher period, but certainly continuing into the 21st century, economic success – as conventionally defined by income and wealth – had become a more important indicator of social standing. The entrepreneur, City dealer or successful business person is a figure of far greater importance than could have been the case during the 1970s. Of course, in many ways this has been a beneficial transition. Economic growth has enabled major improvements in health, life expectancy and the rate of absolute poverty. Often seen as the most sensitive indicator of physical well-being, the rate of infant mortality in the UK has fallen by over 50 per cent since 1981.[26] Between 1981 and 2002, life expectancy at age 50 increased by four and a half years for men and three years for women and this rise is still continuing.[27] Of course, these important improvements may well have occurred without improvements in material prosperity; but the evidence suggests that at least some part of improved health and, indeed, life expectancy in the UK derives from the country's stronger economic performance.[28]

But the transition to a society that rewards economic success with greatly enhanced status has introduced a new compulsion to become wealthy. There is more of a social cost to resisting fossil fuel addiction. I realize that this is a highly contentious point with powerful arguments on the other side; but the unleashing of entrepreneurial dynamism is, in my opinion, likely to inflate fossil fuel demand, particularly in the form of air travel, larger cars and bigger homes to heat. Stepping off the escalator of material prosperity is difficult in a culture which more openly celebrates wealth and the display of material possessions. Self-restraint in consumption becomes more difficult. I think it is no accident that some Nordic countries, still partly gripped by a Lutheran self-control, are making more progress in carbon reduction than we are.[29] Personal consumption in these countries is, perhaps, less important to self-image.

A fully effective capitalism is, I suspect, a highly competitive, brutal world in which corporations are continuously under threat from new participants in their markets, from innovation and new technologies, and from cut-throat pricing from foreign suppliers. It is these conditions which keep companies on their toes. One very senior regulator once said to me that the whole aim of national competition policy was to rid corporations of their autonomy. Effective competition, he said, left companies no discretion – everything they did was dictated by customers and the relentless search for better value.

The UK is a more competitive economy than it was, and in most respects this is good. But it does necessarily mean that companies have even less choice about climate change. They are left with little autonomy and they will only pursue carbon reduction if that is what their customers and their shareholders demand. Their customers are unlikely to pay significantly extra for low-carbon goods, so normal profit-maximizing companies will only reduce emissions if it makes strict financial sense. And since the average institutional shareholder owns a company's shares for a matter of months, rather than decades, it is unlikely that the owner will take a view about the price of oil in 2020 and reward a company for taking investment decisions with a view to that very long-term future.[30]

As a result, today's pattern is for companies to make marginal reductions in fossil fuel use, but only where the effort is justified by the immediate cost savings. The volatility and relatively high levels of fossil fuel prices are certainly increasing the incentive to reduce the use of oil-, coal- and gas-derived products; but the effects only barely show up in aggregate national statistics. So, the consequence of the UK's move to a more competitive, innovative and dynamic economy over the past 25 years has been to give a greater significance to consumption that uses extravagant amounts of fossil fuel, combined with a more responsive corporate sector that marches tightly in step to the drum of customer demand.

This book advances the view that voluntary self-restraint may be the most important way for responsible individuals to cut their own carbon use, combined with some personal investments in lower emissions technologies that are not necessarily financially rational.

But we live in a world that gives huge prominence to the rational pursuit of economic self-interest. The triumph of the Western capitalist model is so complete that the idea that our day-to-day consumption of fossil fuel could have a moral or even religious dimension is seen as deeply eccentric. Even those who recognize the importance of climate change rarely allow themselves to contemplate the idea that market- or taxation-based solutions might not be enough. Self-restraint over consumption is a hugely subversive idea in an economic system which has as its core proposition that greater and greater happiness will follow every increase in our personal incomes and spending.

However, deliberate self-denial is the only way in which individuals can help address the global warming threat. Are there any grounds for hope that people will decide to act out moral decisions in their consumption behaviour, even if it means a higher cost or inconvenience? Are there analogous instances that might give us hope that individual consumers can adjust their perceived needs so as to consume less?

The evidence demonstrates that some limited optimism is justified. Recent history shows that consumers do sometimes make purchases requiring them to pay more for goods or services which embody values that appeal to them. The most ethically conscious consumers will do this even when there is no status attached to the product. Twenty years ago, for example, purchasers of organic vegetables were usually buying them because it seemed right, not because organic foods had a strong positive brand image. In fact, the purchase of organic foods was, to use a loose expression, very 'counter-cultural'. Gradually, however, consumers may move to the next phase. This stage may be the point at which other, less ethically driven, people begin to make the purchase because of some form of cachet or enhanced status derived from using the product. Organic foods have now certainly reached this stage. Eventually, even laggards begin to switch, if only because it is seen as positively evil to continue buying the non-ethical brands. Who now, for example, would knowingly buy cosmetics that were known to be tested on animals?

The move to making low-carbon consumption patterns an endemic feature of the world economy will need to go through these three distinct phases. It does not appear to me to be enough simply to rely on the small number of puritans who dislike consumption of all forms. For widespread personal self-restraint in carbon consumption to become successful, it needs to be developed into a high status activity and, eventually, into the conventional mode of life. The gradual move into being a standard way of living will take generations; but the high costs borne by today's innovators will diminish as low-carbon goods and services decrease in relative price as volumes increase.

It might work as in the following example. Installing ultra-efficient house insulation, for example, is now a goal aimed at by real eco-enthusiasts. It is expensive and does not produce much of a financial return above and beyond normal insulation standards. It is only the socially eccentric who have worried about the 'U' values of walls or other indicators of heat retention. But I suspect that 'eco-housing' of all types is in the process of becoming attractive to the rich and to the famous, even though, in strictly financial terms, it makes little sense. A tightly insulated house might save a few hundred pounds a year in fuel bills, but at a cost of several thousand pounds. Nevertheless, the number of pages devoted to fashionable eco-homes in the pages of the weekend newspapers would indicate growing interest from the elite. Very well-insulated housing will become an object of desirable status, and adoption rates will rise. This will help to push down the cost of extremely good insulation, and, very gradually, ordinary folk will choose to improve their houses for financially rational reasons. It will save enough money to make investment worthwhile. Eventually, not having good insulation will be seen as slightly tacky and somewhat irresponsible.

My optimism is perhaps a little too advanced. But in some areas of food purchasing, ethical brands are making real inroads. One example is the growth of the Fairtrade label. Starting in the Netherlands in 1988 and initially focused only on coffee, the Fairtrade brand mark provides a guarantee that the farmer obtained a relatively high and consistent price for the product. Although still small in terms of its share of the total grocery market, with sales of about £800 million in 2009 out of a grocery market of well over £100 billion in the UK, Fairtrade has had a disproportionate effect. Still growing at over 40 per cent a year in the UK, Fairtrade is an example of how large groups of people are prepared to use moral criteria in their purchasing decisions. The Fairtrade foundation says that over half UK consumers are 'active ethical consumers'. And who could have guessed even five years ago that conventional brands like Nestle's Kit Kat would decide that moving to Fairtrade sourcing would make good business sense?

Recycling is another activity that generally has no direct reward except a feeling of virtue. Actually, it is even less easy to explain than Fairtrade purchasing. At least with coffee or chocolate there may be a sense that the product itself is better. In the case of recycling, voluntary sorting of glass or plastics is time consuming and sometimes slightly unpleasant. It is certainly easier simply to throw the plastic milk carton in the kitchen bin, rather than washing it, crushing it and then storing it in a recycling box for a couple of weeks. Nevertheless, increasing numbers of people do make the effort to segregate their recyclable wastes and do so out of a sense of moral duty.

Recent survey work[31] also shows that activities such as recycling, in which the individual gains little personally from the action, become much more entrenched if organizations such as local councils make active and sustained efforts to improve recycling rates.[32] The lesson seems to be that if people see evidence that their own selfless actions are being matched by other institutions, then their behaviour becomes more determined and committed. This is another example of the 'I will if you will' phenomenon. Social change can proceed very rapidly if everybody is seen to be under equivalent pressure to behave responsibly. Perhaps 10 per cent of people are deeply resistant to recycling, and their behaviour will take a generation to change. But for almost all others, active recycling shows signs of becoming sufficiently embedded to become a social norm. In other words, those failing to recycle, in some areas of the country at least, are beginning to feel under neighbourhood pressure to conform. There is no reason why, over a period of years, the same social compulsion cannot be imposed when it comes to reducing carbon emissions.

Economists often don't understand actions that do not appear to be driven by the pursuit of what is loosely called 'rational self-interest'. The academic and polemicist John Kay, one of the most robust defenders of the power of the price mechanism, wrote this in response to a leaflet about paper recycling from his council:

> *Recycling is our penance for the material advantages of a consumer society. It is no more sensible to ask about its benefits than to enquire whether Hail Marys do the Blessed Virgin any good. The value of saving paper lies in the virtuous feelings it engenders.*[33]

John Kay's thesis in his article was that throwing waste paper away was bad for the environment and, more widely, that recycling was irrational because of the lack of personal economic return. He poured gentle scorn on those who feel a little better as they tug their paper recycling box into the street on collection day. Economists like Kay don't find it easy to empathize with those who make an effort for no return. Members of the dismal profession will always tend to bring up the rear in any campaign to get people to take personal responsibility for global warming, claiming that market mechanisms will work better (even economists acknowledge that they are among the least likely to be cooperative and altruistic in their dealings with others).

Moreover, Kay's assertion that paper recycling is counter-productive is almost certainly wrong. A major review of all the available analyses of the 'life-cycle costs' of paper suggests a saving of over 1 tonne of carbon dioxide for every tonne recycled.[34]

As well as recycling and buying Fairtrade products, UK consumers seem willing to pay more for ethically sound purchases across a wide range of goods and services. Probably the single most advanced ethical market is that for free-range eggs. The New Economics Foundation (NEF) reported that 41 per cent of eggs sold in retail shops were free-range in 2004, up from 33 per cent in 2002 and since then the major supermarkets have gradually decreased the space devoted to battery eggs with Sainsbury's finally abandoning them in mid 2009. The steady increase in consumer resistance to factory-farmed eggs meant that it became politically possible for the EU to ban caged chickens by 2012. At the time of writing in early autumn 2009, Tesco's free-range prices were almost 100 per cent above standard eggs, so the ethical decision has some cost to the household. In the case of eggs, the concerned consumer has nearly won – it is now close to being socially unacceptable, at least in some demographic groups, to eat battery eggs. Stores worried about their reputations will not have them on their shelves. The average household only spends £20 a year on eggs, so the financial sacrifice from buying free-range is not huge. Nevertheless, it is a valuable model for other consumer goods.

Across several different markets, a reasonable percentage of people are apparently willing to act as the shock troops of environmental activism. A study for the Greater London Authority, for example, showed that about 19 per cent of the population were willing to pay an extra £5 a month or more for electricity generated from renewable sources.[35] In a completely different field, a smaller but still significant number – 10 per cent – say that they primarily buy second-hand goods for environmental reasons and 17 per cent made purchases locally in order to support nearby shops.[36] Even in financial services, there are people willing to take costly steps in order to do the right thing; the idealistic Triodos Bank has almost 30,000 customers in the UK even though its interest rates on deposits have historically been well below what customers could achieve elsewhere.

So the evidence is that a small but growing number of people are prepared to make a personal sacrifice in order to buy goods or services that are in tune with their own ethical standpoints. The NEF study also showed a concomitant rise in the percentage of people feeling guilty about purchases that they regarded as 'unethical'. The figure doubled, to over one-third of individuals, between 1999 and 2004. There were also increases in people thinking that their behaviour as consumers could affect the way in which companies behaved and this percentage has certainly continued to increase.

Earlier I suggested that the forces of economic competition meant that businesses were not free to act in environmentally responsible ways unless their customers changed their requirements. But when people do start wanting more ethical choices, successful companies are now likely to react more expeditiously, particularly if their reputation for stocking the eco-friendly items might be under threat. The early switch of Marks & Spencer to entirely Fairtrade coffee and the supermarket chain Waitrose's pioneering move to 100 per cent free-range eggs are small but powerful illustrations of how upmarket retailers are now increasingly anxious to keep their image consistent with the aspirations of their customers. Marks & Spencer's pioneering Plan A, a scheme for making radical reductions to emissions and waste as well as increasing the amount of ethically sourced products, is another example of a nimble retailer understanding that consumer tastes are moving rapidly. The direction of travel is only one way – low-carbon goods and services are going to become more popular and your actions as a consumer can increase the speed of the transition.

In many different markets – whether it is renewable energy or local food – it looks as though about 5 per cent of people are serious activists, resolutely prepared to pay more and endure possible inconvenience to do what they think is right (my mention of inconvenience will be all too familiar to anybody who has had to wash carrots from a local organic box scheme or farmers' market). This 5 per cent is not composed of what marketing people usually call 'early adopters' – normal mainstream people who are quick on the uptake. Today's climate change activists are the very small group who act from moral imperatives, not because they want to get on a bandwagon early.

Getting up from this low level of acceptance to the 40 per cent share of sales at which people appear to start feeling bad about not buying the ethical choice seems to require two steps. First, the items must become fashionable: newspaper columnists must write glowingly of the celebrities who use the product and they must suggest psychic benefits that can only be obtained through extensive use. Fairtrade is clearly at this point in its development. It has an aura of goodness about it even though, to be frank, until recently much Fairtrade coffee has been of indifferent quality. The second, and more important, stage is when prosperous 'early adopters' become committed users and recommend it to their friends. At this point in the marketing of any new product, the promoters can be very confident that the item stands a good chance of eventual success.

I can see several important categories of carbon saving that look as though they might cross the yawning chasm between the nutty activists and the fashionable people who populate our major urban centres. Our solar panels generate regular enquiries from local people wanting to install their own. In an act that might be seen as local one-upmanship, several neighbours have now put up photovoltaic panels with twice the power of ours. This is absolutely wonderful: solar panels might soon become a way of enhancing your local status.

Locally farmed seasonal organic food is another possible target – not only is it good for carbon emissions, it can be sold as healthier and tastier. Better central heating controls, which might save 5 per cent of the emissions from house heating, could also be candidates for entry into the shopping baskets of the rich and famous. They can be attractive electronic devices sitting visibly on the walls which the (male) owners can boast about to their friends. But in my pessimistic moments, it sometimes seems a struggle to see how we can persuade people not to fly as regularly. The idea of avoiding winter holidays in the sun, which are such an effective badge of membership of the high-earning professional classes, is not going to be easy to sell. However, we can certainly hope that the rich will buy carbon offsets to make good part of the damage from air travel. The medieval elite were prepared to buy indulgences from the Pope's agents for their peccadilloes, and carbon offsets can fill a similar niche. In the first edition of this book I wrote that 'it may not be easy to promote the value of smaller cars'. I was too pessimistic. Not only have high fuel prices and company car taxation increased the cost of large vehicles but there has been a definite switch to seeing smaller cars as more attractive than heavy and inefficient larger vehicles. Advertisers focus heavily on the green credentials of nippy little city cars. The swing towards hybrid and even electric cars has undoubtedly begun to gather pace as cars slowly cease to be strong statements of status.

Persuasive research into people's responses to environmental messages shows the importance of establishing strong social norms that reinforce appropriate behaviour.[37] A series of experiments in the US looked at the influence of various different written messages in influencing whether guests reused their towels in hotels or sent them to be washed every day. Washing fewer towels saves hotels money, but also reduces the use of fuels necessary to heat water for washing. The researchers left some messages in hotel rooms that stressed generic goals, such as 'Partner with us to help save the environment'. These texts were less influential in getting hotel guests to recycle their towels than messages that stated an expectation that the user would behave according to a social norm. The most influential message was: 'Join your fellow citizens in helping to save the environment', which got over 40 per cent of guests to reuse towels, compared to a base of 20 per cent when the card said: 'Help the hotel save energy'.

According to the academic researchers looking at the results, the message that worked best was successful because it suggested that the social norm was for the guest to request a reuse of the towels. The lesson drawn for those circumstances when the citizen is asked to be 'good' is to emphasize how many other people are already behaving that way. According to this theory, a statement that 'the vast majority of people don't drop litter' would be more effective at depressing the level of littering than a comment that emphasized that many people do, such as: 'Don't join the litter louts'.

In the case of energy use, it would be more effective to use a slogan that said 'Responsible people are reducing their thermostat settings in winter' rather than 'High temperatures waste energy' or 'Too many people have their house too warm'. This last statement would be particularly counter-productive because it emphasizes that the social norm may well be a wasteful use of energy. It says that other people have excessively hot houses, and therefore may make it seem attractive to run the thermostat high to fit in with the neighbours. Stressing the benefits in terms of social approval of taking the 'good' action, rather than noting the deleterious effects of 'bad' actions, is now a widely understood principle – though surprisingly often ignored in the advertising of consumer goods. Research findings separately show that instructions that tell people what not to do are more effective than those that simply describe the effects of actually doing environmentally destructive acts. For example, a statement that said 'Don't take aeroplane flights because they are one of the most important causes of global warming' would be better than saying 'Those who take aeroplane flights are helping to increase global warming'. Researchers seem to be saying that people absorb a strong injunction not to do something more effectively than they do with simple statements of fact – for example, 'Stop smoking' is better than 'Smoking kills'.

The lesson for those interested in changing human behaviour is that communications messages aimed at fostering better behaviour in response to global warming need to stress how many other people are behaving, as well as to frame the slogan with a strong statement of what not to do. We need to use the dark arts of the advertising agency to help us make carbon saving more fashionable.

Energy saving begets energy saving

Those who have tried to make real cuts in their own carbon emissions all know a little secret. Unlike, say, dieting or giving up tobacco, conserving energy is so easy that it almost becomes addictive. A small effort can cut household electricity bills by 10 per cent and, once achieved, a little twitch on the heating thermostat can save another 10 per cent or so off the gas bill.

Why is this? If reducing energy use is so easy, why didn't we all start earlier? The reason probably lies in the insidious and unconscious growth in our personal energy demand. Energy is both cheap and largely invisible. If I leave the computer on overnight, it doesn't cost me a measurable amount of money and, in fact, it would be very difficult to see from the meter just how much energy I had used. But once I take a decision not to allow appliances to stay on unnecessarily, it is rather simple to turn everything off, and within three months the bills will be lower. If I become habituated to not wasting energy and make it a normal daily activity, it becomes easy.

The painlessness of energy saving is most noticed by people who install their own renewable energy systems, such as solar hot water. The mere act of installing the equipment seems to produce a hugely increased sensitivity to energy use. I noticed this when we put a hot water and photovoltaic system on our roof. The apparent 'savings' from the solar hot water system were about three times what could have been expected. We noticed an implausibly high figure for the reduction in electricity consumption as well. We're still quite large consumers; but we cut our bills by far more than could have been explained by the relatively small quantity of the sun's energy falling on our roof. This was not unusual; the phenomenon has been seen across the world. Before, our usage had been gently drifting upwards – like most British households; but immediately after the panels went up, the meters stopped spinning so fast and haven't increased since. I suppose the most important change for us was a decision not to run the house at 20°C in winter. We moved the thermostat down to 18°, and did notice the difference, but only for a matter of days. Within a few weeks, 18° seemed as warm as 20° had before. The gradual ratcheting upwards must have been a sort of mild addiction; we had needed a 'fix' of rising temperatures to keep feeling warm. But as with, say, strong coffee, one can take a decision to reduce one's consumption and the pain is only mild and temporary.

The upbeat tone of the last few pages has had a purpose. Many people feel a gloomy despair about climate change. Individuals can do so little directly to affect the future health of the global atmosphere. What I have tried to suggest is that there are reasons for optimism. All great social movements were started by determined and slightly eccentric individuals who refused to accept the prevailing social norms. Active carbon avoidance is a principle that is worth pursuing and does have effects on friends and neighbours. It can become a communal activity. The future of the human race is dependent upon sufficient numbers of individuals eventually being persuaded to join the movement.

2

how our lives generate emissions

The UK's yearly national environmental accounts suggest an emissions figure of about 10 tonnes of greenhouse gases per person. This excludes international aviation and shipping. More importantly, it also excludes the footprint of the goods and services imported into the UK. An increasing fraction of the UK's goods are made abroad, often in China, but also in Germany and other countries which specialize in manufacturing. Calculating the emissions that arise in other places in order to make things for the UK market is not a simple task and researchers have produced very different estimates. My rough approximation is that it accounts for about three tonnes per person, adding over a quarter to the UK's real greenhouse gas output.[1]

The calculations in this book suggest that the average individual has emissions from their home and travel totalling about 5 tonnes. This is made up as shown in Figures 2.2 and 2.3.

In addition to home and travel, we need to consider the carbon impact of the things we buy. Over the course of 12 months, the calculations in this book suggest that our consumption adds another 4 tonnes to typical emissions. Food is the largest element, but clothing, paper and consumer electronics are also important. This figure is somewhat less accurate than the numbers for home and travel because we cannot directly measure greenhouse gas emissions for many things that we buy. Nevertheless, the 4 tonne figure is broadly accurate and takes our individual direct and indirect emissions up to around 9 tonnes per person out of the 14 tonne total including imports. This is nearly 65 per cent of the total. The remainder is composed of other activities such as manufacturing, construction, freight transport, and other commercial and public services.[2]

The numbers show all too clearly just how demanding our targets are. If we want to move to 2 tonnes a head, we need to make very substantial changes across the economy and in individual habits. It is simply impossible to achieve the 80–90 per cent cut that we

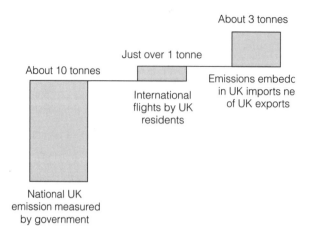

Figure 2.1 *The make-up of average emissions per person*

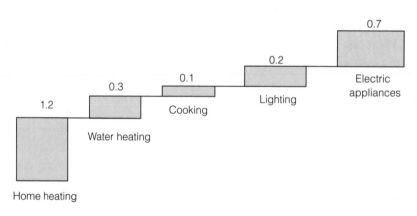

Figure 2.2 *Average emissions from running the home (tonnes)*

need without really substantial improvements both in energy efficiency and, more fundamentally, the way we live our high-consuming Western lives.

The following steps are vital parts of the shift to a lower-carbon economy.

1   huge improvements in home insulation to reduce gas use;
2   near-complete decarbonization of electricity production (so that we get negligible emissions from lighting and home appliances and can switch to electricity for home heating and much transport);

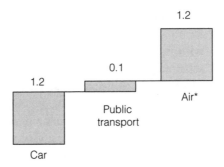

Figure 2.3 *Average emissions from transport (tonnes)*

Note: * Includes a twofold multiplier for non-CO_2 effects

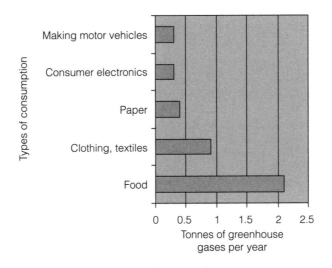

Figure 2.4 *Average emissions from purchased goods*

3   much more fuel-efficient cars, probably powered by electric batteries;
4   large numbers of people deciding not to fly except in emergencies;
5   a substantial move away from livestock farming in developed countries and a switch towards the use of fresh, local and unprocessed plant-based foods;
6   reduction in clothing purchases and a move away from using wool and, possibly, cotton;
7   a substantial reduction in the purchasing of other goods.

This package of measures could reduce the emissions of the typical person to the level that might just meet the UK government's targets for 2020 and beyond. The portfolio mixes substantial lifestyle changes with improvements in technology and investments in energy efficiency. The following chapters try to show how intelligent choices can help householders make substantial and fairly pain-free reductions in energy use.

When the first edition of this book was published, it looked to me as though these changes might help reduce emissions to around 3 tonnes a head, as long as we each made our own investments to 'offset' our own indirect emissions by, for example, investing in communally owned wind farms. Since then, the government has raised its own targets for emissions reductions from 60 per cent to 80 per cent of 1990 levels. This means that we will also need huge improvements in technology, principally in the reduction of emissions from electricity generation. As well as directly allowing us to use electric appliances without a guilty conscience, it means we can switch to home heating by electricity, probably through the use of heat pumps. We can also hope to run most cars on electric batteries by 2030. There is more about this later in the book.

part I

---

direct
emissions

3

home heating

Many people do not realize the importance of home heating in determining how much carbon dioxide we generate. It is, for example, far more important than emissions produced by our use of electricity in the home. Very approximately, the typical UK house uses about 280kWh of gas and electricity per year for every square metre of living space. Space heating represents over 170kWh/year of this total.[1]

The typical house (containing an average of 2.3 people) produces over 2.7 tonnes of carbon dioxide per year just to operate the central heating boiler. This means 1.2 tonnes per person. Heating the house is therefore responsible for nearly 10 per cent of a person's total responsibility for emissions, and about 20 per cent of the greenhouse gases that we can directly control.

What can be done about this? Four measures in particular are worth taking:

1   New boiler: the typical home has a boiler that is about 75 per cent efficient at burning gas and turning it into usable heat in the home. Buying a new condensing boiler with maximum efficiency takes this up to 90 per cent or so. The savings may be as much as 0.2 tonnes per person per year. A new boiler might cost about £1500.
2   Reducing internal winter temperatures will also have a substantial effect. A 1 degree reduction may decrease fuel needs by as much as 15 per cent and takes total emissions per head down to not much more than 0.8 tonnes.[2] (Later in the chapter we try to show why small reductions in central heating temperature can have a major effect). Initially lower temperatures seem unattractive; but the typical householder completely acclimatizes within days to a temperature of 19° rather than 20°C.
3   Better insulation, particularly of cavity walls and roofs, is important. Insulating the house's cavity wall might reduce emissions by 0.3–0.5 tonnes per person. Better insulation is heavily subsidized and will generally cost less than £250 for the cavity walls.
4   Intelligent central heating controls will also help. A good heating programmer will save as much as 10 per cent of the cost of gas used for heating.

Unfortunately, one cannot simply add all of these savings together to get the approximate reduction from taking all four steps. Better insulation, for example, means lower gas need, which reduces the benefit from installing a better boiler. Taking all four measures might cut 40 per cent from the heating bill and reduce personal emissions by 0.5 tonnes.

The first edition of this book commented that gas use for home heating was continuing to rise, despite the effect of improved insulation and better construction standards. The impulses driving up energy use range from the understandable wish to heat our homes better in cold winters, to the rapid increase in the number of households as the UK population expands and household size falls. More households, of whatever size, add to heating demands because each one needs to be heated. The good news is that this increase appears to have tapered off. It may be increasing gas prices or the government's support for better insulation in older homes, but the total amount of gas used by British houses does seem to be starting to fall. We'll find later in this book that this is still not the case for electricity.

One of the main factors increasing gas use was a long-run tendency for homes to be heated to higher and higher temperatures. Average winter house temperatures rose sharply from about 12 degrees in 1970 and hit 18 degrees across the whole house in about 2002. Since most people seem to have a desired comfort level of about 21° or 22°C, house thermostats could yet go higher if gas prices fall back from their current (September 2009) levels.

British homes can be heated by gas, oil, solid fuel or electricity, usually from storage radiators heated by cheaper overnight power. About 80 per cent of UK households are on the mains gas supply and almost all of these use gas for heating. We'll mostly look at the patterns of demand in these homes; but first it is worth mentioning that other countries have much more efficient means of heating their houses. The box on page 43 offers two examples of countries already heating their homes more efficiently, on average, than the UK. Homeowners unable to heat their houses with gas should look instead at electric heat pumps (see page 247). For an electrically heated home (but not necessarily one on the gas network), these pumps should save money and reduce emissions.

Table 3.1 *Measures to reduce carbon emission from home heating*

Option	Reduction per house	Reduction per person	Comment
Install condensing boiler	0.4 tonnes of CO_2	0.2 tonnes of CO_2	Very important if the house is large or badly insulated and the existing boiler is more than ten years old.
Install cavity wall insulation	1.1 tonnes of CO_2 (theoretical maximum for average home)	0.5 tonnes of CO_2	Over a third of UK homes still have uninsulated cavities.
	0.7 tonnes of CO_2 (actual probable reduction)	0.3 tonnes of CO_2	This is a clear first step and makes very good financial sense, particularly for detached homes.
Lower internal winter temperature by 1°C	0.3 tonnes of CO_2	0.1 tonnes of CO_2	It is also important not to heat unused rooms.
Better central heating controls (e.g. purchase of intelligent programmer such as a Dataterm)	0.3 tonnes of CO_2	0.1 tonnes of CO_2	Data is sparse on this, but this estimate seems reasonable.
All measures taken together	1.2 tonnes of CO_2	0.5 tonnes of CO_2	This was a difficult calculation to do and actual results may be at variance with these numbers.

THE HEAT BALANCE OF THE HOUSE

This is a complex section. Its primary purpose is to demonstrate the importance of two things:

1   Domestic boilers use more kilowatt hours of gas than they deliver as useful heat into the house. With an efficiency of 75 per cent, one quarter of the gas used is wasted because it leaves the house as hot exhaust.

2   Houses are heated by many more devices than just a domestic boiler. All of our lights, electrical appliances, hot water, the warmth of our bodies and sun coming in through the windows also heat our homes. Incidentally, this means that some advanced modern houses, such as the Passivhaus buildings mentioned in Box 3.1, can do completely without central heating boilers.

BOX 3.1 – HOME HEATING NEEDS: DATA FROM OTHER COUNTRIES

SWEDEN

A large fraction of Sweden's heating needs are met by district heating plants, usually combining electricity generation and heating distributed in the form of hot water to local housing. Each Swede typically gets 4500kWh/year of heating from such systems. This compares to a total central heating demand of about 6000kWh/year per person in the UK. These district heating plants are efficient and increasingly use low-carbon fuels, such as wood.

GERMANY

The average heat usage by German houses is better than in the UK even though winter temperatures are generally lower. The average German house uses 159kWh/year per square metre. In the UK, this figure is over 170kWh/year.[3] The German Passivhaus Institute is the most effective body in the world at promoting extremely energy-efficient homes, requiring less than 15kWh/year of heating per square metre. For a typical UK house size, this would mean gas consumption of 8 per cent of the current average. The Passivhaus movement has now built 10,000 homes around Europe, mostly in Germany itself. These homes incorporate effective capture of the sun's energy, excellent insulation and a ventilation system that heats the incoming air with the stale air as it leaves the house. The primary importance of the Passivhaus movement is that it demonstrates what can be achieved using thoughtful design. The incremental cost of the Passivhaus elements, such as triple-glazed windows, is said to be €8200 (about £5000) for a new terraced house.[4] British building companies disagree with these figures suggesting that the extra costs are much greater. Nevertheless, Passivhaus building techniques are gradually being adopted all around the world. If the German estimates are correct, the incremental Passivhaus costs would be recouped in lower energy bills in little more than six years for a typical new property. But larger UK building companies have found it expensive and difficult to match the energy efficiency gains achieved on the Continent. Passiv buildings require real care and accuracy when being constructed – not something that the UK construction industry is famous for.

Some readers may wish to skip these pages and just accept my assertion that the average home takes about 14,000kWh/year from the gas main to fire its boiler. This turns into about 10,500kWh/year of usable heat, to which can be added about 6000kWh/year of heat from other sources. So, the house actually gets an input of about 16,500kWh/year to keep us warm, even though the gas bill for heating is only 14,000kWh/year. The purpose of this section is to show how these figures are derived and may only be of interest to people like me, who never believe a number until they have worked it out for themselves. The next few pages give us the background data to enable us to estimate roughly how much energy-saving measures might assist the householder in reducing costs and carbon emissions. After the background work, suggestions for practical measures to reduce home heating costs and carbon start on page 49.

Annual average gas use for home heating adds about 2.7 tonnes of carbon dioxide to the atmosphere. Divided by the typical number of occupants, the contribution of home heating to global warming gases is about 1.2 tonnes a year, or almost 10 per cent of all emissions. If we are interested in reducing our personal responsibility for global warming, household heating matters. And as bills continue to climb, the financial benefit of aiming for best practice is pretty important too.

By how much do gas bills vary according to the type of the house? Accurate figures are not easily available, not least because insulation standards vary so much. But, at the highest level of approximation, typical gas consumption may vary in the way illustrated in Figure 3.1. Readers may find that their own houses are larger than the typical UK property, which is only about 80 square metres, or less than 900 square feet (a total floor area of 30 feet by 30 feet).

Of course, a semi-detached may be small or large, well insulated or draughty, and run at a high or a low temperature. So, these numbers don't actually say much. Nevertheless, they

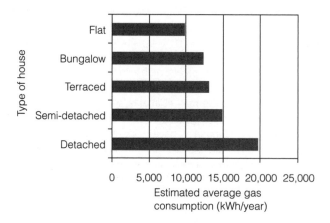

Figure 3.1 *How gas usage for heating may vary with type of house*

Note: These figures are calculated by multiplying the degree of variation of the typical heat loss rate (watts per degree of heating) for the different types of house by the average gas usage of 14,000kWh. These figures should be treated as little better than guesses; but I have included them because many people ask me for an estimate of typical heating bills for different types of houses.

are a useful reminder that house size affects heating bills, as does the number of walls shared with other households. All other things being equal, a large flat of similar size to a small detached house will have lower fuel bills because it is partly insulated by the adjoining properties, whereas all the walls of the house are exposed to the ambient air temperature.

Per household, total gas use (for water heating, cooking and heating) is about 19,000kWh/year. So, on average, heating is responsible for about three-quarters of the total volume of gas demand for homes in the UK.

Unfortunately, the calculation of the energy used to heat our homes is much more complicated than simply assessing the amount of gas that is burned in the central heating boiler. There are five important other considerations:

BOX 3.2 – WHAT DOES 14,000 KILOWATT HOURS ACTUALLY MEAN IN TERMS OF METER READINGS AND COST TO THE HOUSEHOLDER?

Gas meters don't record the number of kilowatt hours a household uses. They actually measure the number of cubic metres, or cubic feet for older meters, of gas flowing into the house. The energy content of this gas can change as a result of very slightly varying pressure or gas composition. Gas supplied from the North Sea is largely methane; but gas from Russia, for example, contains a slightly higher percentage of other hydrocarbons and is a marginally better fuel in terms of the heat generated by a cubic metre. Each period, gas suppliers calculate the energy value of the gas they pump through the pipes, and your bill will specify a 'calorific value' per cubic metre. They then actually charge you for the number of kilowatt hours supplied as a function of this calorific value. To get from cubic metres to kilowatt hours, you need to multiply by about 11.45. For older meters, which record in hundreds of cubic feet, not metres, you need to multiply this again by 2.83.

At the time of writing (September 2009), the price of gas to domestic consumers is about 3.5 pence per kilowatt hour from the largest supplier, British Gas, although you can get it cheaper elsewhere. I am going to use the 3.5 pence figure in this chapter. But, in addition, some suppliers charge substantially more for the first units supplied each quarter. In effect, this is a standing charge which you cannot avoid paying and all the improvements you make as a result of suggestions in this chapter will not reduce this portion of the bill. At 3.5 pence per kilowatt hour, plus the higher prices for the first kilowatt hours each quarter, the average home costs over £500 a year to heat. Add in the costs of water heating and cooking, and the total cost rises to about £700.

1   Not all gas is turned into usable heat. Boilers work with varying levels of efficiency, and the oldest models may well only deliver 60 per cent of the energy consumed. The rest is evacuated to the outside as hot exhausts. The typical boiler in the UK stock is probably about 75 per cent efficient, and I use this average in my calculations. Modern 'condensing' boilers capture a much larger percentage of the heat and deliver about 90 per cent efficiency, although it some circumstances this high figure will not be achieved.

2   Homes typically contain other sources of heat. Electrical appliances act to heat our houses, even when they are sitting in standby mode in the middle of the day. Precisely how much energy our TVs and washing machines replace is a subject of debate; but, increasingly, our houses are full of electrical devices acting as small radiators. Those who say that their houses are entirely heated by gas central heating are, therefore, strictly speaking, wrong. All our homes are also heated by expensive and carbon-intensive electricity, even in summer.

3   The two other key sources of internal heating are, first, what is delightfully known as 'metabolic' and, second, solar. Metabolic heating is you and me, wandering about our houses giving off about 120W in heat. Solar heating from the sun varies enormously, but may be as much as 15 to 20 per cent of the total useful heat demand in some houses, particularly those with large south-facing windows. We are, in effect, living in greenhouses and capture some heat from solar radiation, even in the winter. Passivhaus buildings capture more. (The estimates below exclude the impact of solar radiation when the house is already warm enough in summer. Similar reductions are made for all other indirect sources of heat, although these estimates are subject to considerable uncertainty.)

4   Cooking food also helps to heat the home.

5   Hot water use also serves to heat the home – for example, taking a bath heats the bathroom.

There are various ways of calculating how much heat is used in the house. Using one set of data, the net balance looks approximately as depicted in Figure 3.2. I stress that these are only estimates from one source and, compared to other sources, they emphasize in particular the heat derived from appliances, water heating and solar gain. I will go on to give my own estimates on page 48; but I provide the data in Figure 3.2 because they are derived from a very reputable source.

These statistics suggest that only about 55 per cent of the heating of a home fuelled by gas is from the useful heat delivered by the boiler. The figures are from the stupendously detailed *Domestic Heating Fact File 2003*, published by the Building Research Establishment (BRE)[5] (I have used data from this wonderful source, and its later updates, frequently in the following pages). Other sources, including other BRE texts, suggest that the figure should be nearer two-thirds and, on balance, I think we need to use these different estimates.

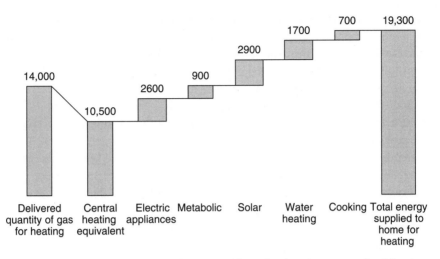

Figure 3.2 *One calculation of sources of heat for the average gas-fired home*

Note: All figures are in kilowatt hours per year (kWh/year) and were calculated in 2001.

Table 3.2 *Average annual heating need for England and Wales, 2005*

Month	Average 24-hour temperature (°C)	Is heating assumed to be on?	Heating need (°C)
January	5.7	Yes	14.3
February	3.9	Yes	16.1
March	6.7	Yes	13.3
April	8.6	Yes	11.4
May	11.0	Yes	9.0
June	15.0	No	–
July	16.3	No	–
August	15.8	No	–
September	14.8	No	–
October	12.6	No	–
November	6.0	Yes	14.0
December	4.2	Yes	15.8
Average	10.1		
Average during heating season	6.7		13.4

Another way of calculating the total heating demand for a typical gas-fired house is to estimate how much energy it would take to heat the home to temperatures that we know are characteristic. In 2001, the average centrally heated home was kept at just over 19°C. For ease of calculation, I have assumed a figure of 20 degrees in my calculation.

Table 3.2 provides the average temperatures for England and Wales during the months of 2005 and the number of degrees of heating necessary to get a house to 20°C. It then assesses the average amount of heating, in degrees, over the period in which the gas boiler would typically be on.

The figures in Table 3.2 show that the heating system (the boiler, and all the other elements that warm the house) had to keep a house an average of 13.4°C above the external temperature for seven months of the year. We know from BRE data that the average UK house loses about 250W (0.25kW) for every degree of difference between the internal and external temperatures. What does this mean? If the inside of the house is 1 degree hotter than the outside, 250W (the equivalent of two or three large old-fashioned light bulbs, or the metabolic energy radiated by two people) will be moving from the house to the outside. So, to keep a 10 degree difference uses 2.5kW, and a 13.4 degree gradient needs 3.4kW.

We can use this figure to estimate how much heating the house will require over the heating season. If, for example, the house needed to be heated for 4000 hours a year, then the total heating demand would be about 13,200kWh/year or so (3.4kW × 4000). Not all of this would be the boiler, of course, and some heat would be provided by the electric appliances and other sources. Add in the losses from leaving the windows open and opening the doors, and I think the average house probably needs total heat, including the boiler, of about 16,500kWh/year.

I therefore propose to use the following numbers in the rest of this chapter:

- Delivered energy for gas heating in the typical house: 14,000kWh/year. This is a little higher than is suggested by national data from the *Digest of UK Energy Statistics.*[6]
- Usable heat produced by the boiler: 10,500kWh/year (meaning that 3500kWh/year are lost to the outside, or, by coincidence, about the same as total home electricity consumption).
- Actual heat needed by house, including the 6000kWh/year from other sources, such as electric appliances, cooking and solar gain: 16,500kWh/year.

Where the range of possible heat demands makes a difference to the calculations in the following text, I have tried to identify the issue and then provide other numbers for comparison.

My calculations assume that 14,000kWh/year is the amount of gas delivered and burned for space heating purposes in the typical home on the mains gas network. Over the course of a typical heating season, lasting perhaps seven months, this is over 65kWh a day, costing about £2.30. What can be done to reduce this figure?

The possible steps can be divided into three main groups:

1 Improve the efficiency of the gas boiler and the controls to the central heating system.
2 Upgrade the insulation in the house or improve the capture of other sources of heat, such as solar radiation.
3 Introduce behavioural changes, such as reduced internal temperatures or ceasing to heat some rooms. Or, indeed, move to a smaller or a better-insulated home.

THE BENEFITS OF A NEW CONDENSING BOILER

Modern 'condensing' boilers convert more of the fuel they consume into useful heat for the central heating system. The exhaust gases, including water vapour, are cooled by a heat exchanger, which extracts useful heat energy. The vapour condenses into water and is drained away. By contrast, older non-condensing boilers push out large volumes of hot gas into the air outside the house, wasting the energy that it contains.

Modern condensing boilers operate at about 90 per cent efficiency. Non-condensing systems are much less efficient. Figure 3.3 provides some estimates of characteristic efficiency for older boilers.[7]

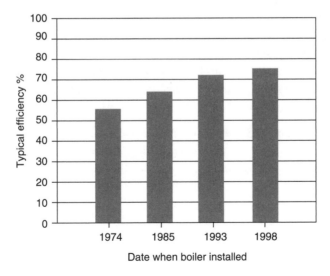

Figure 3.3 *Efficiency estimates for non-condensing gas-fired systems*

Note: Data from Market Transformation Programme (2005) *The Domestic Heating Boiler Energy Model: Methods and Assumptions*, Appendix B, Table 1, p18, Market Transformation Programme, Future Energy Solutions, Didcot, UK (see www.mtprog.com).

So, for example, a condensing boiler replacing a non-condensing version installed in 1985 will increase the efficiency of the use of gas by 23 per cent. For our typical household needing 10,500kWh of heat, the energy value of the gas delivered to the household will fall substantially.

A household switching in this way would save 2333kWh annually, or about 0.4 tonnes of carbon dioxide. The saving in gas costs for a typical house would be about £80 a year at September 2009 gas prices. The savings from reducing costs to heat water (perhaps £20) would be additional.

Recent changes in regulations mean that almost all new boilers now have to be of the condensing type. Therefore, the householder's decision is not whether to buy the slightly more expensive condensing boiler or not. It is *when* to replace an existing non-condensing boiler with a new one. Since boilers often last 20 years or more, the householder's choice may well be a voluntary one. Does it make sense, for example, to bring forward the replacement date of the home boiler by five years in order to get improved efficiency and lower carbon emissions?

The answer depends upon the age of the existing boiler and upon the level of usage in the house. A big house with an old boiler would benefit enormously from replacing the central heating furnace.

The figures in Table 3.4 show the importance of shifting to a condensing boiler if your existing furnace is more than ten years old. In a big house, with a boiler installed in 1993, carbon dioxide emissions might currently be almost 4 tonnes a year from heating alone (a need for usable heat of 15,000kWh/year, but almost 21,000kWh/year of gas burned). A condensing boiler would reduce this by about 20 per cent, or by 0.8 tonnes of CO_2. The savings in cash would not be enormous – about £140 plus, perhaps, £40 for the reduced cost of water heating – but the benefits to the atmosphere are clear and would make a real difference to a household's overall emissions. Of course, if gas prices change, all of the savings will change proportionately.

Table 3.3 *Gas savings from replacing a typical boiler with a condensing variety*

	Typical efficiency	Gas delivered to provide 10,500kWh of usable heat
Traditional boiler installed during the late 1990s	75%	14,000kWh
New condensing boiler installed in 2007	90%	11,667kWh
Saving		2333kWh

The cost of installing a condensing boiler five years before it is strictly necessary depends upon whether you have to borrow money to pay for it. If so, then a typical installation with a full cost of £1400 might result in a five-year interest charge of £560. This cost, divided by the tonnes of carbon dioxide avoided, is shown in Table 3.5.

Table 3.4 *Savings from installing a condensing gas boiler*

	Boiler age	High gas need	Medium gas need	Low gas need
Usable heat needed (kWh/year)		15,000	10,500	7000
Savings from installing condensing boiler (kWh per year)	1974	10,119	7083	4722
	1984	5721	4005	2670
	1993	4167	2917	1944
	1998	3604	2523	1682
Annual savings in cash (3.5 pence per kWh)	1974	354	248	165
	1984	200	140	93
	1993	146	102	68
	1998	126	88	59
Annual saving in CO_2 (tonnes)	1974	1.92	1.35	0.90
	1984	1.09	0.76	0.51
	1993	0.79	0.55	0.37
	1998	0.68	0.48	0.3

Table 3.5 *Cost per tonne of carbon dioxide avoided*

	Boiler age	High gas need	Medium gas need	Low gas need
Cost per tonne of CO_2 emissions avoided	1974	£58	£83	£125
	1984	£103	£147	£221
	1993	£141	£202	£303
	1998	£164	£234	£351

Note: Assumes savings are generated for five years because of the early purchase of the boiler, that the boiler costs £1400, including fitting, and that the householder pays interest of 8 per cent per annum on this expenditure.

For smaller houses, the carbon dioxide benefits of fitting a new boiler look expensive to attain. For bigger houses, the arguments are much stronger, even for houses with relatively recently installed conventional boilers.

But condensing boilers have not been popular. Until the government made it almost mandatory to use condensing technology, the rate of installation was slow. Plumbers complained that they were difficult to fit and unreliable. Others claimed that the postulated savings were difficult to achieve. Householders were wary of the plume of steam that the boiler emitted, not realizing that this steam showed that the boiler was working properly. People have not embraced this technology readily.

The issues behind these complaints appear to have been resolved. Reliability is now said to be good, and the installers are more confident that the boilers really do operate at higher levels of efficiency. The gas companies have made a better job of explaining why the plume of water vapour outside the house indicated that the boiler was more, not less, efficient (because the exhaust gases emitted from the boiler are at a much lower temperature than conventional boilers, the water vapour condenses into steam much more rapidly and closer to the house). Condensing boilers have been the norm in parts of continental Europe for up to 20 years, so it would be amazing if there were genuine problems of reliability.

Nevertheless, boilers are almost invariably bought as distress purchases, when the old stager under the stairs has finally breathed its last. Virtually nobody buys a boiler voluntarily. As a result, active selling of condensing boilers has been limited to a few organizations, such as British Gas. No doubt as a result of high sales costs, these organizations have also tended to offer very high prices. My household received a quote of over £2500 to replace our boiler with a condensing boiler from British Gas, including quotes for some ancillary pipes and valves that are over twice the price of what is readily obtainable elsewhere. Households should be able to get a reasonably powerful condensing boiler for about £1400. The reluctance to change boilers before the old one expires must change: we need to make the plume of vapour outside the house a visible badge of the household's environmental credentials.

OIL CENTRAL HEATING

The advantages of using condensing boilers for homes using oil are somewhat lower than for gas. Oil-fired boilers have traditionally been slightly more efficient than the gas equivalent of the same year, and recently installed non-condensing units are only slightly less efficient than the condensing equivalent. The best advice is probably to wait until your oil-fired boiler really does need replacing and then go for a condensing version. Remember that the boiler itself has a reasonable amount of fossil fuel energy embedded in it.

COMBINATION BOILERS AND BOILERS WITH INTEGRATED SOLAR PANELS

Combination boilers (usually called 'combi' boilers) don't have hot water storage tanks, but for central heating purposes can be considered the same as conventional boilers. An increasing number of suppliers are now also selling new boilers with integrated solar hot water panels for the roof. The hot water will be used for the taps and showers, not for central heating. So they will also not significantly affect the figures in this chapter.

BOILER SIZING

Plumbers will generally install a boiler that is too large for the job that it has to handle. One eco-renovation website comments that in one case the plumber's rule of thumb would have resulted in a boiler of three times the necessary power being installed.[8] No doubt the basis for this conventional rule is that no one ever got sued for installing a boiler that was too big, but that one that is too small would result in continuous complaints that it didn't heat the house.

Getting the right size does matter: boilers work most efficiently if they are working constantly. A boiler that it is too big will be turning on and off every few minutes, reducing its life, but also wasting heat as it fires up, cools down and then fires up again. Probably as importantly, a condensing boiler that is too big in relation to the needs of the house may not actually condense effectively because of the high temperature of the water returning to the boiler. There are good energy-efficiency reasons for not buying a boiler that is too powerful.

Unfortunately, to get the right sized boiler is not a simple matter. In theory, the calculation is easy: you need to work out the heat loss of the house on a very cold winter night and then get a boiler that can deliver this. Across the UK housing stock, this averages about 250W per degree difference between the desired inside temperature and the external figure. Bigger and older houses will lose more. For the average house, and a 20 degree difference between inside and outside temperatures, the boiler should therefore be about 5kW – or 17,000 British thermal units (BTUs) per hour – to maintain the desired temperature. Increase this figure to provide the extra push to get the house to warm up after a cold night and to cover water heating needs, and the average house might need 15kW.

You will find that this is regarded as an absurdly small boiler by plumbers, who will point to the relatively small cost difference between a 15kW boiler and the 30kW variety (perhaps £120). Ignore this and remind your installer that cars with bigger engines use more fuel, even when travelling at the same speed as the smaller-engined equivalent. However, do not ignore the second line of a plumber's defence, which is that a bigger boiler will get a house up from a low temperature more rapidly than its diminutive cousin, the boiler that just meets your heating needs. You will need to make your own mind up about how important this feature is. But you should remember that the best boiler system is one that is appropriately sized, combined with good controls that mean that it fires up when it is needed and not at other times (see the following section).

BETTER USE OF CENTRAL HEATING CONTROLS

Very little research has been done on the impact of improving central heating controls or on getting people to use their existing controls properly. As a result, this section is long on commentary and short on numbers.

Generally, a home has at least five separate control systems that affect fuel use. They are:

1   a wall thermostat;
2   a programmer for the central heating system;
3   thermostatic valves on radiators;
4   a boiler power regulator; and
5   a thermostat on the hot water tank.

The first four of these affect the efficiency of the central heating system, and the fifth influences the cost of a household's hot water.

THE WALL THERMOSTAT

Usually positioned at a central point in the house, the thermostat measures the air temperature.[9] It allows the householder to set a temperature level at which the boiler will turn on, provided that the central heating programmer is set to allow boiler use at that time. The boiler will turn off when the temperature rises above the level set on the thermostat.

Almost all room thermostats are turned up or down by rotating a dial. The typical product is inaccurate and imprecise. Furthermore, the conventional thermostat will tend to cause temperatures to cycle up and down. Most of them are constructed to turn on the heating when the temperature drops a degree or so below the set level, and to turn off when it reaches a degree or so higher (check this on your control: the click that tells the heating to turn off is about 2 degrees above the temperature that tells it to turn on). A graph of room temperature when the thermostat was set to 20°C would show the actual temperature moving in a saw-tooth pattern between 21° and 19°C.

Typical low-quality analogue thermostats (the ones fitted in almost all UK homes) result in inefficient use of gas, even when the owner knows what he or she is doing. They don't, for example, instruct the boiler to start earlier in the morning when the temperature is really low, or cut off when the temperature is rising fast and closing in on the target warmth. These would be obvious and easily programmable features in more sophisticated digital devices. There is no doubt in my mind that this would result in lower fuel bills, if only because users ought to have more confidence in the effects of their thermostat. In general, the theory goes, it would be set lower. (Despite their apparent simplicity, thermostats are not intuitive. For example, I find it very difficult to explain to otherwise highly rational individuals that turning the thermostat up when entering a cold house will not increase the speed at which the house warms up.)

Furthermore, I suspect that intelligent digital thermostats would save energy by allowing households to start heating later in the early morning, and turning it off earlier at night. It would be particularly valuable when combined with programming controls, allowing the users to set varying times for different days of the week.

One UK company produces a device that appears to deliver all of the electronic functions that one would want in a room thermostat.[10] This product, called a Dataterm, is essentially a mixture of a room thermostat and a central heating programmer. It is highly intelligent – that is, for a thermostat – and, for example, can learn how fast an individual house warms up. The claimed improvements are impressive, with two large local authority installations suggesting savings of between 17 and 25 per cent on overall gas bills. Customers quoted on the company's website say that users find it easy to operate.

Comments, reviews and independent data from domestic households are scarce for the Dataterm or other intelligent programmers. Therefore, I hesitate to recommend it; but it does appear to be a highly effective improvement to existing thermostats and will certainly give an improved level of comfort. If it works as it claims, it will allow the user much closer control over temperatures throughout the day.

The device itself is around £250 and installation would probably cost another £80 or so. If it saved 10 per cent of domestic heating bills, which seems a reasonable possibility to me, it would reduce the gas bill by £45 a year at current prices and cut almost 0.3 tonnes off carbon emissions from the typical house. If it lasts 15 years before being replaced, the cost per tonne of carbon saved would be about £70, which makes it better value than installing a condensing boiler (of course, it could be installed in addition to a condensing boiler, in which case the savings would be slightly lower because the percentage gas saving would be similar, but the gas used would be lower). The device would pay for itself in about seven years.

CENTRAL HEATING PROGRAMMER

The programmer sets the times at which the central heating can go on and off. It is, of course, over-ridden by the room thermostat if that device says that the house is already warm enough. Some research carried out for the Market Transformation Programme, one of the UK government's climate change research bodies, suggests that many people have no idea how these programmers work and leave them on all the time, adjusting their internal temperature by yanking the room thermostat back and forward. When they want the boiler to go off, they turn the thermostat down and, conversely, turn the heating on by turning the thermostat to the right.

The readers of this book are probably not quite as crude as this. But even energy-aware folk can be confused by the difficulties of setting a complex modern programmer with its ability to set different start and finish times for different days of the week. I haven't found any estimates of how much might be saved by careful setting of when the programmer turns the heating system on and off. I suspect that saving 5 per cent of the overall fuel bill might be possible by a householder giving very close attention to setting the timings of the programmer to minimize the time that the boiler is working.

In an ideal world, houses would be fitted with intelligent room thermostats that doubled as heating programmers. The Dataterm device described above carries out both functions. But characteristically in UK homes, the programmer is sited in an obscure location, often next to the boiler itself. Unlike the thermostat, which is regarded as aesthetically acceptable, the programmer is not fit for public view. This reduces the chance of it being effectively used to moderate the household's gas consumption.

RADIATOR THERMOSTATS

One would be hard put to find anybody who uses these devices thoughtfully. They sit on top of the inlet pipe into a radiator and allow the homeowner to regulate the temperature in individual rooms. Properly employed, these rotation knobs could be used to maintain slightly lower temperatures in some rooms than in others. It doesn't actually seem to work that way, and they are only ever used (at least in my experience) to turn radiators either fully on or off. The useful gradations of temperature are beyond the skills of most householders, including me.

It is, of course, a mistake to put a thermostatic control on a radiator in the same room as the main thermostat. If the radiator control is set lower than the room thermostat, and the house is well insulated internally, then the boiler will continue working furiously, heating other parts of the house to excessive levels until sufficient hot air leaks into the thermostat room to turn off the heating system.

UPGRADE THE INSULATION IN THE HOUSE OR IMPROVE THE RETENTION OF OTHER SOURCES OF HEAT, SUCH AS SOLAR RADIATION

The previous section looked at ways of ensuring that fuel inputs to the house are efficiently converted to the right level of usable heat. Next, we need to look at how to ensure that this usable heat is retained. The scope for improvement here is considerable. The average UK home is rated E on the European Union's A to G classification of energy efficiency of domestic buildings.[11]

Homeowners can consider six main areas of improvement in home insulation:

1   cavity walls;
2   loft insulation;
3   improvement in windows;
4   improvements in doors;
5   draught proofing;
6   radiator reflectors.

It may be useful to remind ourselves of the main exit routes from the home for our increasingly expensive heat. Figure 3.4 provides approximate figures for heat loss from different parts of a typical house, losing heat at almost 250W for every degree of temperature difference between the inside and the outside.

These figures mean that for a typical house of about 80 square metres (800–900 square feet), the heat from a large light bulb is getting through the walls for every degree by which the house is raised above the outdoor temperature. For a 10 degree difference – usually called a gradient – between the internal temperature and the air outside, the walls lose the heat output from a single-bar electric radiator. Much of that is leaving the house through cracks and what are known as 'thermal bridges' – places where heat is readily conducted from the inside to the open air. Poor construction techniques make these bridges very common even in apparently well-insulated houses. Figure 3.5 shows how heat produced in the house is dissipated through the elements of the building.

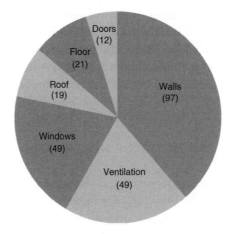

Figure 3.4 *Loss of heat from elements of the typical house*

Note: Numbers in brackets indicate watts per degree temperature difference.

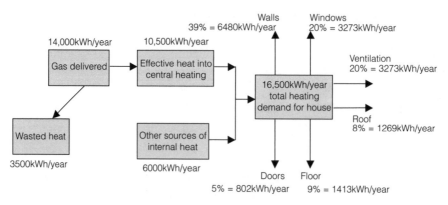

Figure 3.5 *Energy balance for home heating of the typical house*

How much difference would good insulation make? For example, what happens if the heat loss through the walls were to fall to zero? First, of course, the total heat need for the house would decline by 6480kWh/year, meaning that the total input energy required will decline to 10,020kWh/year. The available energy from other sources of heat, such as electric appliances, cooking and solar gain, would remain approximately the same. Therefore, the total need for heat from the central heating would fall by the full 6480kWh/year. Instead of using 10,500kWh/year of heat from the boiler, the house would only need 4020kWh/year. Miraculously, the gas delivered to the 75 per cent efficient boiler would only need to be 5360kWh/year, rather than 14,000kWh/year.

This demonstrates the magnification effect of improved insulation. If wall insulation were perfect and, as a result, reduced the house's total loss by nearly 40 per cent, the need for gas for central heating would fall by over 60 per cent. Of course, insulation can never be completely perfect; but good construction standards – often a failing in new British housing – and sensible techniques mirrored on the European Passivhaus ideal can get surprisingly close.

THE COST OF HEAT LOSSES

What would the average householder save by abolishing all heat loss from the individual elements of the home? Figure 3.6 outlines some figures.

Put in this way, the cost of indifferent insulation begins to look quite minor. Stopping all heat losses through the roof would only save enough each year for one ticket to an expensive sports event. It would, however, reduce annual carbon dioxide emissions by about a quarter of a tonne. Perhaps this sounds like a much more interesting target to aim

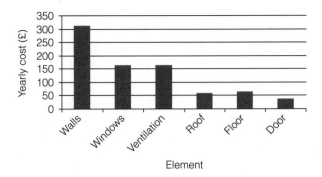

Figure 3.6 *The cost of heat losses*

Note: Yearly cost is calculated at 3.5 pence per kWh. The gas savings arise from the reduction in heat loss, plus the heat loss in the boiler. These savings assume that the boiler is 75 per cent efficient. The savings would be lower if the house had an efficient new condensing boiler and higher if the boiler were old.

for. In some ways, this illustrates one of the problems with climate change – even substantial carbon reductions can look very unimpressive in cash terms.

Cavity walls and other forms of wall insulation

Since walls are typically responsible for 40 per cent of total heat losses, it makes sense to look at this target first.

Walls can be insulated by cladding the outside or the inside with a material that doesn't conduct heat. Heat loss can also be minimized by putting insulating material between the external brickwork and the internal concrete blocks. Since about 1930, British houses have generally been built with an air cavity between these two walls. This makes the house better insulated than if the walls were just brick: air is a relatively poor conductor of heat, and the gap also helps to avoid thermal bridging.

Although air isn't a bad insulator, other materials can be much better. Since the 1960s, energy-conscious homeowners have improved the insulation characteristics of their houses by injecting non-conducting plastics into the gap between the two walls. In 1974, 2.5 per cent of homes with cavities had insulation. By 2001, this had risen to about 32 per cent, and 40 per cent by 2006. However, even today, 10 million UK homes have wall cavities that could be insulated, but leak unnecessary quantities of expensive heat to the outside world. This is almost 40 per cent of all UK housing.

Effective cavity wall insulation does significantly affect energy demand for domestic heating. Nevertheless, it has only recently become mandatory for new buildings, even though the cost of adding a proper insulator during construction is vanishingly small.

Until building regulations were tightened in 2002, even larger properties, which have the most to gain, were usually constructed with a thin insulating membrane between the external and internal walls, rather than the full infilling of the complete gap. Perhaps this doesn't seem to matter very much – the number of new houses built each year is less than 1 per cent of the existing stock; but the cost of systematically lagging behind best practice has left UK housing among the worst insulated in Northern Europe. (Many houses in places such as Spain are insulated to even lower standards. This is not necessarily a particular problem in winter because of the higher temperatures, at least in southern Spain, but poor insulation hugely increases the demand for air-conditioning in summer.)

The precise savings produced by cavity wall insulation are difficult to determine, depending, as they do, upon the quality of the installation and the characteristics of the uninsulated wall. The most reliable estimates I can find suggest that good insulation installed in a wide cavity (more than 60mm, or 2.5 inches) will reduce the heat losses compared to the uninsulated wall by about two-thirds[12] (these figures were provided to me by a manufacturer of insulating material, but seem to be consistent with other sources of information).

If typical losses through walls are 40 per cent of the total heat dissipation from a house, the simple calculation might suggest that total gas demand would go down by about 26 per cent. This would be an underestimate for the reason we established in looking at condensing boilers; central heating tops up the other sources of heat gain in a house, such as electric appliances. Therefore, filling the cavity in the wall will actually reduce gas demand by a larger percentage than the insulation improvement might indicate. Table 3.6 provides my estimates.

Cavity wall insulation makes most sense for big detached houses. In these cases, gas demand may fall by a huge amount. In Table 3.7, the saving for a big house will be over 2 tonnes of carbon dioxide – as well as a substantial amount of money.

These numbers are spuriously precise. They are intended to be indicative because we cannot really know the characteristics of the typical house with a high gas need. Nor can they accommodate the tendency of people with well-insulated houses to run their heating at a higher level. It is a well-established fact that people take insulation improvements in what the engineers call greater 'comfort', or higher temperatures throughout the dwelling.

And the cavity wall insulation won't necessarily be perfect. There will be gaps and places where the insulation doesn't reach. So, data from suppliers that estimate the impact of better wall insulation will often be lower than these figures. Good cavity wall insulation will also have the effect of reducing the amount of solar energy warming the house on a sunny winter's day. This will tend to reduce the savings in gas consumption; but the effect will be minor for most houses. Conversely, in the summer, proper wall insulation will reduce the internal temperature increase coming from solar energy and will therefore keep the house cooler, reducing the needs for fans or other cooling devices.

Table 3.6 *Very approximate gas usage savings from installing cavity wall insulation*

	House with high gas need	House with average gas need	House with low gas need
Delivered gas (kWh/year)	20,000	14,000	9333
Usable heat output from gas boiler at 75% efficiency (kWh/year)	15,000	10,500	7000
Other sources of heat gain[a] (kWh/year)	9000	6000	4000
Total heat (kWh/year)	24,000	16,500	11,000
Reduction from cavity wall insulation[b] (kWh/year)	10,667	5760	2933
Percentage saving in gas bill	53	41	31

Notes: [a] I assume that if a house has a high gas need, it probably also has more substantial sources of heat from electric appliances, solar gain and other non-fossil fuel sources.
[b] Larger houses will generally lose a larger fraction of their heat through the walls. Therefore, I have used a larger percentage than average for the loss from walls. Consider a big detached house standing in its own grounds and compare it to a mid-terraced house. The terraced house will lose relatively little through its walls because of its neighbours; but the detached house will have a high ratio of wall area to the size of the home. These calculations include an estimate of this effect.

Table 3.7 *Potential savings from cavity wall insulation*

	House with high gas need	House with average gas need	House with low gas need
Gas saving (kWh/year)	10,667	5867	2933
Tonnes of CO_2 averted	2.0	1.1	0.6
Financial saving at 3.5 pence/kWh	£373	£205	£103

In late 2009, most homeowners can have their cavity walls insulated for £250 or even less by contractors working for the main energy companies. These costs are heavily subsidized, and many people claiming state benefits will actually be able to get lower prices, or even obtain the installation free. These subsidies are a result of the government insisting that domestic gas and electricity suppliers pay a portion of the cost as part of their obligation towards improving energy efficiency.

The ratio between cost and benefit is strikingly favourable to large houses. The payback period for a big detached house is less than one year. At the other extreme, the payback for a small mid-terraced house might be two or three years.

Assume that all of these houses have another 50 years of life. The cost per tonne of carbon saved is as low as £2 for a big house and £6 for a small terrace. These are strikingly low figures compared to almost any other carbon-reduction technique. Even if the full cost, including the subsidy from the energy supplier, is included, the numbers would only approximately double.

This point is not well understood and needs to be forcibly made. The single most important contribution that the UK could make to carbon dioxide reduction is to improve the heat retention of the walls of domestic properties. What is the scope for the UK as a country to use this lever to cut emissions? About 10 million homes have cavity walls, but no insulation within these walls. The typical house will see annual savings of 1.1 tonnes if the insulation is done well and the homeowner does not turn up the thermostat to compensate. This means that 12 million tonnes of carbon dioxide emissions could be avoided annually by a national endeavour to insulate walls. This is about 2 per cent of the UK total.

If there were a national programme of insulation, handled like the North Sea gas conversion in the 1960s, for example, the cost per household might reduce to £300, excluding any subsidy. The total cost might run to £3–3.5 billion. This would be about £5–6 per tonne of carbon dioxide. This is an almost absurdly good payback – and well below the European market price for carbon dioxide permits of about £13 a tonne (September 2009).

So, why doesn't the government institute a national scheme for insulation? A large-scale scheme need not be compulsory. It could, for example, allow householders to opt out. A national programme of wall insulation could see the installers move methodically down streets so that people would see at first hand how simple and non-intrusive the process is. Even if only 90 per cent of homes allowed the insulation to take place, the savings would be huge. Indeed, there is no other single thing, excluding a large-scale transfer to nuclear power, that would have such an impact on greenhouse gases. So, why is the government prepared to allow such slow progress in reducing the number of UK homes with poor – and easily rectifiable – energy efficiency?

The first reason is probably a fear of the logistical problems of handling such an endeavour. A project that sought to carry out £300 of works on 10 million homes spread across the UK would bring innumerable problems of fraud, poor performance, dissatisfied householders and unexplained delays. The press would be merciless, but that is no excuse.

BOX 3.3 – CAVITY WALL INSULATION: OUR PERSONAL CASE HISTORY

We live in a house built in 2001, before recent improvements to building regulations. The walls have a cavity and a thin insulating membrane that covers the inside of the internal block wall. The gas bills for our house are not particularly low; so I investigated adding full cavity wall insulation. My calculations suggest that the house did not even meet UK building regulations in force in 2001. This is, unfortunately, typical; house builders do not seem to construct their houses with appropriate insulation standards, even by the extremely undemanding UK regulations.

Unfortunately, I was told by the cavity wall insulation firm that because we have the thin membrane – rather than simply an empty cavity – installers will not be able to put in proper insulation, except at a very high price. So we are stuck with our poor insulation standards forever, or at least until installers find a satisfactory way of blowing insulation into the cavity.

A second concern would be the political consequences of improving the insulation standards and thus lowering the heating bills of roughly half the UK's homes, while ignoring the rest. Why should poor pensioners living in Victorian terraced housing with no wall cavities not also see their gas bills reduced?

These issues seem solvable to me. A national scheme to insulate all cavities over a three-year period would, indeed, cost more than it should. It might be beset by corruption, excess bureaucracy and inefficiency. And there would be complaints from people in energy-inefficient housing that their bills remained unaffordable. Nevertheless, compared to almost any other scheme, a determined national initiative on cavity wall insulation is a first-rate use of money. It is a pity that we don't appear to have the political will to make it happen.

Approximately 7 million homes cannot use cavity wall insulation, either because they are part of blocks of flats or because the house walls are made from solid brick. Most houses built before the 1930s did not have a cavity wall.

The heat loss from the walls of older houses, particularly larger detached properties, is even greater than for homes with uninsulated cavities (after all, the cavity does have an important insulating effect). It therefore makes sense to contemplate covering either the outside or the inside of the wall with an insulating material. Either technique can improve the heat loss from walls sevenfold and make the wall better insulated than all but the very best-insulated cavity walls.

The cost runs to about £45 and £65 per square metre for external cladding (the cost is probably ten times as much as cavity wall insulation). For a typical semi-detached house, this would mean between £3500 and £5500. My calculations suggest that the typical gas bill for such a house would be reduced by about £270 after installing external cladding, with a saving of over 1.7 tonnes of carbon dioxide per year; but figures from the trade association of external cladding firms are slightly lower. Payback periods are therefore far longer than for cavity wall installation.

Internal cladding – achieved by fixing battens of cladding to the wall – provides equally effective insulation, but is much cheaper than external work. A do-it-yourself job can be done for about £450, and the saving should be as much as external cladding. Internal cladding therefore has a payback of about two years. Internal cladding lasting 30 years might reduce carbon dioxide emissions by 50 tonnes, meaning that the cost per tonne is £10 or less. The only reason that we do not see heavy promotion of this insulation technique is that it reduces the size of the rooms and therefore decreases the area of the house. Unfortunately, the value of space in British homes is far greater than the worth of good insulation. A semi-detached house with a floor area of 80 square metres (about 900 square feet) might sell for £240,000 in the south-east of England. If the internal insulation caused a loss in internal area of 1 per cent, the resulting diminution of market value might be far greater than the cost of the installation itself. Very expensive living space may not make it easier to decide to add insulation.

Roof insulation

In the typical home, 7 per cent of heat losses are through the roof. In 1970, the figure was 17 per cent, and in the last 35 years the energy flowing out from the roof has fallen in absolute terms by almost three-quarters. The reason is the increase in the percentage of homes that have properly insulated lofts. From about 40 per cent in 1970, the share of homes with at least some insulation in the loft has risen to about 95 per cent (this figure excludes flats and other properties not immediately beneath a roof).

For a home left without any loft insulation today, the prospective savings are at least as great as cavity wall insulation. So, loft insulation should be part of any systematic national programme to improve insulation standards. But the number of homes left without any insulation is small, and the aggregate national saving in carbon dioxide emissions will be much less significant than the impact from wall improvements.

For most homeowners, therefore, the issue is whether to lay thicker insulation in the roof space. Early loft insulation usually only used 2.5cm (1 inch) of insulation, and owners might need to increase the thickness of coverage. Another 4.5 million or so houses have only 5–7.5cm (2–3 inches) of insulation. For these people, and owners with even less coverage, would it make sense to increase the covering to 15cm, which is the thickness usually present in lofts today (2006 regulations for new buildings actually require a figure of 25cm)? My calculations suggest that with typical boiler efficiencies, the savings for a medium sized house will be about £30 a year at gas prices of 3.5 pence per kWh, though it would be somewhat more for a house with only 2.5cm of insulation. When done by professionals, the cost might be between £200 and £250, making the investment attractive, but not overwhelmingly good, even if gas prices increase further. The carbon dioxide savings will average about 150kg a year. Over a remaining 50-year life of a house, this amounts to 7.5 tonnes, or about £30 per tonne of carbon dioxide avoided. But you can usually put in loft insulation yourself reasonably easily.

Buy material for loft insulation which itself has good environmental credentials. Wood fibre insulation or sheep's wool products can offer equally good insulation performance to the standard glass fibre and use very little energy in their manufacture.[13]

Glazing improvements

About two-thirds of homes now have at least some windows with double glazing, although the number with all windows properly insulated is no more than about 40 per cent. Window insulation matters. A home with single glazing may well lose more heat through the windows than it does through the walls. This is particularly likely to be true if the walls are cavity filled.

But sorting out the windows is likely to be extremely expensive. A study of the costs of double glazing conducted by the Office of Fair Trading showed that the average price to replace eight or nine windows averaged about £500 a window.[14] To refurbish the windows of an average house might therefore cost at least £5000. The calculation of any savings is made more difficult because of two factors. Putting in double glazing will reduce the solar energy that warms the house – less will get through the windows in winter (of course, therefore, double glazing helps to reduce the internal temperature of a house in summer). Second, double glazing does seem to be installed by householders deliberately in order to be able to run the house at a higher temperature. These complications make it more complex to assess any likely savings from double glazing, either in cash or carbon terms.

Analysis shows that good double glazing reduces the heat loss through windows by about two-thirds. But note that even the best double glazing leaves the typical window still losing more heat than the same area of uninsulated wall. And so-called four season-glazed conservatories, which allow use even in winter, are absolute disasters in terms of heat loss. These glazed conservatories, often completely open to the living areas of the house, are now very difficult to build without breaching building regulations.

The maximum saving that could be hoped for from converting single glazing to good double glazing in a typical house is about £150 a year, equivalent to about 1 tonne of carbon dioxide.[15] Double-glazed windows may last, perhaps, 25 years, meaning that the cost of averting 1 tonne of carbon dioxide is about £200. Even if the full £150 yearly cash benefit is gained, this is of limited interest as a return on a £5000 investment. The saving will, anyway, be reduced by the impact of lower solar energy gain through the windows and a tendency to use increased internal temperatures. Perhaps the true saving will be less than £100, or 2 per cent of the cost. Of course, double glazing does make a house more attractive, with less window condensation and more even temperatures throughout the year, so there are other good reasons for installation. For those unable to afford full double glazing, the logical choice may be to insulate windows on the northern side of the house because south-facing single-glazed windows will capture more solar energy in winter.

Doors

Although external doors are only responsible for about 5 per cent of the heat loss from the house, it can be more economical to improve this aspect of insulation than, for example, to install double glazing. An ordinary solid wood door is a very poor insulator, leaking heat at twice the rate of an uninsulated wall.

Installing two first-rate insulated doors, front and back, may, however, cost over £500 and save no more than £15–£20 a year. Carbon savings are likely to be about 100kg a year, with the cost per tonne of carbon being about £200 if the doors last 20 years. This looks similar to double glazing; but in this case the saving may not be lost in higher internal temperatures or loss of solar energy gain.

Floors

Where possible, insulating material should be placed on stone, concrete or tiled floors. If wood floorboards are accessible, gaps between them should be filled. If cellar access is possible, it may be beneficial to place insulating material, such as appropriately fire-retarded recycled newspapers, underneath the floorboards. If done on a do-it-yourself basis, better ground-floor insulation may be cost effective, although I've found it difficult to get good estimates.

Other minor measures

In addition to these measures, it may be worthwhile installing reflective panels behind radiators. These redirect some of the heat that would otherwise flow outwards through the external wall. This is particularly important if the walls of the house are solid, as heat can flow freely outwards. One website says that the carbon dioxide saving resulting from this measure can be as much as 200kg a year for a once-off cost of £45.[16] Other commentators seem much less optimistic about prospective savings.

Ventilation

For completeness, we need to mention ventilation, which is responsible for about 20 per cent of the cost of heating a home. Ventilation doesn't just mean draughts. Air needs to flow in and out of a house in order to provide the necessary oxygen for its inhabitants. Even

BOX 3.4 – MEASURES TO CONSERVE HEAT

These very useful comments are from the Oxford City Council website:[17]

1   Eliminate draughts and wasted heat by fixing draught-proofing to exterior doors. Remember that some ventilation is important.
    Cost: around £5.

2   Buy an insulating jacket for the hot water cylinder. This needs to be at least 75mm thick.*
    Cost: around £10.
    Saving: £10 to £15 per year.

3   Insulate your hot water pipes to stop heat escaping from them.
    Cost: around £1 per metre.
    Saving: around £5 per year.

4   Stop draughts and heat from escaping by filling gaps under skirting boards with newspaper, beading or sealant.
    Cost: around £25.
    Saving: £5 to £10 per year.

5   Letterboxes and keyholes can let in draughts. Fit nylon brush seal or spring flap, and put a cover over the keyhole.
    Cost: around £5.

* Even if you already have some lagging, add more if needed to make it 75mm thick.

the best-insulated house needs to sustain enough airflow to turn over the complete stock of air in the house every hour or so. This means that each hour the heating system has to heat all of the air in the house, from the external to the internal temperature (in the German Passivhaus design, this is done by passing the incoming air through a heat exchanger that uses the warm air that is being extracted from the house).

As George Marshall puts it in his inspiring and encyclopaedic website The Yellow House (www.theyellowhouse.org.uk):

> *Any house that does not have air passing through it is fundamentally unhealthy. Ventilation is vital to replace moist, stale air with fresh, clean air. The problem is that ventilation can also account for up to a third of the heat loss of the house.*

Just as 'weeds' are plants we don't want, 'draughts' are ventilation we don't want. The trick is to control the passage of air such that it is just enough to meet the ventilation needs and has an efficient route through the house.[18]

The Yellow House gives useful detailed instructions for simple methods to get the right amount of ventilation in a home and to cut unwanted draughts to a minimum.

Using solar gain

To varying extents, all houses function as greenhouses, trapping heat from the sun. New houses can be built that maximize the gain in energy from this source, and simple principles can result in major savings in energy cost and carbon dioxide emissions. The very best examples of new houses can have very low needs for space heating because of their mixture of high levels of insulation and effective trapping of winter sunlight. In order to avoid overheating in summer, these 'eco-homes' also need to have a high thermal mass – that is, the ability to retain heat within the structure and slowly release it to the interior space.

What can owners of existing buildings do? The easiest and most effective method of capturing solar energy is to install a south-facing three-season conservatory. The homeowner can build what is, in effect, a greenhouse on the south side of the house, trapping heat in the spring and the autumn. Solar energy heats the air in this room, and on sunlit days, the door to the main body of the house is opened, allowing the energy to flow into the living rooms. In the dull days of winter, the door to the house is shut.

Solar conservatories work in three different ways. Godfrey Boyle's excellent book *Renewable Energy*[19] gives the following figures:

- Fifteen per cent of the value is gained because the solar conservatory effectively acts as additional insulation for the house.
- Fifty-five per cent comes from the warming of the air that circulates through the rest of the house.
- Thirty per cent comes from solar energy entering the house through conventional conduction across the external wall.

In total, Boyle says that a solar conservatory added to a badly insulated house in Milton Keynes saved about 800kWh a year (£30, or 150kg of carbon dioxide), so they are never likely to be cost effective. Moreover, the fashion for installing three-season conservatories in the 1960s and 1970s quietly developed into the building of conservatories that function as all-year-round rooms, with no barrier to the rest of the house.

REDUCING HOUSE TEMPERATURES

The simplest way to reduce bills and the carbon emissions from home heating is to reduce temperatures. This obvious fact tends not to be mentioned in textbook analyses of the impact of heating on greenhouse gas emissions. Commentators are afraid of being labelled masochists. This is unfortunate because if we are to grasp the enormity of the climate change challenge we need to understand that some sacrifices may well be necessary. The path from a 14 tonnes per person society to one in which carbon dioxide emissions are no more than 2 tonnes will not be easy. We can build new houses that are vastly more energy efficient than the ones we are building today, and the occupants of these homes will be able to keep their houses hot. The rest of us may need to accept that our house temperatures will have to be reduced or that we spend the money necessary to massively improve the insulation of our homes.

Internal winter house temperatures rose steadily from the 1970s until quite recently. By 2001, average winter internal temperatures were about 19°C up from as low as 13°C three decades earlier. (The rise may now have stopped, probably because of the near doubling of household gas prices since 2001.) Better insulation standards, the wider availability of central heating and increases in disposable income have meant that homeowners choose to run their houses at internal winter temperatures that would have been almost unheard of a couple of generations ago. Most observers think that if heating were affordable householders would like to run their homes at 21°C. This figure is already reached in typical Swedish homes and the ideal temperature in ultra-insulated German Passivhaus homes seems to be about 22°C.

Of course, average external winter temperatures have also risen as a result of global warming and now average about 7°C in the heating season – although 2008/2009 was colder than this (by contrast, as recently as 1981, admittedly a cold year, the average winter temperature was as low as 5.1°C). The typical winter rise since the 1970s of about 1 degree or so – all other things being equal – would have allowed a 1 degree rise in internal temperatures with no extra fuel cost. But the actual rise since 1981 in internal temperatures has been about 5 degrees.

Instead of running the house at 19°C, what would be the impact on fuel bills of setting the thermostat for a target of 18°C? With a boiler efficiency of 75 per cent, turning the thermostat down by 1 degree will reduce the total amount of gas delivered to the average house by about 1750kWh/year, or about 12.5 per cent of total usage. This would save over £60 and about 330kg of carbon dioxide. A reduction of 2 degrees would double these numbers.

How difficult is it to reduce internal temperatures once a family has got used to walking about in shirtsleeves in January? The evidence is that the adoption is remarkably easy and swift. Acclimatization is aided by adding several layers of clothing, of course. What about the health impact of lower temperatures? The evidence I have seen is that as long as the interior of the house remains above 16°C, there is no impact on physical well-being. Below 16°C and the risk of respiratory infection does seem to rise.[20]

Heating fewer rooms

Until recently, gas prices were sufficiently low for households to consume energy profligately. Even for a family on average income, the total heating bill was not sufficiently large for economizing to have been an attractive option.

But choosing to heat only those rooms in active use does make sense for the carbon-conscious householder. Holding half of the house – the first floor, perhaps – at 3 degrees below the level of the main living rooms makes substantial sense. Turning off radiators in upstairs rooms, and closing the doors, will save some portion of the gas bill. If internal insulation is bad, as it is particularly in new houses, this will mean substantial leaks of heat from the warm to the cold areas, which will reduce the saving. But careful use of radiator thermostats should enable the owner to capture savings of at least as much as can be gained by taking the whole house down by 1 degree.

Living in a smaller house

Data are sparse; but the limited evidence I have found suggests that moving from the average detached house to a terraced property might save 6600kWh of gas heating, cutting bills by about £250 and carbon dioxide by 1.25 tonnes. Although very few people would want to make this move, it would be an effective means of cutting personal emissions.

Buying a newly constructed house

New houses have much better insulation standards than the bulk of the UK housing stock. There is earnest debate among experts about exactly how good modern standards have turned out to be. Real houses tend to have much higher heat losses than predicted by the complex models used by builders and architects. They are less well constructed than predicted, with more leaks and bridges between the outside air and the interior. Householders run these houses at higher temperatures than expected.

Some 'ultra low-energy' dwellings reported on by the Association for Environment Conscious Building had total energy consumption (gas and electricity) of about 160kWh/year per square metre. This compares with 278kWh/year for the UK average and probably means that space heating costs are less than 50 per cent of the typical homes. This is a substantial improvement, but nowhere near as good as can be achieved by using international best practice. We need to continue to force the UK's government and its construction industry to improve the lamentable insulation characteristics and construction standards of British homes. Building regulations have been tightened so that new dwellings will have to be 'zero carbon' by 2016. These rules are resisted by parts of the construction industry, claiming that the targets are impossibly expensive to meet. There will undoubtedly be some backtracking from government between now and full implementation of the regulation but, by the middle of the next decade, the building trade will have to be making homes to massively higher standards than they do at present.[21]

What about electrically heated houses?

About 10 per cent of homes are heated using electricity, usually via storage radiators. These radiators consist of large heat stores, often made of ceramic bricks, which absorb energy during the night and release it during the day. Users subscribe to electricity tariffs that are lower during the night-time hours. Storage radiators are 100 per cent efficient: all of the heat they produce goes into raising temperatures, unlike gas boilers that have to exhaust some of their heat to the outside.

Electric heating is generally said to be more expensive and less efficient at meeting a house's needs. Our need for heating is sometimes difficult to predict because temperatures change quite rapidly – so a house with storage radiators can be cold by the end of the day. Electrically heated homes tend to be smaller than average and use less energy for heating. My rough calculations suggest that the typical electric heating system uses about 7000kWh a year, compared to 14,000kWh for a gas or oil system. Since electricity is over twice as carbon-intensive as gas, it might seem that these homes typically result in higher carbon dioxide outputs than the bigger gas-fuelled homes. However, electrically heated homes are generally taking their power during the night, when electricity demand is low, and the bulk of electricity is being generated by the nuclear power stations. Some people say, therefore, that electric heating using storage radiators is not a particularly carbon-intensive activity.

Electric underfloor heating, rather than storage radiators, is a feature of many new flats. Because it tends to provide a better sensation of warmth, it is used even in large luxury flats – and advertised as a major advantage over hot water radiators and a gas central-heating system. Sadly, these systems are likely to be both expensive to run and to produce a large carbon footprint. One source suggests that it will use about 15 per cent less energy than a conventional radiator system; but since electricity is over three times the price of gas, and over twice as carbon-intensive in the UK, the cost and carbon emissions will be significantly higher than for hot water radiators.[22] Electric underfloor heating is attractive and fashionable, and is a good example of how economic progress tends to increase greenhouse gas emissions.

Wherever and however you live, home heating consumes huge volumes of fossil fuel energy. Reducing this is one of the major steps towards a lower-carbon life.

BOX 3.5 – HOME HEATING ENERGY REQUIREMENTS: DATA FROM OTHER COUNTRIES

Home heating energy requirements obviously vary enormously between countries, depending upon average winter temperatures. The average across the European Union's (EU) 15 pre-expansion member states is about 14,000kWh/year, and the most recent data I can find shows the number increasing slowly since about 1995. New dwellings are much more energy efficient, with the most recently constructed homes in the EU having a heating consumption of less than half this total. Increasing sizes of new dwellings – a feature of many countries, but not the UK – added at least 5 per cent to the average heat use in new homes.[23]

Adjusted for temperature differences and for the average size of houses, the UK has one of the highest energy uses for heating in Europe, with Belgium and Ireland being slightly worse. The Nordic countries and the Netherlands are the best, with temperature and size-adjusted consumption running at about 60 per cent of the UK.

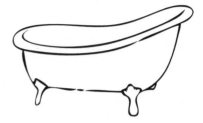

4

water heating and cooking

Hot water use is creeping upwards as more powerful showers are installed in homes. The average person now uses over 50 litres a day. The emissions from this can be relatively easily reduced by half by taking shorter showers, and not baths, and using slightly lower temperatures. The net impact might reduce the emissions impact of water heating to 0.2 tonnes per person per year. The household cost of water heating could be cut from about £140 per year to little more than £70.

Cooking should be carried out by gas, not electricity. The absolute amounts to be saved are not huge. Cooking uses less than 1000kWh/year in the average home and this number is probably falling as more prepared food is bought and larger numbers of people eat out. Best practice would be to cook as much food as possible in a pressure cooker, which saves large amounts of heat, and to use the microwave to cook pre-prepared foods.

H eating the home, examined in the previous chapter, accounts for the majority of a household's gas consumption. The other two uses are the production of hot water and cooking. This chapter looks at both of these less significant activities.

WATER HEATING

Water heating uses 4000–4500kWh/year in the typical home with mains gas. This is about one third of the gas used for space heating. Nevertheless, in terms of kilowatt hours water heating is more important than the entire electricity consumption of the home. However, the cost of water heating will be lower because heat is generally provided by gas, and not by the more expensive electricity. And because a kilowatt hour of gas produces less than half the emissions of a power station generating a similar amount of electricity, the emissions from using gas are far lower. This chapter assumes that both cooking and water heating use mains gas.

Although water heating is currently only a fraction of the energy demand for heating a home, advances in insulation and air-tightness in new houses mean that water heating may eventually become the dominant source of domestic emissions. As the legislation stands today, new homes built in 2016 will require almost no central heating, while emissions from water heating remain much as they are today. One study projects that over three-quarters of energy use for heating will eventually be devoted to water for showers, baths and hot water taps.

The average person uses about 55 litres of hot water a day. Total domestic water use, now about 160 litres a day – hot and cold – is probably still growing slightly although increased metering has helped restrain wastage. The US uses about twice as much water per person, and France slightly less than the UK.

Households use hot water for baths and showers, for hand washing, for dishwashing and, in rare cases, for use in the washing machine (although almost all new machines are now exclusively cold fill). Of the total hot water use, I estimate that about 40 litres goes on baths and showers.[1] Other uses are relatively insignificant unless the household washes its dishes by hand in running water.

The actual amount used in a household will be substantially affected by whether the household members use baths or showers. Full-size UK baths have a capacity of 200–250 litres. Researchers assume that people typically use about 80 litres of hot water for a bath, but use only 30 litres in ordinary mains pressure showers. Of course, this depends upon the length of time spent washing in the shower.

By contrast to conventional showers, the high-pressure variety using pumps to increase water flow rates can use up to 16 litres per minute, so that even a five-minute shower may be as bad as a bath using 80 litres. This is greater than the total daily UK hot water need for the average person. The welcome tendency for people to have a shower every day will continue to increase the amount of hot water used. By the way, power showers of this high flow rate are frowned upon in the more water conservation-conscious US and cannot be sold to federal government installations. In the UK, they are major contributors towards excessive water use and high water heating costs.

After taking into account boiler inefficiency and losses in the pipework, the typical house probably uses about 4200kWh/year of gas to heat water in the home. At 3.5 pence a kilowatt hour, this costs about £150 (see Table 4.1).

What can be done to reduce the cost of heating water? There are three main options:

1   Improve the efficiency of the boiler. New condensing boilers will operate at 90 per cent efficiency, not the 75 per cent that I estimate is typical of the UK. This might save 700kWh/year, or nearly 140kg of carbon dioxide. The financial benefit would be about £21 a year (this is additional, of course, to the savings that would also accrue in heating the house from using a condensing boiler).
2   Water temperature can be reduced. This is either a behavioural change – learning to have cooler showers – or perhaps reducing the thermostat temperature on the hot water tank.
3   Water volumes can be reduced. The most efficient thing to do would be to move from having a bath to a shower. Assuming that this is a daily event, the reduction from one person doing this might be 20 litres a day, or up to 700kWh/year. The carbon savings will be about 140kg per year and the financial benefit about £25. The cost savings may be small; but this is a worthwhile benefit to the atmosphere.

What can be done about existing power showers? The easiest action is to change the shower head to one that constricts the flow of water. These water-saving devices create thin needle-sharp streams of water that generally do not seem to have much appeal for users. Possibly a

Table 4.1 *Gas demand for water heating in the typical household*

Number of litres of hot water used per person per day	55 litres
Energy needed to heat 1 litre by 1°C	0.0011kWh
Temperature elevation needed (10–60°C)	50°C
Total energy need for an individual's daily hot water	3.03kWh
Persons per house	2.3
Total water heating demand	6.96kWh per day
Days in year	365
Total per year	2539kWh
Boiler efficiency	75%
Gas need	3385kWh/year
Plus loss from hot water tank and pipes	800kWh/year
Total gas need	4185kWh/year

better solution is the mixing of air with the water, which can leave the apparent volume of water the same, but does significantly reduce flow rates.[2] The usual figures quoted are savings of about 7.5 litres per minute. These shower heads seem effective and the cost is relatively low at about £70. Over the course of a year, the reduction in use from having one person move from a power shower to a more miserly air-mix shower might be over 12,000 litres of hot water. For a home with a water meter, this will save at least £20 in water charges and slightly more in gas bills for each person. The reduction in carbon dioxide will be about 140kg. In a house with four people, these savings are significant and will pay back the initial cost in well under a year.

COOKING WITH GAS

Where possible, cooking should be done by gas. Although gas ovens typically use a little more energy to cook the same amount of food, the lower carbon dioxide output from a kilowatt hour of gas very much outweighs this difference in efficiency. One hundred kilowatt hours of gas cost £3.50, but up to £13 if delivered as electricity. The carbon dioxide produced is well over twice as much. (Of course when electricity generation moves to low-carbon sources, such as wind or nuclear, the carbon-conscious household should move back to cooking with electricity).

Nevertheless, a surprising number of people use electricity for cooking, even if they have access to gas. Only 37 per cent of UK homes have gas ovens and 55 per cent have gas hobs, compared to the 80 per cent who use gas for heating.[3] Curiously, the percentage of families cooking with gas varies enormously across Europe. The market research company GfK reported that 100 per cent of cookers sold in Germany in 2005 were powered by electricity; but in Spain, 75 per cent were gas.[4]

Is it worth buying a gas oven if the house currently uses electricity for cooking? If gas cooking typically uses 800kWh/year, compared to 700kWh/year for electric cooking, the saving from switching is less than £70 a year. The carbon dioxide saving is about 150kg. The embedded energy contained in a free-standing new cooker is probably about 600kWh, or perhaps 250kg of carbon dioxide.[5] So, the carbon payback for a new free-standing gas cooker is less than two years. The cash payback would be about four years on a simple new model; but a heavier range-style model would have a less attractive return because of the greater embedded energy in the steel of the appliance. Of course, if the cooker needs replacing, then it is worth plumbing in a new gas oven rather than an electric version.

Data are sparse, but the average family seems to use the oven about 200 times a year. Some sources suggest even lower figures. The gas consumption per use is probably about 2kWh over a typical 46-minute cooking period. The gas burners on the stove are used more often – perhaps 400 times a year – and the energy use each time probably averages about 1kWh. As an experiment to check this number, I've just cooked 200g of pasta in 1 litre of water, and it took about 0.5kWh of gas, although purists might say it was still a little undercooked.

Moves to improve the efficiency of gas ovens are muted, partly by the relative unimportance of cooking as a user of gas, and partly by the slow decline in the amount of home cooking. The figures given above suggest that household gas cooking uses about 800kWh/year, at a cost of about £30, and carbon dioxide output of about 150kg. Per person, therefore, gas cooking only costs about £12 a year. The typical household using gas and electricity uses about 23,000kWh/year in total – so cooking is only 3–4 per cent of total household energy use. Across the world, homes using gas for cooking tend to use somewhat more than the UK – the International Energy Agency offers a figure of about 1000kWh/year for the typical use of a gas cooker.[6] Another source suggests that cooking is responsible for just under 5 per cent of total energy use in homes in the 15 European Union member states, somewhat more than the UK.[7]

What information there is suggests that the most efficient gas ovens are about 25 per cent better than the average appliance in homes today. But the lack of an agreed test procedure and the absence of any energy labelling on gas ovens (not so for electric) mean that consumers are unable to search for the most efficient appliance. Even if information were easily available, ditching an old gas oven for the most efficient new model would be expensive. An expenditure of about £400 for a nice new cooker might save 200kWh and almost 40kg of carbon dioxide a year. If the cooker lasted 20 years, this implies a cost of £500 per tonne of reduced carbon. This is a much higher figure than, say, the typical carbon reduction cost from an investment in a new condensing boiler.

Our estimates of energy use in British ovens may even be a little high. One source puts the total energy consumption from cooking at about 850kWh/year, including microwave use and kettles.[8] Deducting kettles (150kWh/year) and microwaves (65kWh/year) suggests a cooking usage of about 650kWh/year. Gas cookers will typically be somewhat more than this, with electricity rather less. For comparison, one survey suggested a figure of just over 500kWh/year for electric cookers in France.[9]

We know that the use of cookers is probably falling slowly in the UK. But we should not infer from this that energy consumption from all food preparation activities is necessarily falling. Paul Waide from the International Energy Agency notes a strong and continuing rise in the energy use of small food-related appliances in the US. His research suggests that even automatic coffee machines are continuing to take more and more electricity, even though they have been a fixture in US homes for decades.[10] Major growth is also forecast in small appliances as diverse as waffle irons and electric grills. In the US these small appliances currently use about two-thirds as much energy as that consumed by all UK cooking activities, although, of course, the US does have a population five times as large.

Perhaps surprisingly, given the continuing importance of cooking in some family homes, cooking accounts for little more than 1 per cent of carbon emissions directly caused by our activities. And at £30 a year, the incentive to do something about the cooking bills is limited, however virtuous you are. Furthermore, much cooking is done in the heating season, when the cooker is effectively replacing energy that would otherwise be provided by central heating. Indeed, because the oven is almost always only in use when its inhabitants are in the home, it is a remarkably efficient provider of heat in the living rooms. A boiler toiling away in a remote cupboard and only working at 75 per cent efficiency may well offer less good value than the incidental impact of cooking a meal in the winter.

Nevertheless, it makes sense to carry out simple steps to improve efficiency. Using a big enough pan to cover the flames, not heating too much water, covering the pan with a lid – these are all pieces of good advice. The only significant energy-reducing appliance is the pressure cooker. This will reduce the gas expenditure to cook most foods by about 50 per cent – some sources claim an even higher figure. The energy saving comes from two principal sources: the higher boiling temperature and the entrapment of steam, rather than its loss to the open air.

Some low-carbon gurus now recommend buying induction hobs for cooking. These devices typically use about 30 per cent less electricity than conventional hobs. But they cost a lot of money (up to £500) and it is better to use gas if you are concerned about greenhouse gas emissions.

The debate about whether microwave ovens save energy will run and run. Some sources suggest that they are remarkably efficient. Other reports are less sanguine. At first sight, it seems obvious that microwaves are more energy sparing; they actually directly cook the food, rather than warming up the large cavity of an oven. However, Nicola King, one of the stalwart researchers from the government's Market Transformation Programme, reported on cooking times for various standard UK foods (ready-prepared lasagne, porridge, baked beans and the like). Her results show that energy use was not predictably lower than hob or oven, although chilled ready meals were much more efficiently warmed up in a microwave. Photographs attached to her presentation also demonstrated that microwaved food almost always looks far less appetising than meals cooked in an oven.[11]

In Chapter 10 on the food production chain later in this book, I suggest that the growth in ready meals is inflating the energy demands of food manufacturers. I also estimate that food manufacturing may be responsible for three times as much carbon output as home cooking. It is certainly not true to assume that the swing to manufactured food and away from home-prepared meals is necessarily saving energy.

5

• •

lighting

Governments have been increasingly determined to reduce the electricity used in domestic lighting. The incandescent bulb is grossly inefficient; only a small fraction of the power it uses is actually converted into light rather than heat. During 2009, UK retailers withdrew the highest wattage incandescent bulbs from sale and by 2012 most old-fashioned bulbs will no longer be available in shops as a result of European legislation.

Currently, the average house uses about 750kWh/year of electricity for lighting, and this will fall to about 200–300kWh/year if all light bulbs are converted to energy-saving varieties. The cost would be about £80 and the yearly saving perhaps £60, with a household reduction of well over 200kg of carbon dioxide. Per person in the typical 2.3-member household, the saving would be over 100kg, or less than 1 per cent of total carbon output.

There needs to be a caveat to these figures. Light bulbs act as miniature radiators. Energy-saving bulbs emit less heat, so the demands on central heating will be greater. Perhaps one-third of the claimed savings in carbon may be lost because of the increased need to heat the house in winter. However, more careful use of lighting – turning them off when not in the room, for example – might restore the savings.

The last two chapters have been concerned with gas consumption in the home. The next two chapters are about electricity use, starting with lighting. Despite the attention paid to electricity by energy advisers, it is less important than gas use in terms of greenhouse gas emissions.

The average UK house has about 25 light bulbs. Each of these bulbs is used for an average of just over an hour a day. At a typical wattage of 75–80W, the home therefore uses about 750kWh/year for lighting, or about 20 per cent of total domestic electricity use. This figure is slightly higher than the average for industrial countries. The International Energy Agency reports that lighting was only responsible for about 14 per cent of domestic electricity consumption in its member countries.[1]

UK usage generates about 400kg of carbon dioxide per household per year. Spread across the typical numbers of people per house, this is about 170kg a head, or little more than 1 per cent of total average carbon emissions. Spoken of in this way, lighting doesn't seem that important. But it is still 9 million tonnes of carbon dioxide a year, and reductions are perfectly easy although consumer resistance has, so far, been marked.

Lighting use has been far less extensively studied than domestic space or water heating. Estimates of lighting use are still far from robust, and data sources are often in conflict. I have tried to generate my own estimates in the section that follows. My guesses are made in September 2009, just as the EU restriction on the sale of 100W incandescent bulbs comes into force. As the UK population is gradually obliged to switch away from conventional bulbs, the numbers will change (see Table 5.1).

Of the total of 25 bulbs, most analysis of domestic lighting has found that in a typical house about four light bulbs are in high-usage locations. These might be used an average of 2.5 hours per day taken across the year. Medium-usage bulbs number about six. These average a use of about one hour a day or somewhat more, while the remaining 15 or so might commonly be used for about half an hour a day. Across the year, this means that each bulb averages about an hour of use per day (Table 5.2).

Table 5.1 *Summary of potential savings in lighting use*

Energy-saving measure for average house	Cost	Impact on CO_2 output per person per year
Replace all remaining conventional light bulbs with energy-efficient equivalents	£80 to buy bulbs, but save £55 a year from lower bills	0.1 tonnes
Replace all remaining conventional light bulbs with energy-efficient equivalents and estimate the heat replacement effect	£80 to buy bulbs, but save £35 a year from lower bills	0.07 tonnes
Reduce use of lighting in secondary locations by 25 per cent	None: this will actually mean that the bill for replacing light bulbs will fall, albeit by a minimal amount, as well as reducing electricity bills	0.08 tonnes

Table 5.2 *Distribution of light bulb usage in a typical house*

Type of usage	Number	Average use per day
Light bulbs in high-usage locations	4	3 hours
Medium-usage locations	6	1.25 hours
Low-usage locations	15	0.5 hours
Total	25	About 27 hours' usage in total per day

Source: various, including data produced by the Market Transformation Programme

Larger houses have more lights, and those lights tend to be of higher wattage. Studies in the US show that detached houses use about twice as much energy for lighting as do flats or apartments. In the UK, lighting use is also strongly associated with income. A survey of low-income households showed an average of 10 light bulbs, while a similar piece of research showed that middle- to high-income homes had 32. A comparison of these two

UK surveys shows that the higher-income households had almost twice as many bulbs per main room as the less wealthy homes. It is a small example, but again shows that increasing prosperity has a sharp effect on fossil fuel consumption.

Published data show that the number of hours during which lights are on varies greatly during the year, from under three hours in June to about nine hours in December. Furthermore, more lights are used at any one time in the dark hours of December than in high summer, suggesting that the total demand for electricity for lighting in a house may vary by far more than a factor of three across the days of the year.

Nevertheless, the main issues for those interested in minimizing their carbon emissions are transparent: how do we reduce the wattage of the lights we use and the number of light bulbs in use at any one moment? First, we need a few paragraphs on technology.

THE VARIOUS TYPES OF LIGHT BULBS

UK homes have a choice of two main types of bulb – incandescent or fluorescent. In an incandescent bulb, the passage of electricity heats a thin metal element which then emits light. This is the old technology, originating in the 19th century. It is hugely inefficient, with almost all of the energy passing through the bulb being radiated as heat. Most light bulbs in homes are still of this type. Ordinary incandescent light bulbs can be dimmed and are cheap and easy to replace.

Halogen bulbs, whether they operate at 12 volts (V) or 240V, are of the incandescent type. They are more expensive, last longer and give slightly more light output per unit of electricity consumed than the conventional incandescent bulb. But they still get very hot – wasting most of the energy they use.

Fluorescent bulbs are much more efficient. In a fluorescent bulb, an electric arc is created between the two ends of the lamp. The ultraviolet output from this arc excites mercury compounds on the wall of the tube, which in turn stimulate the internal phosphor coating to fluoresce, or create light.[2] Fluorescent lamps range from tubes several metres long that illuminate factories and offices, to increasingly tiny bulbs that can be used in almost all domestic light fittings. In technical language, small domestic bulbs of this type are called compact fluorescents (CFLs); but to most consumers they are just 'energy-efficient bulbs'. These smaller bulbs consist of much longer bulbs folded over one or more times. Sometimes they are even encased in a spherical glass container to resemble more closely a conventional incandescent light bulb. Fluorescent tubes are more expensive than incandescent bulbs, last perhaps ten times longer and generate four to five times the illumination per unit of electricity consumed.

In a few years' time, we might be starting to replace our compact fluorescents with light-emitting diode (LED) lights in the home. These bulbs are similar, for example, to those already used to power cycle lamps. LEDs are semiconductor devices that turn electricity directly into light, with very little generation of heat. Their power consumption is usually less than 10W and can be as low as a fraction of a watt. These bulbs are currently very expensive (up to £40), usually only illuminate a small arc, and don't deliver a very attractive light. But LEDs are improving fast and prices will decline rapidly. In our off-grid family cottage in Wales, they already provide adequate reading light powered by a battery replenished by a solar panel. Eventually, I'm sure, lighting will be largely derived from LEDs – but not quite yet. In fact by the time this book is published, it will be worth trying to replace kitchen or bathroom halogen ceiling lights, which are often 35 watts or more, with powerful LEDs. You may need new transformers as well for low voltage bulbs. At today's LED prices, I'm afraid the financial returns will be quite poor.

CULTURAL FORCES

Forty years ago, English homes were generally lit by pendant lights hanging from a ceiling in the middle of a room. Reading light was provided by standard lamps positioned near chairs. As prosperity has increased, so has the number and wattage of lights. Where a room had two lamps in the past, it might now have four. These four lamps are often positioned around the room, and the central hanging lamp is moving out of fashion. In smaller rooms, such as kitchens and bathrooms, the tendency to disperse light fittings has moved more rapidly. Refitted kitchens are generally equipped with large numbers of 20W halogens in glass-fronted cabinets and above the work surfaces. Forecasts suggest that the number of light fittings in the typical home will continue to increase.

Until the recent switch to CFL bulbs gathered pace, the amount of energy used by lighting was tending to increase, probably by about 1 per cent a year. The amount of lighting used is rising for two main reasons. Smaller households tend to use more electricity per head for lighting – there are fewer people to share the light. So, the decreasing average household size in the UK, resulting from family breakdown and from increasing numbers of people living alone, tends to increase the electricity demand for lighting. More generally, householders want the level of illumination across the house to be higher than they did in the past. Well-lit houses are seen as more welcoming, comfortable and pleasant to be in. An ageing population also needs more light to carry out its day-to-day activities. People need much more light to read by as they get older.

Unfortunately perhaps, lighting is also a form of social display. A prosperous household demonstrates its wealth partly by broadcasting its light into the street and towards adjoining houses. Few households deliberately constrain their consumption of lighting; lights are left on even when rooms are empty. This is not an entirely trivial point – the generations that saw illumination as expensive or wasteful are gradually being replaced by those who know no such inhibitions and regard lighting as essentially cost-free, or at least as being so cheap as not to be worth the effort of reducing use. The average yearly cost of household lighting is about £100 at late 2009 electricity prices, so this indifference is unsurprising. It is simply not enough to get people to take slightly inconvenient actions to reduce their energy use.

As societies get richer, there is a strong upward tendency in the amount of light that they demand, and this is going to be extremely difficult to choke off, even with continued steep rises in the price of electricity. International Energy Agency work suggests that lighting intensity rises proportionately far more as national income increases.

THE IMPACT OF COMPACT FLUORESCENTS

Compact fluorescents have been one of the most important energy-saving innovations of the past 25 years. Their scope to reduce electricity consumption is, at least in theory, substantial, although we can see no evidence yet in the UK that the electricity used for lighting has begun to decline. Although the typical home now has several CFLs – often provided free by electricity companies – the reduction in energy use has been outweighed by the increased numbers and wattages of other lights bulbs in the house. It may be worth mentioning that the efficient bulbs handed out so cheaply do actually cost £5 or so to buy from the manufacturers but are subsidized by the utility firms as part of their legal obligation to improve energy efficiency.

Before the rise of the highly subsidized programme to encourage UK residents to use energy-efficient bulbs, retailers sold about 180 million ordinary incandescent bulbs a year. During 2009, that number has probably fallen by at least a third, with CFLs making up the difference. A highly publicized offer from supermarket chain Tesco saw over 6m bulbs sold in one month in early 2009 in its shops. This drive will eventually push down electricity use in lighting but there is little evidence of any effect yet.

Table 5.3 shows how CFLs compare with other types of light bulbs. The figures in this table show that CFLs are inferior to strip fluorescents in terms of working life and light output per unit of electricity used, but are much better than incandescent lamps, whether ordinary light bulbs or halogens. The average number of CFLs in a house is now about five, usually in higher-usage locations. This means that about 100–120 million CFLs are in use today, or about 20 per cent of the total light bulbs in UK homes. If, on average, they are used two hours a day – because they tend to be in high-usage locations – they are supplying well over a quarter of the light in UK homes and this will rise sharply as the homeowner is forced to replace failed incandescents with higher efficiency bulbs. But the EU legislation doesn't ban small halogen bulbs, such as those used in kitchens and bathrooms, even though these bulbs are only marginally more efficient than the old-fashioned variety. The full effect of the phase-out of incandescents may be smaller than the government hopes for.

Unless there is a rapid switch to LEDs, which may become up to three times as efficient as CFLs within a few years, the decline in the amount of electricity used for

Table 5.3 *Comparison of the main types of lighting*

	Light (lumens) per watt (W) of electricity	Typical length of working life (hours)	Index of light quality[a] (100 is optimal)
Standard incandescent	12	1000	95
Low-voltage (12V) halogen	15	3000	95
Mains-voltage halogen	20	2000	95
Strip fluorescent	80	15,000	75
Compact fluorescent	50	10,000	85
Light-emitting diode (LED) light bulbs	Eventually 150	Up to 100,000	Not yet certain, but some lamps can achieve 80 already

Note: [a]Colour rendering index (CRI): a measure of how well the light enables a person to see colour accurately. Any figure over 80 is usually regarded as acceptable.

lighting may be quite slow. The improved efficiency of CFLs will be counterbalanced by an increase in household light fittings, the social tendency towards higher levels of lighting in rooms and also outside the house and the gradual demise of generations that were used to religiously switching off the light when leaving the room.

SO WHY HAVE COMPACT FLUORESCENTS NOT TAKEN OVER FASTER?

Until a couple of years ago, CFLs were only suitable for larger light fittings. We all experienced the disappointment of trying to put compact fluorescents in standard light fittings, only to find that the tubes bulged over the top of the shade. But CFLs can now be found that fit almost all types and sizes of light fitting, including kitchen spotlamps. They need take no more space than the equivalent incandescent, although the smaller sizes have not yet arrived in the main shopping chains. A number of voluntary organizations and local authorities now operate what are called 'light bulb libraries'. Large numbers of different types of bulbs are made available for trial in the home. House-owners can experiment and see which bulbs deliver the best light and work successfully in their light fittings. The appropriate bulbs can then be bought from specialist retailers, usually on the internet.

CFLs remain more expensive than the equivalent incandescent, although the price differential has fallen markedly. An ordinary light bulb might cost 60 pence; but an (unsubsidized) CFL alternative could cost seven times as much. Of course, the bulb will last ten times as long, so the cost per hour of use is much lower. And the electricity cost is about one quarter. So, over a year, replacing a 60W bulb with a 15W CFL will save about £1 per hour of daily use. The typical bulb is on for an hour a day; therefore, only in locations of heavy use will the purchase be obviously financially advantageous to the homeowner. By the way, CFLs do take more energy to manufacture than ordinary bulbs, but this difference is more than outweighed by their longer life.

It is a suspicion rarely voiced by those who want us to switch to fluorescents, but most householders seem not to particularly like CFLs. Today, they don't flicker and hum like the first generation; but they can still take a minute or so to warm up to full light and don't seem to deliver quite the lighting power that is claimed. Their colour rendering is also slightly less appealing (see Table 5.3) and, as a result, they make the room somewhat less friendly and warm. These pessimistic conclusions are fiercely attacked by the government's Energy Saving Trust, which ran a blind test in a shopping centre. The Trust set up two identical living rooms and asked people to say which room had CFLs and which one used conventional incandescent bulbs. Most people couldn't tell and when asked the majority actually preferred the light from the energy-efficient bulbs. But the grumpy letters to the newspapers suggest otherwise.

If you did decide to switch to 100 per cent energy-efficient bulbs, what would be the impact of switching all of your bulbs to the CFL variety?

MAKING YOUR HOUSE 100 PER CENT COMPACT FLUORESCENT

Here are the figures for a reasonably typical house that already uses four CFLs and has a total electricity use for lighting of about 750kWh:

- Assume four CFLs in the house already. These might use about 40kWh/year.
- The 21 other bulbs are of the incandescent type, providing 23 hours of daily light in total.
- These 21 bulbs average 85W each and, in total, use about 710kWh/year. Total energy demand for lighting is 750kWh/year.
- Replacing the incandescent bulbs with CFLs would save about 550kWh/year and reduce total lighting demand to little more than 200kWh/year. (Switching to LEDs when they become competitive in terms of cost and light quality should reduce this figure to no more than about 100kWh).
- The saving would be about 15 per cent of total household electricity use.
- This equates to a household saving of well over 200kg of carbon dioxide.

The saving from switching to all energy-efficient bulbs would reduce your electricity bill by about £65. The 21 extra bulbs will typically last more than ten years at the relatively low rate of use implied in this calculation. Even if they were mostly unusual varieties, and therefore not subsidized, the total cost is unlikely to be more than £100. Over ten years, the carbon dioxide saving would be 3 tonnes. So the returns from switching to 100 per cent energy-efficient bulbs are good – about £35 per tonne of carbon reduction. The savings are therefore relatively small, but cheap to achieve compared to most of the choices addressed in this book.

In France, which has low electricity consumption for lighting purposes (about 450kWh/year), a 1998 survey showed that a household switch to compact fluorescents reduced electricity use by almost 75 per cent.[3] An Italian study showed that replacing the six most highly used bulbs in the house captured 85 per cent of the potential savings.[4]

BOX 5.1 – ELECTRICITY CONSUMPTION FOR LIGHTING: DATA FROM OTHER COUNTRIES[5]

Electricity consumption for lighting varies hugely. US houses use almost 2000kWh/year, whereas Greek homes take less than 400kWh/year for lighting purposes. The average European household uses about 560kWh/year, compared to the UK figure of 750kWh/year. The UK's relatively high total is partly accounted for by the longer hours of night in winter than in Southern Europe. But Denmark, a country on a similar latitude to the UK, had a consumption of only 426kWh/year, largely because it uses many more efficient lamps. Germany's figures are very similar to the UK. According to another source, across the EU, lighting takes about 19 per cent of domestic electricity demand, excluding heating and cooking, compared to my estimate of about 20 per cent in the UK.[6]

But note that the actual carbon savings must be reduced by the 'heat replacement effect'. Having inefficient light bulbs helps to heat the house in winter. Since lighting is largely used at the same time as the house needs heating, perhaps 70 per cent of the waste heat from incandescent bulbs replaces heating fuel. If the house is heated by gas, then at least 1kWh of heating from electricity replaces 1kWh of gas in the heating season. However, gas is a much less carbon-intensive fuel than electricity, so there are still substantial carbon dioxide savings from not using incandescent bulbs to heat your home. I calculate that the net impact, even after the heat replacement effect, of switching entirely to CFLs for an ordinary house is more than 160kg of carbon dioxide a year, or about 70kg per person.

Actually, I think we should ignore the heat effect in estimating the carbon dioxide savings from switching to energy-efficient bulbs. Lighting tends to be used at times of the highest energy demand – early evening in winter. At these times, the carbon content of electricity generation is at its highest. Most power stations will be working, including the highly polluting coal-fired stations, and the average CO_2 emissions from 1kWh hour of generation will be higher than, say, in the middle of the night when it might be just the nuclear fleet, with zero measured emissions. And, second, a house that switches to all CFLs will almost certainly be much more conscious of lighting use – we can expect that actual hours of use will fall.

6

household appliances

The biggest users of electricity around the home are the tumble dryer, the refrigerator and the washing machine. New fridge–freezers – provided that they are not American-style behemoths – can save up to 50 per cent of their energy use. If you feel you must use a tumble dryer, buy a gas-powered one or one with a heat exchanger. The extra cost will be perhaps £150 and the carbon saving is about 100kg per year.

The next greediest device is the television. The rule here is simple – buy a small liquid crystal display (LCD) screen to replace your old cathode ray tube-based TV. It will save the household 60kg per year in emissions, or about 25kg per person in the average 2.3 person family group. Big flat-screen TVs are prodigious consumers of electricity – avoid them.

Sky boxes are insidious users of power, even when not actually working. If you can get rid of digital satellite or cable, do so and replace it with Freeview. Buy a box with low standby power consumption, or make a religion of turning the box off at all times when not in use.

Other steps to improve electricity use can easily reduce consumption by another 10 per cent (simply turning everything off at the wall when not in use may save 10 per cent by itself in the average household). In an ordinary house, emissions from electricity can be reduced to below 0.6 tonnes per person with very little cost in terms of lifestyle.

A nnual electricity use by the typical household that uses mains gas for its heating is about 3700kWh, or 'units' in conventional usage. Deducting approximately 750kWh/year for lighting leaves about 2950kWh/year for other appliances, or approximately 1.5 tonnes of carbon dioxide. Until recently, this figure was rising inexorably here and in other countries. In the Netherlands, for example, electricity use in the home rose by 2.8 per cent a year in the period 1995–2002.[1] Greece easily matched this figure for the 1990s. But in the last few years, domestic consumption of electricity appears to have reached a plateau in the UK. It isn't falling yet, as the increase in the number of appliances in the home balances out the better efficiency of new machines and household gadgets.

The estimates in Table 6.1 of the cost per tonne of carbon dioxide saved assume that the house has an existing appliance of typical household efficiency, bought eight or so years ago. It compares the electrical consumption of the best new appliance with this figure.[2] This produces a cost per tonne of carbon dioxide saved, and the numbers are all high. For people who have already decided to buy a new machine, the figures will be lower because, in these cases, it would be more appropriate to calculate the incremental cost of the best new machine over a typical model in the shops today. These figures are given in the text.

The cheapest way of reducing carbon emissions is to use appliances less frequently, to minimize standby losses by disconnecting devices and to buy smaller machines, particularly TVs. These points are discussed extensively in the following sections.

'WET' APPLIANCES

'Wet' appliances are those we use to wash or dry clothes, or to clean our dishes. The International Energy Agency reports that they 'typically account for 20 to 30 per cent of both the energy consumption and the water consumption in the average European home'.[3]

Table 6.1 *Electricity use by the major home appliances*

	Average today (kWh/year)[a]	Best practice (kWh/year)	Approximate cost of new machine to achieve best practice (£)	Cost per tonne of CO_2 saved (£) [b]	Comment
Washing machine	270	200	300	570	More important to fill properly than to buy new machine
Tumble dryer	400	240	490	410	Spin efficiency in washing machine vital
Dishwasher	300	200	250	330	More important to fill properly than to buy new machine
Fridge	250	120	200	210	Keep in cold place
Fridge–freezer	500	280	230	140	
Freezer	350	240	300	360	
Kettle	150	100	35	280	
TV (two to three per home)	500	400[c]	Depends on size	–	Important to buy small LCD screen
Small appliances	500	500	Various	–	
Consumer entertainment	100	100	Various	–	Most electricity used in standby
Computer	150	75	400	2100	Laptop better than PC
Standby losses	400	100	Not available	Easiest saving to make	
Wall transformers	80	40	Not available	–	

Notes: [a] The typical home does not have all of these appliances, so the total electricity consumption in the table is greater than the average for all households.

[b] Assumes 15-year life, except computer and kettle (5 years).

[c] Based on three 26-inch screens.

Washing machines

Washing machines are to be found in about 95 per cent of UK households and are used an average of 270 times a year, or five or so times a week. Most machines can operate at at least three temperatures, and estimates have been made of the frequency of use during the year. These are shown in Table 6.2.

The typical washing machine now gurgling and splashing away in a British home uses about 1kWh per wash. So, in total, washing consumes about 270kWh/year, or just under 10 per cent of all electricity consumption, excluding lighting. About 80 per cent of this electricity is used to heat the cold water up to the wash temperature and to keep it there. In energy terms, one can think of a washing machine as little more than a device for heating water by electricity.

Almost all washing machines now sold in the UK are filled from the cold tap and don't have a connection to the hot water system. Machines fed by hot water would tend to be more efficient because it costs less – in money and carbon dioxide – to heat water using gas rather than using electricity in the washing machine. Some cunning individuals have worked this out and use their rooftop solar panels to preheat the water before it goes into the machine.

The electricity taken by the washing machine typically costs about £35 per year and results in about 140kg of carbon dioxide emissions. In addition, of course, washing machines use large amounts of water. A wasteful older machine, perhaps ten years from purchase, might get through 100 litres of water per wash, or 27,000 litres in a year. In a home with a water meter, this might cost £50 in charges from the supplier. So, perhaps surprisingly, the cost of the water may well be considerably more than the cost of the electricity. The canny consumer will be right to look even more closely at water consumption figures than at electricity usage when the household needs a new washing machine.

Table 6.2 *Number of washes in a typical UK home*

Temperature (°C)	Washes per year
90	5
60	83
40	186
Total	274

Source: Defra, Market Transformation Programme (2006).

Technical advances mean that today's machines use less energy and fewer litres of water. These improvements have been encouraged by a reasonably effective energy labelling scheme mandated by the European Union (EU). Top-class washing machines with a 6kg washing capacity now use about 0.6–0.7kWh per 40°C wash. Strangely, the EU energy standards measure the electricity consumption at 60°C, not 40°C, and typically the figure for this test, legally required to be visible on all new washing machines, is now slightly in excess of 1kWh. So, when buying a 6kg capacity washing machine, look for a figure of about 1.0–1.1kWh per wash on the label, and proportionately less for a 5kg machine. As a rule of thumb, the best performing appliances will use under 0.17kWh per kilogram of washing in a full machine.

Please don't be confused by the coincidence of the typical 1kWh figure both for typical consumption by an older machine working away in a house and the required figure to achieve a good 'A' rating for a new machine. The typical cycle today is at 40°C. For a 40-degree cycle, a new machine might actually use about one-third less electricity than is shown on the EU energy-efficiency label, which is assuming a 60°C wash.

New machines are substantially more efficient than washers bought some years ago. The saving from simply switching from an eight-year-old machine to a new washer will be approximately 0.3kWh per 40-degree wash, or something like 85kWh/year. This might reduce your electricity bill by about £10 and your household carbon dioxide by less than 50kg. It is therefore very difficult to encourage the householder to buy a new washing machine when the carbon savings are so small. Furthermore, a new washing machine is a fairly substantial piece of equipment and requires a lot of energy to make. It may be better to wait for your old machine to wear out.

However, water consumption is now a lot lower than for older machines. Good models can deliver their washes with less than 50 litres, or no more than half the most inefficient older models. The metered householder – now about 25 per cent of the UK total – will see savings of perhaps £25 a year. This may actually be a better financial reason to buy a machine a couple of years early than the savings in energy. (Note that there will be some indirect savings in carbon dioxide from the water company not having to push the washing water to the customer and to process it when it comes back through the sewers. Based on figures from Southern Water, the carbon dioxide savings at the water company from a householder switching to a new washing machine may be about 12kg a year.)

Are washing machines going to get much more efficient? Probably not: the savings are now largely captured and the majority of the electricity used by the machine is now utilized to heat the water. We're close to the limits imposed by the laws of physics. In theory, the trend towards increasing the washing capacity of the typical machine might yield some efficiency savings – fewer washes will be required. But the energy benefit of washing a larger weight of clothes in one wash rather than two will almost certainly be outweighed by an increased tendency to run the machine when it is not full. Therefore buying a machine which can wash 9kg, rather than 6kg, may actually result in less energy-efficient operation. Be aware of this – and buy a machine whose size is best suited to your household needs.

Do the key figures for washing machine performance vary much across Europe? One German study indicates very similar results to those used in this section.[4] The researchers estimated that the average German washing machine was 14 years old when taken to a recycling centre. The typical retired washing machine was about 40 per cent less efficient in energy terms than new models and consumed twice as much water.

I suspect that most people only look at the energy-efficiency rating of the *washing* cycle of a new washing machine. This may be the wrong decision: we should actually pay as much attention to the rating of the efficiency of the *spin* cycle in the washing machine, especially if the household intends to dry the clothes in a tumble dryer. Why? A good spin cycle reduces the amount of residual moisture in the clothes. This reduces the energy needed to subsequently dry the clothes in a tumble dryer. Just as, in energy terms, a washing machine is little more than a device for heating water, a tumble dryer is a machine for evaporating it. Evaporating water is expensive – perhaps three times more energy-intensive than washing the clothes in the first place. So if you regularly use a dryer for your clothes, it will reduce your electricity bills if you have a washing machine that spins fast and drives off most of the water.

The moisture level of clothes coming out of a washing machine, and therefore how much energy they require to get completely dry, is largely dependent upon the maximum spin speed of the machine and the number of holes in the drum through which the water can escape. Generally speaking, a washing machine requires spin speeds of more than 1400 revolutions per minute (rpm) to achieve the 'A' grade for spin efficiency. Manufacturers will need to charge more for spin speeds of 1400rpm compared to a 1000rpm version because the drum will need to be stronger to cope with the greater centrifugal forces.

How much will a good spin cycle in the washing machine reduce the energy needed to run the tumble dryer? Compare two washing machines, rated A and C for spin efficiency:

- The A-rated washing machine will leave 3kg of dry weight of clothes with no more than 1.35kg of water.
- The C-rated washing machine will have no more than 1.89kg of water.
- The difference is 0.54kg of water. This will take approximately 0.9kWh to evaporate (this includes an estimate of the energy losses in the machine and is not just what physicists call the 'latent heat of evaporation', which is about half the total).
- Not all of the average household's 270 washes a year will be spun at the top speed. Generally speaking only a small number of programmes, such as those for cotton, will use the full speed. So, the total saving in drying costs from getting a machine with a more efficient spin cycle will probably be less than 120kWh. This equates to about £15 of electricity cost and about 60kg of carbon dioxide.

BOX 6.1 – HOW MUCH EXTRA DOES IT COST TO GET GOOD SPIN EFFICIENCY?

In July 2009, the John Lewis website was selling 55 models of washing machine.[5] All of the washing-only machines were graded A or A+ for washing efficiency. Only 13 of the 55 were rated A for spin efficiency. (This is a small improvement since 2006 when I last calculated this number). Almost all the rest were B.

Is it worth buying machines with an A grade for spin efficiency? Although a small number of cheaper washing machines achieve the A standard and cost less than £300, the majority of A rated machines are priced at more than £400. The premium over good quality washers with B rated spin efficiency seems to be about £80. Of course, the buying decision is going to be complicated by the sort of features that a family wants and various other considerations, but it is probably worth spending the extra money to get good spin speeds if you have to use a tumble dryer to get the clothes dry. Over a ten-year life, the better machine will save about £150 and reduce carbon dioxide emissions by the best part of a tonne. Some consumer websites offer a contradictory view, saying that the higher stresses caused by a fast spin speed means that the washing machine will not last as long, outweighing the savings from getting dryer clothes.

Although a good spin cycle may be important to some households, filling the machine with full loads is probably more helpful in reducing energy use. The limited evidence that I can find suggests that the typical washing machine is used about twice as often as it should be. Rather than filling the typical wash with about 2kg of clothes – a figure that *Which?* apparently found in a household survey – it should be perfectly possible to aim for at least 4kg per wash. This might reduce the number of washes by 50 per cent. The reduction in energy use would not be as great as this, but could still be substantial. Savings of 100kWh/year would probably be possible, reducing emissions by 50kg or so.

Of course most of us have a poor sense of how much clothes weigh. So next time you use your washing machine, put the washing on the kitchen scales. This will give you some idea whether you are you filling the washing machine close to its capacity or whether you are regularly wasting energy, heating up water for a bigger load than will actually be used.

It may also be that we could choose to wash our clothes less frequently. This might not be quite as bad as it sounds. Rather than wear lightly coloured clothes, likely to be marked on one wearing, we could switch to deeper colours, upon which the impact of day-to-day activities would be less visible. But since this book is aimed at ordinary people seeking to remain part of conventional society, I won't suggest switching entirely to dressing in rarely washed polyester fleeces or hand washing of garments in the nearest river.

Tumble dryers

Tumble dryers are a good example of the developed world's continuing tendency to use more electricity without really noticing it. These machines have become standard items in middle-class homes over the past 30 years, adding significant amounts to energy consumption. They make life easier and have replaced the often inconvenient and troublesome use of the clothes line or the airing cupboard. Two types of machine predominate: the venting type, which evacuates the hot damp air to the outside, and the condenser, which keeps the heat in the house and transfers the surplus water to a storage tank in the machine.

BOX 6.2 – COOLING THE HOUSE BY DRYING CLOTHES IN IT

To get water to evaporate and change from being a liquid to a gas requires prodigious amounts of energy. We see this around us in a number of different ways:

- A kettle that is boiling isn't raising the temperature of the liquid beyond 100°C. Almost the entire energy from the kettle's element is being used to evaporate the water. But it still takes a long while to boil away the kettle's contents.
- Sweating is highly effective at keeping us at the right temperature. The evaporation of the water from the skin takes energy from the body, and even quite small volumes of water maintain the human body at very close to its correct temperature.
- Draping wet clothes around a fire to get them dry also uses a large amount of energy. It takes about 0.8kWh of energy to evaporate 1 litre of water. This will cool the room. To maintain the temperature at the desired level in the heating season, the central heating system will have to replace this loss.

Of course, when water vapour condenses back into a liquid, the heat energy is recaptured by the room. But even the best-insulated modern houses rotate the air in a house every hour or so. So, most of the energy from condensation will be lost to the house. Or perhaps the vapour will condense onto cold windows, where it will be partly lost by conduction to the outside world.

The important point is this: drying clothes inside a house will always cause a heat loss. The only way to avoid this is to dry them on a line outside the home. On wet winter days, this is impossible. The net energy effect of drying clothes in a tumble dryer in winter, above and beyond what happens by drying clothes over radiators or in an airing cupboard, may be not much more than half the gross energy cost of the operation of the dryer.

Of course, most home heating is carried out by gas; but dryers use electricity. Because the carbon cost of gas is less than half that of electricity, this still means it is much better to dry clothes in the home than it is to put them in the dryer.

In the summer, the rational householder uses washing spread about the house to help keep the building cool. A tumble dryer does not have this effect. A few wet towels placed around a hot room will have a significant cooling effect in the warmest months.

Most of us using tumble dryers have a strong intuitive sense that these machines – useful though they are – are prodigious consumers of electricity. The 40 per cent of homeowners who have tumble dryers will not be surprised to learn that they use about 400kWh of electricity a year, costing somewhere around £50. For an otherwise average household, the purchase of a tumble dryer would increase home electricity bills by over 10 per cent. In these homes, the tumble dryer will typically be eating considerably more electricity than the washing machine (400kWh/year versus 270kWh/year), though it will be used far less often.

But the arguments about the wickedness of tumble dryers do somewhat exaggerate the problem. It's not just the usual benefit that comes from the appliance heating the house in winter, but also that drying clothes inside a house will always use energy, even if they are draped over radiators.

Condensing dryers take about 10 per cent more electricity than venting products. Because all of the heat from the condensing dryer remains in the house, and thus reduces the need for central heating, a condensing machine probably costs less to run even though they appear to use slightly more energy.

Vented tumble dryers are actually worse for the energy balance of the house than you might think. When the machine is working, hot air is pushed out from the room containing the dryer. This means that new, cold, air will be pulled into the house. This increases the load on the central heating system.

The typical home uses the dryer about 150 times a year. The machine is generally loaded with about 3kg of clothing (and the associated moisture, of course). The cycle typically uses about 2.7kWh and costs 35 pence. Tumble dryers operate at around 2kW, meaning that the machine is typically on for between an hour and an hour and a half each time it is used. Studies show that about 35 per cent of households with dryers use them all year round, even when it is warm, windy and sunny outside.

Rather surprisingly, the authorities seem to have put little effort into improving the energy efficiencies of these products. Perhaps the scope for reducing electricity consumption is too small, or the differences between different machines too marginal. In any event, today's dryers seem to use more electricity than ten years ago. This observation may, however, be derived from homeowners using the machines to achieve a dryer finish than they were previously accustomed to. This slight change in behaviour would, of course, be consistent with what we observe in other areas; the relatively low cost of electricity, particularly expressed in terms of household disposable income, means that normal rational people will use electricity more and their own labour less. This is still true even at today's increased prices. To a person unconcerned by global warming, a cost of perhaps 50 pence to dry clothes is nothing compared with the effort to put out the washing, peg it onto a line and then return to collect it.

Almost all washing machines sold in the UK now achieve an A rating (for energy efficiency, but not for spin effectiveness); but I could find few tumble dryers that got better than a C, though I am sure they must exist. What should the concerned homeowner do about tumble dryers? The purists, of course, are united on this issue. We should wheel them out of our kitchens and go back to drying clothes on an outside line or in the boiler cupboard. We should use clothes that dry easily and, dare I say it, wash them less often. Some very green people whom I know take this principle a little too far.

These radical solutions will not generally appeal, perhaps even to those who recognize the severity of the climate change problem. Nevertheless, we do need to understand that tumble dryers are one of the many types of relatively new machines that provide the upwards momentum to household energy use. We can't reduce our carbon dioxide emissions if we add new appliances as fast as we increase the efficiency of others.

What can be done without too much disruption? We can use the machines less often and stop the cycle when the clothes are almost dry, rather than ready to put in the cupboard. The final drying can occur in front of a radiator, or over the hot water tank. A clothes line in summer will leave the clothes with a fresh feel, and a dry, sunny and windy day in winter will get the clothes dry faster than we might think. We can also ensure that the dryer is in a warm room because otherwise it will have to raise the temperature of the air in the machine by a larger amount, and the heat it generates will be wasted.

To get significant improvements in the carbon emissions resulting from the use of tumble dryers, we have two main options. Neither is perfect:

1 an electric tumble dryer with a condenser and a heat pump to recycle the heat;
2 gas-powered condenser dryers.

Electric condenser dryers with heat pumps

The primary reason that most tumble dryers in UK shops only achieve a 'C' energy rating is that a lot of the heat used in the machine is wasted. A heat pump system that improves the efficiency of the dryer is perhaps the easiest way of achieving significant reductions in electricity use. The heat pump recaptures some of the energy, but it adds considerably to the price.

As far as I can see, there is only one heat pump dryer available in the UK market. Made by AEG Electrolux, it claims to reduce energy use by over 40 per cent over a very long drying programme. This model – the AEG T59840 – was sold online in August 2009 for about £550. An AEG model of similar characteristics but without a heat pump, the T58840, sells for about £440, so the premium for the heat pump is about £110.

None of the websites I looked at seemed to understand the importance of the heat pump in reducing energy costs to the consumer. It is a difficult story to understand and communicate; but over a typical year the savings will be about 160kWh (perhaps £20) and the emissions reductions about 80kg. Over a 15-year life, the machine will save almost a tonne and a half of carbon dioxide in return for a £110 higher purchase price. This makes it a good way of reducing emissions, particularly in a big household that uses a clothes dryer frequently. In terms of cash payback, at August 2009 electricity prices, the incremental cost will take about 5 years to pay for itself in the average household.

Gas-powered dryers

Gas-powered dryers are more efficient than electric dryers in the same way that gas heating produces less carbon than electric heating. It uses a primary fuel source (gas), rather than a source which has itself been converted from gas and then transmitted to the home (electricity). In the US about a quarter of all dryers are powered by gas.

One manufacturer makes gas-fuelled dryers for the UK market. This company – Crosslee – makes the White Knight brand and claims savings as much as two-thirds of the cost of running an electric dryer. From the information that the company provides, the energy consumption of the gas dryers seems very slightly higher than for electric models; but because gas is very much cheaper than electricity per kilowatt hour, the cost is much lower. At current electricity and gas prices, the typical user will save about £30 and 100kg of carbon dioxide a year by using gas.

Crosslee's gas dryers are not widely available, but can be bought from some websites. The prices of the dryer itself are not out of line with conventional models and may actually be slightly cheaper than electric dryers with similar features. The issue, of course, is plumbing gas to the machine. Let us assume that it costs £150 to get an installer to fit the dryer. If it lasts 12 years, it will save 1.2 tonnes of carbon dioxide and the cost per tonne saved will be about £125. This makes it quite a good investment but the AEG heat pump dryer is better.

Combined washer–dryers

Many people seek to save space by combining washing and drying in one machine. Research suggests to me that there is a slight cost in energy efficiency from buying one machine rather than two (this is the opposite finding to the comparison for fridges and freezers on page 108). The average washer–dryer on the John Lewis website had a combined consumption of 5.1kWh for a full cycle. If a good washing machine has usage of 1.1kWh (for a 60°C wash) and a condenser dryer about 3kWh, the incremental cost is about 1kWh per use.

Dishwashers

Readers will not be surprised to know that academics at a German university have carefully compared the energy and water consumption patterns of hand dishwashing and machine washing.[6] Which method of washing dirty dishes used less energy? The core conclusion of this very interesting work is that the hot water used by the average European to hand wash a full dishwasher load of dishes would take 2.5kWh to heat. Since new dishwashers today require just over 1kWh for an entire 65°C cycle, the researchers conclude that dishwashers are energy efficient. Unfortunately, this is probably not a robust conclusion:

- A dishwasher uses electricity to heat water to wash the dishes. 1kWh of electricity equates to about 0.5kg of carbon dioxide emissions.
- In a household using gas for water heating, 2.5kWh of heat requires about 3.3kWh of gas to be burned in a boiler that is 75 per cent efficient (this is about the average figure for the UK). This produces about 0.63kg of carbon dioxide.
- Dishwashers look slightly better. But they have to be full for the benefit to be realized. If half empty, or as badly loaded as they typically are in our household, then the energy cost is the same. In this case, hand washing would be more effective in energy terms.
- The situation is made even less clear by the findings of the German researchers on British habits when it comes to washing dishes. The Germans observed that the British subjects used far less water than average to clean the dishes (they also left them dirtier than any other nationality). So, the balance tips even further in favour of hand washing.
- In our household, doubts about the efficacy of our dishwasher mean that we actually pre-wash some of the dirtier plates in running hot water. This makes it even clearer that we would do better by washing by hand, as long as we did so in a bowl of hot water and not under a constantly running tap.
- As a final thought, the standby power used by dishwashers when not in use also adds to the advantage of hand washing (but, to be really picky, a dishwasher also helps to keep the kitchen warm, and so replaces some gas heating).

Energy-efficiency buffs always say that it makes sense to use a dishwasher. But actually the evidence doesn't really bear this out as clearly as it seems. Although a typical dishwasher uses quite small amounts of water – as little as 14 litres in new models, or about one-quarter of that used by a good washing machine – the fact that this water is heated by electricity means that carbon dioxide and energy costs may be higher when compared to hand-washing water heated by gas. This would be particularly true in a household with a high-efficiency condensing boiler for water heating, or if the householder has a surplus of solar-heated water in the summer.

George Marshall's eco-renovation website, www.theyellowhouse.org.uk, has a go at dishwasher manufacturers for not having hot water feed models that would allow the householder to power the dishwasher with water heated by gas. Of course, he is right; but we are all now too used to being able to turn on the dishwasher whenever we want, and not just when the boiler has heated hot water.

About 28 per cent of UK households have automatic dishwashers, a much lower number than in most European countries. On average, the household uses these appliances about 250 times a year, or about five times a week (this number appears to be falling as households eat less at home). The installed population of dishwashers typically uses about 1.2kWh per cycle, implying a yearly electricity consumption of about 300kWh. Buying one of the newest models might reduce the consumption by one-third, saving 100kWh/year, or 50kg of carbon dioxide, and with a financial benefit of £13. Provided that the householder's old dishwasher is working reasonably well, there is little financial reason to switch to a new model as the cost per tonne of CO_2 saved is over £400.[7]

Dishwashers clean plates more effectively than all but the best hand washer. But, as we have seen, they aren't necessarily more energy efficient. The implications for committed dishwasher users are clear: the machines should only be used when absolutely full. When the cycle is finished, the machine should be turned off in order to minimize standby power consumption.

Some research data suggests that the typical user only manages to fill the dishwasher to half its capacity before turning it on. In our case, this is certainly true. The shape of our plates makes it difficult to fit in a full load, and we would certainly benefit from buying new tableware. But the saving in cash terms from being able to run the dishwasher less frequently might only be £10 a year, not enough to pay for the cost of new plates and cups. If the householder has surplus hot water from solar panels, then it makes a lot of sense to break the habit of using a machine and to wash the dishes with the free hot water in the months of high summer. The water is certainly abundant enough in June and July in our house.

As with many electrical appliances, most of the potential energy-efficiency savings were captured at least five years ago. Improvements are now marginal. So, once again, the crucial change may not be to buy a new and more energy-efficient machine. Rather, it is probably to use the existing machine in a way that maximizes its effectiveness, using it less frequently and in an intelligent way that reduces its total energy use.

'COLD' APPLIANCES

Major improvements have taken place in the energy efficiency of fridges and freezers over the last ten years. The EU Energy Labelling Scheme has been very effective at improving the typical energy consumption of new machines. In 1995, the average fridge–freezer in the shops would consume over 600kWh of electricity a year, or about 20 per cent of total electricity consumption, including lighting. The ten cheapest fridge–freezers in John Lewis in summer 2009 are projected to use an average of 295kWh, a reduction of over 50 per cent.

Industry studies suggest that the total electricity consumption of cold appliances, including all types of fridge and freezer, has fallen by about 25 per cent in the last ten years.

This is a rare success story; efforts to improve efficiency have worked, and have not been entirely compensated for by an increased size of appliance or by a greater number of fridges or freezers in the home. If there is an energy-efficiency success story, this is it.

The dramatic improvements in energy use have come largely by improving the insulation of the doors and walls of cold appliances. Very approximately, 80 per cent of the running costs of an appliance are due to heat coming in through the external covering. Only about 10 per cent comes from the energy cost of opening doors, and the remaining 10 per cent from the impact of cooling the food that is placed in the fridge or freezer. Still greater efficiency is possible in the insulation of walls and doors, so we should see a slow decline in the energy consumption of new machines.

Household ownership of cold appliances

The average UK household owns about 1.5 cold appliances. Almost all households have either a fridge or a fridge–freezer. Slightly less than half of all homes also have a separate freezer.

The total electricity consumption from these devices averages about 500kWh/year. A house with just a new fridge, and no freezer, may have a lower usage of perhaps 160kWh/year, while a home with ten-year-old fridge–freezer and a separate freezer might be using over 1000kWh/year, or over one-quarter of total average electricity consumption.

As with UK school exams, merely getting an A grade for energy efficiency is not necessarily good enough. The range of A performance is so wide. It is worth looking for A+ and A++ machines, although they are generally few and far between in the UK retail market.

The electricity consumption figures above are calculated by running the machines in a laboratory at a consistent temperature. They do not pretend to be an accurate assessment of actual electricity consumption when the machine is in ordinary domestic use. For example, the tests do not involve any opening or closing of the fridge door. However, independent studies have shown that the laboratory tests are reasonably accurate predictors of actual electricity use. Although the tests do not simulate real household conditions, the laboratory is kept at a high temperature compared to the typical home. This has the effect of increasing electricity consumption because of the larger heat difference that the appliance has to maintain between the cold inside and the warm outside.

Testers in other countries do attempt to model the real use of cold appliances more accurately. Japanese tests, for example, include a measurement of the effect of opening and closing the fridge door 50 times a day. Not surprisingly, other testers regard this as excessive and have tended to use 25 door openings as their standard. However, the time between opening and closing is set at 10 seconds, which anybody observing a small child trying to decide between four flavours of yoghurt will know is hopelessly insufficient.

The main tips for reducing energy use

Whether or not the household fridge is a new, shiny, curved stainless steel appliance or a grubby enamelled veteran, good practice can reduce energy use. The most important advice is probably to try to put fridges and freezers in the coldest room in the house. Placing the appliances in an unheated storeroom may save over 30 per cent of electricity costs according to one European study. Putting the machines in a cold room minimizes the work they have to do to maintain a low temperature (this advice is the opposite from that for washing machines and dryers, which benefit from being in a hotter room). It may be an obvious point, but all fridges and freezers also need to be kept out of the sun. Some machines will not work properly when kept in a place that gets particularly cold, such as an uninsulated garage. Very low winter temperatures may mean that the machines' thermostats will not operate correctly.

The second important step is to run the appliances at the highest possible temperature consistent with food safety. According to a French study, the typical freezer is set 3 degrees below the recommended $-18°C$. It may be worth buying a thermometer to check that your appliances are achieving the right temperature.

The external coils that dissipate the heat extracted from inside the fridge or freezer should also be kept free of dust and dirt and need to be properly ventilated to allow the hot air to escape easily. If the seals on a fridge door are beginning to perish, it is almost certainly time to trade it in. Of course, there is an extra worry now; the coolant in fridges is often itself a powerful greenhouse gas – usually known as hydrofluorocarbon (HFC) – and this gas needs to be carefully removed to avoid it entering the atmosphere. When buying a new fridge, it is now thought to be preferable to look for a hydrocarbon-based coolant, usually going by the designation R600 or HC600a.

Fridge–freezers

Table 6.3 shows that the scope for reducing electricity consumption by replacing an old fridge–freezer is more substantial than for almost any other home appliance. The most energy-efficient fridge–freezers I can find that are easily available in UK shops in August 2009 are made by Indesit. The BAAN10 and BAAN12 machines use 284kWh/year, at least according to the John Lewis website. These machines are not obviously more expensive than their less efficient equivalents with comparable internal space and electronic features. The cheaper machine in this range (the BAAN10) is on sale for about £250, and though less expensive fridge–freezers can be found at other shops, this A+ model does not look expensive by comparison to less energy-efficient brands.

Anyone buying the ultra-efficient Indesit machines will save over 300kWh/year compared to the average ten-year-old device. At today's electricity prices, this is worth

Table 6.3 *Approximate figures for the electricity consumption of typical cold appliances*

	Percentage of household ownership	Average machines in shops ten years ago (kWh/year)	Reasonably efficient machines 2009 (kWh/year)
Fridges (short and tall)	42	300	160
Fridge–freezers	63	600	320
Freezers (upright and chest)	40	420	250

£40 and the carbon dioxide saving is 150kg a year. So, all other things being equal, the average home electricity bill will fall by over 8 per cent simply by replacing an old fridge–freezer with the best new one. In other words, you may even notice the difference in your electricity costs by buying one of the Indesit models. There are no other types of appliance of which this could generally be said when comparing with a ten-year-old equivalent.

The main disadvantage is that the range is not 'frost-free' and ice will occasionally need to be scraped from the interior of the freezer compartment. Most other appliances currently on the market are advertised as frost-free – this means that they have a cycle that will periodically defrost the freezer coils. Machines of this type are inherently less efficient than the small number of models on the market today that are not frost-free. Buying a frost-free fridge saves some effort and inconvenience, but may add 50–60kWh to annual consumption, or roughly 25kg of carbon dioxide. This is another instance of convenience being traded for energy efficiency.

Fridges

Small stand-alone fridges can now be strikingly efficient. Whereas the Indesit BAAN range of fridge–freezers has yearly electricity consumption of 284kWh, the very best A+ fridges can achieve figures as low as 120kWh or less (for comparison, this is less than the power consumption of many of the older generation of Sky boxes and no more than about 3 per cent of the typical household's electricity bill). The internal capacity of the most efficient fridges is small; but even full-size fridges now use as little as 160kWh/year or so.

Buy an efficient small fridge and the benefit of switching from a ten-year-old model may be as much 200kWh/year or £26. These models cost around £200, so the payback is eight years at August 2009 electricity prices. Over a fifteen-year life, the saving will be about 1.5 tonnes of carbon dioxide, implying a cost per tonne of carbon of about £130.

Freezers

There are stand-alone freezers in about 45 per cent of UK homes; there is a small swing towards upright freezers. A decade ago, the way to run an energy-efficient household would have been to have a chest freezer kept in a cold room, such as the garage, surrounded by sheets of extra insulation. A small fridge would be kept in a cool place in the kitchen, well away from sources of heat such as the cooker. Advances in insulation, particularly in fridge–freezers, have made this a much less common arrangement.

A good energy-efficient large freezer, with a capacity of more than 150 litres, should use no more than about 240kWh/year. Smaller worktop height freezers should be obtainable with a consumption of no more than about 200kWh/year. So, where possible, buy a smaller freezer, or fridge, rather than a larger version.

The next question is: which is more efficient – a fridge and a freezer, or a fridge–freezer? A full-height fridge–freezer, standing about 1.80m tall, might typically have 180 litres of refrigerated capacity and 80 litres of freezer. A good model might use less than 320kWh/year. A very good free-standing freezer that gives 80–100 litres useful space would use 180kWh/year and a 180 litre refrigerator might consume 160kWh/year. Added together, the consumption of even very good individual machines will almost certainly be greater than a fridge–freezer.

Table 6.4 gives the details of the very best models that I could find as of August 2006 on the John Lewis website, and compares their cost and energy consumption. This table indicates that it is currently unlikely that separate machines could meet the efficiency of the combined fridge–freezer and still be competitive in the shops in terms of cost. In the example, the two machines would cost £200 more than the single and would not save any energy. The usable capacity would be less. All in all, running two separate machines is

Table 6.4 *Getting the best possible energy efficiency from fridge–freezers, refrigerators and freezers*

	Model name	Height (m)	Price	Capacity (litres)		Energy consumption (kWh/year)
				Fridge	Freezer	
Fridge–freezer	Indesit BAAN12S	1.75	£279	180	110	284
Fridge	Bosch KTR18P20	0.85	£219	154		117
Freezer	Siemens GS12DA 70GB	0.85	£299		97	179
Fridge plus freezer			£518	154	97	296

bound to use more electricity. Of course, the numbers will change as retailers and manufacturers rotate their models; but this conclusion seems fairly robust.

The marketing of energy efficiency

Searching for the 'most efficient' machines is difficult. I could find no UK retailer with an internet site that allowed me to search for these appliances by their energy-use characteristics. As importantly, the quality of the descriptions of energy use and of energy efficiency, more generally, are absolutely dismal. Since good retailers do what their customers want, this must reflect a lack of interest. Whether we like it or not, the market seems to be telling us that consumers do not regard energy efficiency as particularly important. They have to be told about electricity costs, and don't actively want to know about this topic. While the EU energy labels have undeniably pulled down average energy consumption (alongside the very clear threat to ban inefficient machines), pressure from consumers is apparently non-existent. Is this consumer indifference rational? Are consumers right not to actively search for the best machines? Let's look at the variety of energy consumption figures at the main price points for fridge–freezers. Instead of going to the John Lewis website, this time I looked at Comet in March 2006.[8]

At the time of the research, Comet had slightly more than 100 fridge–freezers on sale. They ranged in price from £150 to a jaw-dropping £2000. The mid-point is about £450. The expected energy consumption ranged from just under 200kWh/year to almost 500kWh/year.

The more expensive machines were generally slightly bigger than the cheapest appliances, but the difference is not great. The least expensive fridge–freezers were typically at least 70 per cent of the size of the biggest. The prices per litre of internal capacity in the fridge or the freezer rise sharply. But does spending a few more pounds mean that energy consumption is better? The answer was clearly and unambiguously 'no'. There is absolutely no relationship between the price per litre of capacity and the machine's energy consumption. Whatever people are paying for when they spend – say, £800 on a fridge–freezer – it is certainly not better energy efficiency.

Anyone looking for energy efficiency should concentrate the search on the smaller fridge–freezers. Going from a 300 litre capacity machine to a 400 litre will typically add about 60kWh/year to electricity consumption, so it makes sense to try to buy a moderately sized appliance. A 300 litre fridge–freezer (over 10 cubic feet) is a reasonably big machine. The buyer should probably follow a simple rule – look to buy a 300 litre machine that uses less than 300kWh/year and costs less than £300. No appliance quite met this specification on the Comet website; but several come close and careful shopping around will get you a machine that fits these targets.

BOX 6.3 – THE EXAMPLE OF AMERICAN-STYLE FRIDGE–FREEZERS

When researching this case study, I found that Comet sell a range of huge American-style fridge–freezers. These monsters started at £300 and went up to a scarcely believable £7500. With one exception, they were graded 'A'; but almost all of them used over 500kWh/year, or nearly twice the best-performing conventional fridge–freezer. The biggest and most expensive machines consumed the most electricity, with the champion using almost 700kWh/year, but still capturing the 'A' rating because it is so huge. American-style fridges are gaining market share in UK homes, partly because of their convenience and partly because they represent a mark of affluence. We can be sure that the downward trend in emissions from home refrigeration would be rapidly reversed if more UK homes had the space and the money to install these energy-hungry appliances.

But does it actually make sense to do this search? How much better efficiency do you get by a careful search compared to walking into the store and buying the first 300 litre machine you come across? In the case of Comet, a randomly chosen machine of approximately the right size would have an energy consumption of 338kWh/year.

Therefore, random choice might cost a buyer 40kWh/year or so (338kWh/year minus the target I suggested of around 300kWh/year).[9] The saving in yearly energy bills is potentially only £4. This means £52 over a ten-year life and a carbon dioxide benefit of about 200kg.

When what economists call 'search costs' are high – and it took me five hours to enter all the Comet data into a spreadsheet and do the calculations – no economically rational individual will focus his or her attention on energy use. It is simply too costly to look through the 100 or so models on the Comet website merely to save £4 on the yearly electricity bill.

Intuitively, most human beings recognize this. They will not spend much time over small savings. Because energy is still very cheap in relation to the cost of time, it is not worth seeking out the most efficient machine. Energy labels might help; but all bar a few fridge–freezer models on the Comet website were rated 'A'. It doesn't help much to have such indiscriminate targets. But imposing stricter requirements to attain the A grade is opposed by manufacturers, particularly if it is accompanied by any move to penalize larger appliances. At the moment, the biggest fridge–freezers can still be classed 'A' even though they have much higher electricity consumption than smaller machines. The grades are allocated on the basis of energy use per unit of refrigeration capacity. But from the perspective of the national consumption of electricity, we need to discourage electricity use, even if it means reducing the size of appliances. We ought to base our labels on the absolute value of energy consumed.

The introduction of EU labels on electrical appliances has clearly had some success. It pushed the pace of technical innovation and removed the most egregiously poorly insulated 'cold' appliances from the market. Now that all appliances are of a reasonable standard, technical improvement will be quite slow (this is also true for washing machines and dryers).

BOX 6.4 – LARGE APPLIANCES: DATA FROM OTHER COUNTRIES

Large appliances ('wet' and 'cold' machines) consume about 1100kWh/year in the average UK home. Other European countries are generally a little higher than this, in part because of higher ownership levels of appliances, such as dishwashers. Germany's levels of consumption are lower than the UK after adjusting for ownership levels; but Sweden and France are higher, at 1400–1500kWh/year. Large appliances typically represent about 45 per cent of household electricity consumption for all appliances and lighting. In the UK, the comparable figure is less than 40 per cent. As in the UK, improvements in refrigerator efficiency are pushing down electricity use; but European dishwasher use is rising and dryers now absorb two or three times the energy that they did in 1985.[10]

Therefore, the fight has got to move from labelling to reducing the size of appliances and the number that we have in each home. This is an enormously challenging political issue.

KETTLES

Kettles are responsible for a surprising amount of energy use. Almost all households own one, and they typically use them over 1500 times a year, with an average content of about 1 litre of water. The energy used per home is probably about 150kWh/year, or approximately 5 per cent of the total electricity consumed excluding lighting. To put this in perspective, the cost to boil 1 litre of water is no more than 1.5 pence at today's electricity prices.

Kettles are efficient devices for converting electrical energy into heat. Therefore, improvements in technology are unlikely to significantly cut energy use. In fact, the evidence suggests that kettles are demanding more electricity, not less. Three forces are at work:

1   In recent years, kettles have moved from 2kW to 3kW heating elements. Although kettles operating at 2kW are still on sale, the bulk of the market is now composed of more powerful 3kW devices. Why does this matter? After all, it will simply mean that it is quicker to boil 1 litre, but the total amount of energy will remain the same. The issue is a behavioural one. A 2kW kettle boils 1 litre of water in about three minutes, compared to two minutes for a 3kW model. Waiting three minutes for a kettle to boil is, of course, almost equivalent to an eternity, so the tea drinker is relatively careful about boiling approximately the right amount of water. A 3kW kettle boils 33 per cent faster, and the incentive on the user not to overfill the kettle is proportionately reduced. So, the kettle is filled less accurately and hot water is wasted. And at less than 1 pence per litre of boiled water, you have to be very worried about global warming to carefully measure how much water you need.

2   Having at one time been simply a functional and utilitarian device that sat on a gas stove, the kettle is now regarded as something of a fashion item. They come in brushed metal, with pastel panels. A recent trend sees them coordinated with kitchen toasters for maximum visual effect. In addition, they have lights to flicker or glow and 'keep warm' buttons that ensure that the contents are always hot – thus further reducing the time to deliver boiling hot water. These add to energy consumption. One estimate says that a kettle being 'kept warm' uses a constant 66W to maintain the temperature.

3   A further fashion trend is for kettles to spread further in the base, much like the British population itself. Ten years ago, jug kettles were cylindrical. Now they are often far wider at the bottom than at the spout. Why is this important? It means that for many kettles the minimum fill is much greater than in the older machines. Where it was possible to run a kettle just with one cup of water, it now often requires two.

These three things make it more and more difficult, in physical and behavioural terms, for the user to make the effort to reduce the amount of water boiled to the minimum. Where before we might carefully fill the kettle to suit our immediate need, we are now almost encouraged to be wasteful.

One solution is to reduce the possibility of the user overfilling the kettle. The Eco Kettle is divided into two compartments. When the user wants to boil one cup of water, he or she presses a button and precisely the right amount of liquid drops from one compartment to the other, and is then boiled. Because the amount of water boiled is more accurately tied to the user's needs, much less is wasted. Initial studies on this machine suggest that it saves about 30 per cent on energy use.

Does it make sense to buy this machine? It retails for about £35 and has a 3kW element and a 1.5 litre capacity, which is a bit low compared with the 1.7 litre machines that clog the market. The nearest equivalent conventional machines are between £15 and £20.

BOX 6.5 – HOW TO BOIL WATER

Even simple tasks can demand some detailed calculations. The maximum efficiencies of the main methods of boiling water are as follows:

- The electric kettle converts about 80 per cent of electricity used into energy that heats the water.
- The similar figure for a light pan on a gas hob is about 40 per cent.
- The figure for a microwave is about 55 per cent.

If users filled the electric kettle with just enough water to make their tea, the kettle would clearly be better than the microwave for boiling water (the kettle's efficiency is higher than the microwave's). But is this a realistic conclusion? Probably not. Studies of consumer behaviour suggest that people usually use about twice as much water as they need when filling a kettle. Water gets boiled, doesn't get used and then gradually falls back in temperature.

Therefore, a mug of water placed in the microwave should be compared against the equivalent two mugs boiled in an electric kettle. The greater efficiency of a kettle isn't enough to compensate for the wastefulness of most users in overfilling the kettle. But many new kettles don't indicate how much water they contain. So people guess and will tend to err on the conservative side, putting too much water in the kettle.

What about the gas hob? More heat is wasted using gas: the efficiency is less than electricity. But does this mean that it would be wrong to use the stove? No: on the grounds of expense and carbon emissions, water should be boiled using gas (see Table 6.5).

So, for the very careful person, boiling a kettle on a gas stove is better than using an electric kettle. But the differences aren't great and could be outweighed by many things. Electric kettles turn themselves off, for example, while kettles on a hob will be left while boiling. Sometimes gas kettles aren't placed efficiently on the stove, with some of the heat being wasted. On the other hand, electric kettles may be more susceptible to efficiency-reducing lime scale. Electric kettles may also be 're-boiled' more often if the user has gone away and wants to reheat the water.

Assume for one second that the raw calculations are correct: the cost per litre is, indeed, nearly twice as much for electricity as for gas. What will be the yearly savings of moving to a gas kettle? If the average household use is 1500 litres, the saving might be around £10 – and the carbon dioxide abatement less than 30kg. What person in her right mind would switch to gas merely to save this small amount of pollution? The extra time taken to boil a kettle on a gas stove is perhaps two minutes a time, or over 20 hours a year. No British person values time at as little as 50 pence an hour, which might be what it would take to rationally justify using gas instead of electricity for boiling water.

It is far more important to fill the kettle accurately with what the user needs, de-scale the element with vinegar regularly and only boil once. Some of the sources I have consulted suggest that herbal teas and fresh coffee taste better with water just below boiling temperature, not with water at 100°C or above.

Table 6.5 *The costs of boiling water*

Fuel	Amount used to boil 1 litre (kWh)	Price per kWh (pence)	Cost per litre of boiled water (pence)	CO_2 emitted per boiled litre (kg)
Gas	0.25	3.5	0.9	0.05
Electricity	0.125	12	1.5	0.07

So, a careful shopper might be spending an extra £20 on the Eco Kettle. If it does, indeed, save 30 per cent of electricity use, it reduces the typical electricity bill by about £7 a year. The payback is therefore about three years. Since many kettles don't last this long, it is not necessarily a good financial investment. If it lasts five years, then the carbon dioxide savings in the average house will be about 125kg, and therefore the price to save 1 tonne of greenhouse gas is about £280. This makes it quite expensive in carbon terms, although it is an appealing device for those offended by obvious waste. However, it will not appeal to those who like the energy-guzzling 'keep warm' feature in other kettles. It has to be said that many reviewers on comparison shopping sites also strongly question the quality of the Eco Kettle's design.

Does it make sense not to use conventional electric kettles at all and, instead, rely on an old-fashioned semi-spherical whistling kettle on a gas hob?

TELEVISIONS

TVs in the home are major users of electricity. The typical household uses about 500kWh/year powering the multiple televisions around the home. This is over one-sixth of all electricity consumption, excluding that for lighting. It exceeds the figure for tumble dryers, normally thought of as the worst energy guzzlers in the home. The average number of TVs in the home is rising. Now over 2.4, it will probably rise to about three TVs by 2020. In other words, the home typically has more TVs than inhabitants and this imbalance is likely to become marked as the number of people per house continues to fall.

Each television uses about 200kWh/year. When working, old-fashioned cathode ray tube (CRT) televisions use about 80W, although this varies somewhat according to the size of the screen. TVs are typically being used more than six hours a day, although they may not be watched all of this time. They are, of course, increasingly used as background entertainment and as radios in many homes with digital set-top boxes.

Government projections show typical household electricity demand to power televisions rising from about 500kWh/year now to well over 600kWh/year at the end of this decade.[11] To put this in context, this increase alone will add well over 1 million tonnes of carbon dioxide to UK emissions (this assumes no change in the energy efficiency of TV sets). The rise in household demand is driven both by increasing numbers of television sets and a rise in their power consumption. New sets bought today absorb a lot more power than those bought five years ago. The rapid increase in liquid crystal display (LCD) screen sizes now in the shops suggests an even faster increase in total electricity demand from televisions.

Technology changes

Ten years ago, almost all televisions sold in shops used cathode ray tubes (CRTs) to display the picture. Now flat screen TVs using liquid crystal or plasma technologies are ubiquitous. An LCD screen of 17–20 inches consumes little, if any, more power than a similarly sized CRT model. But as LCD TVs get bigger, their power consumption goes up more than proportionately to the screen size. Thus, a 30-inch LCD screen will consume well over twice as much as a 20-inch display. By the way, this is also true for typical flat-panel computer screens.

And TV screens are getting bigger all the time. Screens of over 40 inches are now common. Prices are strikingly high, but are continuing to fall rapidly as LCD manufacturing technology improves. At the moment, 40 inch screens typically consume over 160W, and this power usage will probably not fall markedly over the next few years. The degree of the problem posed by the growth of the size of domestic LCD screens is illustrated by an Australian survey which showed that the typical new LCD TV consumed 50W in 2003, but 92W in 2005. This increase in the average size of TV screens will continue for several years. Plasma screens, which are sometimes said to give the highest picture quality have even worse power consumption patterns. The largest devices can take over 300W.

There is some relief in sight. Within a few years we will (probably) see the replacement of LCD as the dominant technology by new display techniques that use very little power. The most likely candidate is something known as an organic light-emitting diode (OLED). Light-emitting diodes (LEDs) are already used for lights such as those on bicycles and may eventually spread into the home (see Chapter 5). LEDs use much less energy and TV displays employing this technology are already in the shops. Within five years, perhaps, new TVs will use significantly less electricity than at present. But by that time, most UK homes will have two or three (long-lasting) large-screen LCDs or plasma TVs.

Typical usage patterns

The average person watches TV for about three and a half hours per day; but surveys seem to suggest that TVs are left on for about six hours. In the remainder of the time, the TVs are almost invariably left on standby, when the electronics in the machine are still on, but merely ticking over. In this state, the TV might take 3–5W, although in the survey I did in August 2009 most new machines used less than 1W.

For a typical CRT TV, still probably the majority of TVs in UK homes, the position is approximately as outlined in Table 6.6.

How does this change if you add a monster LCD TV to your home entertainment options? If the new LCD TV replaces the old CRT, the increment to household energy consumption is 130kWh/year (about 60kg of carbon dioxide, or £160). On the other hand, if, as is more likely, the old screen ends up in another room, still being left on some of the time, the total increase in energy consumption might perhaps go up to double this level.

Is it reasonable to assume that the typical new LCD TV is as large as 40 inches? Perhaps not; but 20 per cent of the models on sale at Currys in August 2009 were this size or larger. Of course, actual sales are likely to be biased towards cheaper TV sets; but as prices fall, 40 inches is going to be a pretty conventional purchase. As in many other ways, technology and rising prosperity are tending to increase our need for electricity in the home. Although it might cost almost £45 a year to run a large LCD TV, those who paid out more than £600 to buy it are unlikely to be very sensitive to the price of electricity.

Table 6.6 *Power consumption for a full-size old-fashioned TV*

	Time (hrs)	Watts (W) used	Total (kWh/year)
Hours of use per day	6	80	175
Hours of standby per day	18	4.5	30
Total	24		205

Table 6.7 *Power consumption for a typical 40-inch LCD TV*

	Time (hrs)	Watts (W) used	Total (kWh/year)
Hours of use per day	6	150	328
Hours of standby per day	18	1	7
Total	24		335

BOX 6.6 – DOES IT MATTER WHEN YOU WATCH TV?

Domestic electricity consumption varies by a factor of two or three during a typical day. The peak is reached at about 6.00 or 6.30 in the evening, when people are home, cooking is taking place and the TV is on. After this time, electricity use fades away slowly. A disruption to this pattern is caused by breaks in extremely popular television programmes. At this time, demand shoots upward. Important events on TV in the later evening sometimes produce a spike in electricity demand that exceeds the highest level of demand at 6.00 pm. These jumps are usually predictable events, and the TV companies give the National Grid notice of expected peaks. Nevertheless, at these times the grid has to bring into production power stations that are relatively costly producers of electricity. Today, these stations tend to be coal fired, although this depends crucially upon the relative prices of gas and coal. Coal generation produces two to three times as much carbon dioxide as gas for every unit of electricity generated. So the (perhaps excessively) concerned householder needs to bear in mind that watching TV at moments of great national interest, such as the death of a much reviled character in a soap opera, will tend to cause higher levels of carbon pollution than watching it when electricity demand is low and the least polluting fuels are being used. Moreover, coal power stations have to be warmed up – literally – in order to be ready for the moment the kettles are turned on at the end of a particularly gruesome episode of Coronation Street. This also wastes carbon dioxide. The really carbon-phobic household would always seek to watch TV at times when the base-load electricity generators – nuclear, hydro and wind – provide the majority of our electricity. Or, since VCRs or other recorders typically use much less electricity than TVs, record Coronation Street and watch when other people aren't using their TVs. 'Shaving the peak', as it is known, is a good way of cutting the carbon output from electricity generation. Other countries pursue much more active policies to even out electricity demand than the UK, and the effects can be substantial.

The impact of the growth of LCD TVs

About 6 million TVs are sold in the UK each year.[12] When householders buy a new television, some old TVs are retired; but the total number in UK homes is probably rising by over 3 million a year. If the average increment to household consumption is 200kWh/year from the purchase of a new LCD TV, the 6 million TVs sold will add about 0.6 million tonnes of carbon dioxide to the atmosphere every year, about a tenth of 1 per cent of UK emissions.

Why has this been allowed to happen unchecked?

There are no labelling schemes of any importance covering TVs. In fact, you have to look hard to get information on energy use from retailers' websites. The well-developed labelling schemes for washing machines and other appliances have had some effect and are highly visible reminders of the energy implications of a poor purchase. But consumers have no such assistance when buying a television. This is remarkable; sales of consumer electronics have introduced a new buoyancy in home electricity use that is outweighing the energy savings in other areas, such as refrigerators. It is TVs, satellite decoders and digital recorders that are responsible for pushing up domestic electricity use; but very little is done to alert or restrain the public. Other countries have introduced voluntary labelling schemes; but in the UK the problem is ignored. I suspect that policy makers have simply not yet realized the effect of increasing the size of LCDs on household energy use.

Nevertheless, we need some action. Consumers eager to avoid higher electricity bills need to buy small-screen LCD TVs, turn them off when not being watched and throw out any old CRT appliances. And we can all read books rather than watch the TV.

SMALL APPLIANCES

Modern living demands a range of little devices that burn huge quantities of electricity, but only for a few minutes a day. Anything with a big motor or a large heating element will be taking 1–2kW to do its work. Table 6.8 focuses on four appliances.

How much are these appliances used every week? I have not been able to find good estimates, so I'll make up my own. I think irons might be used for 90 minutes in a typical house, vacuums for 60 minutes, toasters for 40 and microwaves for 20. With this pattern of use, these appliances together take somewhat over 300kWh/year. Of course, this will vary hugely with the size and type of household. But if my estimates of usage times are right, the iron is a particularly intense user of electricity. On its own, it might be using over 150kWh/year.

Table 6.8 *Power consumption figures for four small appliances*

	Typical consumption when in use (W)
Irons	2000
Vacuum cleaners	1800
Toasters	1000
Microwave ovens	1500[a]

Note: [a] The typical microwave seems to take about twice as much power as it delivers in useful energy to warm food

The new type of iron, in which steam is generated in a separate container, uses somewhat more energy than the conventional steam iron. However, retailers claim that the time needed for pressing is up to 50 per cent less. Perhaps this is so; but it would be one of the rare appliances where power increases actually reduce total energy consumption.

Microwave ovens deliver about half their energy use in useful heating to food. So a machine advertised as 800W may actually be typically taking over 1.6kW from the mains. Nevertheless, for some types of food they are effective and energy efficient. The following summary is from a US website:[13]

> Take the simple matter of baking a potato. You start out with a very hot heat source: a gas burner or a set of electric coils. You heat up the inside walls of the oven, the grill, the pan and all of the air trapped inside. Just to bring the oven up to the required 400 degrees [Fahrenheit] takes four to five minutes. You then overwhelm the potato with a massive onslaught of heat from all sides. The potato, heating from [the] surface inward through conduction, requires an hour to bake. Cooling down time for the oven is an additional three to four hours.
>
> On the other hand, the microwave oven starts instantly – like a radio – from a cold condition. The minute you turn it on, the potato begins to absorb heat throughout its entire bulk. It's baked ready to serve in four or five minutes – the same time it required to bring the conventional oven up to working temperature. And when you turn off the microwave oven, it's cool. There's no wasted-heat hangover.

This seems to make good sense, although I very much doubt that a decently sized potato will be cooked in four or five minutes – 15 minutes is more like it.

You'll see estimates of microwave efficiency that suggest they save up to 90 per cent of the energy that might be used by a conventional oven. Of course, it is not always this simple. Cooking a large quantity of potatoes in a gas oven won't be quite as inefficient as a couple of small specimens. Nevertheless, the point is broadly that if we are solely interested in energy efficiency, microwave cooking is used far too little.

Table 6.9 shows that a toaster is quite efficient as well, at least by comparison to a gas grill. Other small appliances may take about 100–200kWh/year in total. They will vary enormously by household. For example, we use our bread-maker almost once a day and it probably consumes up to half a kWh in each cycle. (By the way, this is only slightly more than a large commercial bakery.) Other homes will use high-consumption appliances such as hair dryers or wine chillers. The hair dryer is a good example of an appliance that is using more and more electricity. New models often use 2kW, up from half this level a few years ago. Six minutes a day of active use means 35kg of carbon dioxide a year.

The person interested in energy efficiency will seek to minimize the use of these products and be boringly diligent at taking the plugs out of the wall.

Table 6.9 *Toasting a piece of bread using electricity or gas:*
A comparison

	Electric toaster	Gas oven
Time taken	3 minutes	5 minutes
Energy used	0.05kWh	0.24kWh
CO_2 produced	22.5g	46g
Energy cost	0.6 pence	0.8 pence

Notes: The piece of toast only weighed about 80g. This experiment
may overestimate the relative disadvantage of cooking with gas since
the large grill was cold at the start of the experiment. Further pieces of
bread would take much less time to cook, although this effect would
also operate in the case of the toaster.
Source: personal experience of cooking two pieces of toast for lunch,
22 March 2006.

CONSUMER ELECTRONICS

Entertainment

Of the electronic entertainment devices in the home, the TV is usually the most important
consumer of electric power. But in an increasingly large number of households, other electronic
appliances now take more electricity than home TVs. There's every reason to suppose that
within ten years the power consumption of the ever-growing number of electronic
entertainment products in the household will significantly augment total electricity use.

As is becoming increasingly well understood, much electricity use in these devices
occurs when they are apparently not in use. 'Standby' power, usually utilized to keep the
product ready for use at a moment's notice, means that the appliance may be using up to
20W when not in use. This sounds an insignificant amount of energy; but, over the year,
this will amount to over 175kWh, or over 80kg of carbon dioxide. More and more homes
have large numbers of these products, and growth will almost certainly continue at an
unchecked rate.

Table 6.10 shows how much electricity typical home electronics products consume
when in use and when on standby. These estimates should be treated with caution: the
standby function, in particular, varies enormously in terms of power use from model to
model and manufacturer to manufacturer.

Some homes will possess all of these appliances, while others will only have one or two.
Therefore, generalization is difficult. From published data on hours of use, it is possible to
estimate with reasonable accuracy how much each type of appliance adds to electricity usage.

Table 6.10 *Power consumption in use and in standby mode for consumer electronics*

	Power use when on (W)	Power use in standby mode (W)
Sky	17	16*
Sky+ (hard disc recorder)	24	16*
Cable	17	16*
Freeview	10	7*
VCR (video cassette recorder)	22	8
DVD player	10	1
DVD recorder	20	2
Radio (digital or analogue)	8	0
Home theatre	200	1
Games console	60*	5

Notes: New consumer electronics generally have lower standby power figures than suggested in this table. The asterisked figures in particular are for older devices that have been in homes for some time.

What do these figures suggest for total power consumption from consumer electronics in people's homes? I've set up four stereotypes: the addict, the heavy consumer, the moderate user and the home that hasn't quite caught up with the 1990s yet (see Table 6.12).

It is easy to see the consequence of the household's choice of home entertainment appliances. There's a tenfold variation between the addicts and the homes stuck in the 1980s with a VCR and a few radios. The aficionados use a megawatt hour (1000kWh) just to power their gizmos and I haven't included the little devices, such as MP3 players and clock radios plugged in around the home. And much of this is invisible in the sense that it occurs when the machines are not in use, but are sitting quietly humming in standby mode. VCRs are relatively rarely used; typical estimates suggest that eight times as much power is consumed by a VCR in standby than when it is in use.

Pressure from consumer groups, retailers and the media has obliged manufacturers to dramatically reduce standby power in many types of consumer electronics. Most new devices have much lower power losses than even a few years ago. The cost to the manufacturers was small but it wasn't until people began to rail against the losses from

Table 6.11 *Energy consumption of consumer electronics*

	Hours of use	Hours of standby	Energy use when on (kWh/year)	Energy use in standby (kWh/year)	Total energy use (kWh/year)
Sky	6	18	37	105*	142
Sky (two rooms)	5	19	62	222*	284
Sky+	6	18	53	105*	158
Cable	6	18	37	105*	142
Freeview	5	19	18	49*	67
VCR	1	23	8	67	75
DVD player	1	23	4	8	12
DVD recorder	6	18	44	13	57
Radio	2	22	6	0	6
Home theatre	6	18	438	7	445
Games console	4	20	88	37	124

Note: *Older devices actually in the home; new machines will usually have a much lower figure.

Table 6.12 *Energy usage by the four stereotypical households for consumer electronics*

	Energy used actively (kWh/year)	Energy used in standby mode (kWh/year)	Total energy used (kWh/year)	Home contents
Stuck in the 1980s (light)	23	76	99	VCR, DVD, two radios
Moderate	99	296	395	Sky, Freeview, two VCRs, four radios, DVD
Heavy	207	256	463	Sky+, two Freeview, two DVDs, games console, four radios
Addict	739	377	1116	Sky+ (multi-room), two Freeview, two DVD-R, home theatre, games console

standby a couple of years ago that the improvements really started. This is a good indication of how determined and consistent campaigns can dramatically affect manufacturers' choices and result in significant savings.

The switch to all-digital TV broadcasting in the UK, which will be well underway by mid 2010 may boost electricity use as households acquire new set-top boxes to decode the signals. The first generation of these boxes was very power-hungry, but improvements have now brought electricity use to much lower levels, even in very cheap machines. But, elsewhere in the house, power levels are still increasing. Take one example: the games console. Microsoft's Xbox® 360 is said to take 160W of electricity when in use. It replaced the older version of the console, which only needed 70–80W. The older Sony PlayStation® required 50W and the new one up to 190W. Progress in games technology means, at least for the moment, very substantial increases in power to drive the realistic graphics on screen. A player using the Xbox® 360 for four hours a day – and leaving it plugged in when not in use – will use 330kWh/year, compared to about 150kWh when using the earlier model.

So Xbox® 360 is an important additional consumer of electricity. But the electricity bill will be perhaps £40, or less than the cost of one new game. The trade-off is clear – there is virtually no incentive for manufacturers independently to reduce energy use. Computer gamers buy machines based on the quality of the graphics in the games and on the speed and realism of the gory action. At today's energy prices, neither Microsoft nor its customers will seek to reduce power consumption if this entails any diminution whatsoever in the quality of the gaming experience. Energy is still too cheap.

Of course, the new home theatre devices are just as much of a problem. These packages, combining powerful speakers and DVD/audio players, can use huge amounts of energy to power. But they are clearly a product whose time is coming: in March 2006, Comet stocked 13 different packages, all of which were major users of electricity when in use. By August 2009, it had 27 different home theatre bundles on its website. The lesson is all too obvious: advances in consumer electronics are very likely to mean continuing increases in power sucked from the mains. But because TV is such an important part of everyday life, no government finds it easy to meddle with power consumption.

Computers

Similar forces are at work in home desktop computers. Increasing processor speeds tend to increase electricity consumption. More electricity use increases the heat given off by the chip, which means a bigger fan. This also takes more power. Top of the range PCs can use 200W – equivalent to two large incandescent light bulbs – when in full activity. Even when droning along, not doing very much, these machines use over 100W.

Computers have various different states of alertness. A PC whose processor is working hard, probably processing graphics, will use more electricity. But even when the machine is just turned on and a screensaver is hopping around the screen, it is probably still using 100W.

It surprises most people, but the computer is still consuming electricity even when it is turned off. Unless the plug is pulled out of the socket or turned off at the wall, the machine is typically burning about 8.5W – or 55kWh/year if it is 'turned off' for 16 hours a day.

Modern PCs are bad news for carbon emissions; but there's little economic incentive for people to do much about the power drain. For the typical user, it is hardly likely to be worth unplugging the machine rather than leaving it with the screensaver overnight. The saving might be as much as £25; but even a new and uncluttered machine might take five minutes to move from turning on to the point where the key programmes are all working. So, leaving the machine on probably saves 1000 minutes a year of valuable working time. The electricity cost of this time is no more than 2.5 pence a minute. In the economist's language, the 'rational' individual therefore doesn't turn the computer off. Even at today's high prices of electricity, the exchange rate between money and carbon dioxide is so unfavourable that no one has sufficient incentive to reduce their carbon dioxide emissions in return for more cash.

This is not just a problem in Western economies; the price of fossil fuel is so low that even newly industrializing nations will use coal and oil rather than human labour. And for many people, this is the end of the matter. The price mechanism has spoken and most people simply follow its signals. Human beings who behave differently and try to conserve energy even if it is not worth the effort are labelled as eccentrics and cranks. I hope that some of the readers of this book might see a moral quality in saving energy; but most people simply respond passively to the price of energy compared to the value of their own time. No one can blame them – but the consequences for emissions are increasingly severe.

Some manufacturers have now begun to produce energy-efficient PCs. The British company Very PC makes desktop computers with a power consumption in use of no more than about 70W. The company has done this through the careful choice of components and only including the functions that the user expects to need. For example, most home users don't need fast graphics processors and just equipping the machine with simple hardware means power use is reduced.

Laptops are even better. In fact the laptop is the only consumer electronics product in which power use is very carefully managed. Laptops are probably twice as energy efficient as desktop computers. Because users value the length of time before the computer needs to be plugged in for refreshment, the laptop has been engineered to use as little power as possible (this is the case even when the computer is powered by the mains and not just when it is working off the battery).

Should you work with the laptop plugged or run it off its battery? This partly depends upon whether you set your computer to dim its screen when working off battery; but, in general, it makes sense to run it from mains electricity because there are electrical losses in charging and discharging the battery. One study saw 20 per cent efficiency losses from running off the battery rather than the mains, although it commented that this was much better than observed with other battery-charged devices.[14]

About 70 per cent of homes now have a PC, and the energy consumption in these households will be tending to rise as a result of computing. The growing use of computers for internet access and the playing of films and video is increasing power demands. The increasingly ubiquitous broadband modem or router, now present in over half UK homes, is another small cause of rising emissions.

The rules for computers are reasonably simple. Use a laptop rather than a desktop. Turn off machines when you can, and ensure that the plug is removed from the wall (or the wall switch turned off). Set the computer (via the control panel in Microsoft operating systems) into low-energy or 'hibernation' mode when not in use. When possible, don't use processor-intensive activities. And don't be in a hurry to upgrade to the latest machine with a faster processor. It will probably use more energy. Networking of computers is relatively cheap in energy terms; but excess peripherals should be turned off completely when not in use. If you continue to use a desktop, rather than a laptop, ensure you have an LCD ('flat') screen rather than a CRT (one that looks like an old TV). As we discussed when talking about TVs, these are more energy efficient for the same size screen.

STANDBY LOSSES

It is not just consumer electronics that waste power when in standby. Most of today's appliances are using electricity even when they are apparently turned off. Sitting waiting to be used, these devices are burning a few watts in standby state. Almost everything with any electronics uses electricity whenever it is plugged in at the wall. One sophisticated toaster that termed itself 'eco-friendly' used 8W when not in use, probably doubling the total electricity consumption over the course of the day. Many people's reaction to this is of understandable outrage. Since the first edition of this book was published in 2007, progress has certainly been made. Public pressure means that new appliances now tend to have much lower standby losses than older equivalents. This is good, but I sometimes wish manufacturers had targeted the energy consumption of consumer electronics when they are actually in use. The potential savings are almost certainly greater.

Some household gadgets, such as mobile phones, also use little black transformers that plug into a socket. These chargers, or 'wall warts', as they sometimes used to be called in the US, also use electricity even when they are not working. And when they are being used, they often don't efficiently convert mains power into the lower voltages that the appliance is designed to handle. Some of the oldest transformers still in use lose over 50 per cent of the power in the form of heat.

The average UK home probably has at least 20 devices that consume electricity when on standby. They range from telephone answering machines to smoke alarms, microwave ovens and digital set-top boxes. Even that recent addition, the domestic bread-maker, is chewing up current. One obvious symbol of their continuous drain of electricity is the little light that stares at you at all times, day and night. However, it isn't just the red light, or even the clock on the oven, that is consuming electricity, but also the slow trickle that is needed to keep the electronics ready to switch on without a second's delay.

In the office where I have written this book, I can see ten small green lights without turning my head. They indicate appliances that are using electricity even when they are not doing any useful work. There's a laser printer that might actually run off 20 pages a day, but which I am sometimes too lazy to turn off when I have finished using it. A cordless telephone sits erect in a small cradle. A new and unreliable system for linking the three computers in the house via a network has a total of a further five unblinking bulbs. When my own computer is turned off, the screen tells me it is still ready by showing a weak yellow signal. Some of these lights I can turn off; others stay on all the time. But even though I nag others in the household about turning appliances off at the mains, I myself sometimes cannot be bothered to spend the 30 seconds or so shutting everything down at night and then powering it up again in the morning. New gadgets are becoming available that will turn the power off from these devices when they haven't been used for a set period of time.

Typically, the electronic devices consume 3–4W of power while not working (the light itself is a small fraction of this electricity consumption, but usually signifies that background electronics are working, too). So, a house with, say, 15 devices is burning 50W every hour of the day for no obvious purpose. That's over 400kWh/year, or more than 200kg of carbon dioxide per household. The cost is over £50 a year. Most experts think that about 10 per cent of all the domestic electricity that we use is wasted in this way, although the number is probably now falling gradually.

Even the simplest device is now equipped with electronics that need power dribbling through. And we have more and more such devices in the home. Almost every person over ten has a mobile phone and the charger is usually permanently in the socket. The number of set-top boxes will continue to increase, perhaps rapidly. Battery-powered devices such as electric toothbrushes, cordless power tools and hand vacuum cleaners are all rapidly penetrating UK homes. Our five-person household could never be called a home of gadget fans; but when I counted I found that we have over 30 appliances that will use standby power when plugged into the mains. Most of these have been acquired over the last five years. Unsurprisingly, the International Energy Agency says that standby power is already responsible for roughly 1 per cent of global carbon dioxide emissions.

The standby mode, whether used by the device itself humming quietly in the corner or, in addition, by the wall block that delivers its electricity, will always require a small amount of power. But most of today's devices use far more than is necessary. The high power usage levels are partly a function of laziness in design and partly because low standby power levels require slightly more expensive components. To its great credit, the satellite company Sky made the decision to adopt high standby standards in all the new boxes it installs in homes. Because of the size of Sky's business, this move will eventually make a measurable difference to domestic electricity use in the UK. But it will be many years before all the old boxes are removed from homes.

Today's most efficient devices use substantially less than 1W when on standby. For example, a good mobile phone charger uses between 0.25–0.5W when not charging the phone. Televisions can also be less than 1W. However, the typical appliance still runs at several times this level. If the appliance uses a wall wart, you can tell whether it has a significant power loss by touching it with your hand. If the transformer is warm, the appliance attached to it is using a measurable quantity of electricity.

Governments have latched onto the importance of the standby power issue. Around the world, energy-efficiency bodies are pushing manufacturers to introduce maximum standby power limits of 1W. European compliance is, however, entirely voluntary and progress here is probably even slower than in the US. Contrast this tolerance of high wastage of electricity with the position in the US, where President Bush signed an executive order in 2001 obliging the US federal government to buy only appliances with standby losses of 1W or less. Australia and South Korea have also formally adopted a target of 1W standby power.

The US also has a much better energy labelling system than in Europe. Here we rely on a complex categorization that gives each appliance a letter from A to E. The US Energy Star programme, by contrast, simply sets a single target. If the appliance meets the criterion, it can use the Energy Star logo. If not, it can't. To get an Energy Star designation for a wall transformer, the device must lose less than 0.75W for a major appliance. The limit is even tighter for a transformer for a small appliance. The requirements were introduced in early 2005. These limits are perfectly manageable, and manufacturers will probably fall into line. No such pressure exists for companies selling into the UK market.

BOX 6.7 – STANDBY LOSSES: DATA FROM OTHER COUNTRIES

According to a 2002 study, the average German home has continuous standby losses of 45W (the figure means that an average of 45W is being used at all times simply to keep appliances ready for use).[15] This equates to just under 400kWh/year. Add in standby losses in the non-residential sector and the figure rises to about 4 per cent of German electricity consumption, at a cost of about 14 million tonnes of carbon dioxide.

Danish homes lose 10 per cent of their electricity to standby consumption and Japan has a similar figure. Estimates from other European countries are 5–10 per cent of total domestic electricity use. The UK is a relatively poor performer, probably because of the greater penetration of inefficient digital set-top boxes.

Transformer losses

As I mentioned earlier, all wall transformers lose electricity when in standby mode. It is usually not much, but it is measurable. The transformers, generally, are also not particularly efficient at converting mains electricity into lower voltages. Many older transformers, recognized by their large regular shape, operate at no more than 50 per cent efficiency. Newer, less wasteful transformers can achieve efficiencies of more than 90 per cent or so (laptop transformers are generally very good). These power supplies are also much smaller and are often irregularly shaped, rather than cuboid. Older transformers are about the size of six or eight matchboxes put together, and are often so large that they block the adjacent wall socket. The more efficient types occupy perhaps one-quarter of the space so that you can easily recognize which type you are using.

The losses from the older type of transformer are enormous. The appliance itself might use 10W or 20W, and the transformer effectively doubles this. For some appliances, the transformer almost has to be on all the time, but is used for ten minutes a day. A cordless telephone would be a good example. A few years ago, the Energy Saving Trust in the UK published evidence that the average UK home has five wall transformers, which jointly consume 18 per cent of the energy used by domestic electronic appliances.[16] The number has probably fallen slightly since this result was reported.

What do we do?

The recommendations are reasonably clear and easy to implement:

- **Turn off all appliances at the mains – or pull out the plug – when not in use.** For the average appliance, this will save roughly 3–4W. This is a simple recommendation for things such as mobile phone chargers. For other devices, such as clock radios, for example, it is clearly nonsensical. Larger and larger numbers of appliances come equipped with digital clocks that flash crossly and require resetting every time the device is turned on. Try to buy versions of these products that don't have lights, displays or clocks. They do exist.

  Some people will also protest that turning off appliances is not always advisable. Users of the early personal computers were told that turning the machine off would shorten the life of the hard disc. This was probably true; but modern computers are now typically engineered to withstand 40,000 start-ups and shutdowns. Talking of computers, don't be confused into thinking that the screensaver conserves electricity. It doesn't. It is there for entertainment, not energy saving, and the screen generally continues to use the same amount of power as when the display is actually in working mode.

Look round the house. You'll probably find many appliances that constantly use electricity without telling you. That nice new bread-maker that you leave plugged in? 2–3W. The inkjet printer? 5W or so. And so it goes on – you can probably reduce your background electricity consumption by 25W without any problem at all simply by walking from room to room (perhaps saving £25 a year). The simple rule is that if the machine doesn't need to be plugged in, it shouldn't be. People often ask me about light bulbs – these don't take any power when not in use. You can leave them plugged in.

- **Where possible, avoid buying products that use external power transformers ('chargers').** Where the product isn't available without these transformers, such as mobile phones, make sure that you buy one that uses a small non-cuboid transformer (any irregularly shaped charger is probably better than the big cube transformers that are still used on some appliances). In general, mobile phone manufacturers have come into line and their transformers are very efficient. But other manufacturers are still using power supplies that lose a lot of energy when they are powering a device and considerable amounts when they are inactive. The Energy Saving Trust identified cordless phones and digital radios among the categories of electronic devices that used poorly designed transformers.[17]

- **Own fewer devices.** Buy less electronics. This is the real winner. More electronics in the home means more power consumption. A hard-headed assessment of whether it really is necessary to run a third TV, another DVD player or a new cordless power tool will sometimes force the concerned buyer simply to reject the new purchase.

- **Consider buying a device that tells you exactly how much electricity the house is using every second.** These simple displays demonstrate the amount of power appliances are using in standby and the huge impact of turning on tumble dryers and other electricity guzzlers. The Owl energy monitor costs about £25–30.[18] Several people I know who have bought this machine report their shock when watching these displays and seeing the impact of a kettle or a hair-dryer being turned on. This surprise may wear off but some studies suggest that providing a constant visual reminder of how much electricity is being used helps restrain household energy use.

7

car travel

The average car in the UK emits about 170g of carbon dioxide every kilometre. Typical new cars are only slightly better than this average. Change your car for a small (or medium-sized) diesel with manual transmission and you can get this number down to below 120g per kilometre. Such a car doing typical mileage will cut the emissions per person down to 0.8 tonnes from 1.2 tonnes.

Reduce this small car's mileage down to, say, 7000 miles (11,300km) a year, rather than the UK average of 9000 miles (14,500km), and the figure drops to just over 0.6 tonnes. Hire a car or belong to a car club, and the number falls ever further. Other choices, such as buying a hybrid electric car, can help to reduce emissions, but at a high financial cost.

Domestic cars, typically weighing well over a tonne, will always use large amounts of energy to move around the country. This is a simple outcome of the laws of physics, and we should distrust those who claim that any new type of car will somehow avoid being bound by the usual rules. Although the average fuel efficiency of a new car continues to rise, the increase in the number of cars washes away much of this improvement. To get rapid improvement in the future we will need to switch to electric cars, which do not suffer from the inherent inefficiencies of internal combustion engines. Battery-powered cars capable of being driven long distances without being recharged will not become widely available until 2012. Before then, the typical car user can reduce his or her carbon dioxide emissions by 50 per cent by making some simple choices.

Despite the widespread impression to the contrary, car use is only increasing very slowly in the UK. The number of cars on the road continues to rise; but the average mileage per car is flat, or even slowly reducing. Nevertheless, private car transport is already responsible for over 12 per cent of total carbon dioxide emissions. Per UK citizen, cars contribute about 1.2 tonnes of emissions per year, and for each car, the figure is around 2.6 tonnes. Car journeys represent a higher proportion of all land travel in the UK than any other European Union country except Lithuania and this figure shows little sign of falling.[1]

Individuals and families face an array of alternative choices for reducing the emissions for which they are responsible. One way is simply to drive better and to look after the car. A good driver can make substantial improvements in petrol consumption by avoiding rapid acceleration, driving at below 70mph, keeping tyres well inflated and replacing the oil filter regularly. But most of this chapter is concerned with the main options for permanently reducing emissions from car travel. Broadly speaking, these options divide into four groups:

1 driving fewer miles or using a lower-emission car;
2 using lower-emission fuels;
3 harnessing technology to get better fuel consumption.

Reducing emissions from driving isn't primarily a matter of using improved technology. The simplest things have the most effect. Halving the miles driven will halve emissions. Combining this with driving a small, efficient diesel car, preferably with manual transmission, might reduce consumption by a further third. This would cut the typical impact of using a car from about 2.5 tonnes down to about 0.8 tonnes and reducing per capita emissions to well below half a tonne. This effect is much greater than can be accomplished just by using lower-emission fuels, such as liquid petroleum gas (LPG) or diesel. We've also heard a great deal about biofuels, such as ethanol or biodiesel; but the emissions impact of these fuels remains extremely controversial. Because of the enormous amounts of fossil fuel used in the growing of crops for biofuel, the emissions savings may be non-existent. Getting better fuel consumption by using a hybrid car, such as the Toyota Prius, is extremely helpful; but once again the effect is not as great as simply driving less in a smaller car.

Table 7.1 looks at the main alternative ways of reducing emissions from personal car travel. It tries to show that there is no easy technological solution to carbon emissions from

Table 7.1 *The main options for reducing emissions from car travel*

Option	Main impact on typical CO_2 emissions*
Hybrid car, such as Prius	Reduce emissions by 1.1 tonnes
Liquid petroleum gas (LPG) car	Reduce emissions by 0.35 tonnes
New efficient car	Would only reduce emissions if old car it replaces is at the end of its life
Drive less	Just cutting out short journeys isn't enough to make much difference
Smaller car	A small diesel with manual transmission can halve emissions compared to a 2.0 litre petrol car
Auto versus manual	Switching from automatic to manual transmission typically saves 0.3 tonnes
Diesel versus petrol	A small manual diesel car offers savings of up to 0.8 tonnes
Electric car	Reduces emissions to about half the level of a small manual diesel
Car clubs	Joining a car club typically reduces car use by two-thirds, saving perhaps 1.6 tonnes
Biofuels	Complex calculations, but no convincing evidence that agricultural biofuels reduce fossil fuel use; cars using old frying oils are, however, very close to zero emission

Note: *Compared with an average car doing 9000 miles (14,500km) and adding 2.4 tonnes of CO_2 to the atmosphere each year.

cars. The two best routes forward are either to drive a small car fewer miles or to use the only genuinely near-zero emission vehicle – a car powered by used oil from a fish and chip shop. Eventually we'll be able to drive electric cars powered by renewable energy – another way of getting reduced emissions – but this isn't on the horizon yet.

This chapter looks at how responsible people can cut the carbon dioxide that comes from driving cars. Some people can simply give up their car; but others do not readily have this option. Therefore, the analysis tries to provide guidance as to what people can do to reduce emissions without giving up the car altogether. It quantifies some of the main options by their effectiveness in challenging global warming and in terms of their cost per tonne of carbon dioxide saved.

But first let's run through the ways in which we can drive better:

- Don't accelerate hard.
- Try to drive so you never have to brake (because you waste energy getting the car up to the speed from which you were required to brake).
- Keep the tyres inflated and replace filters frequently.

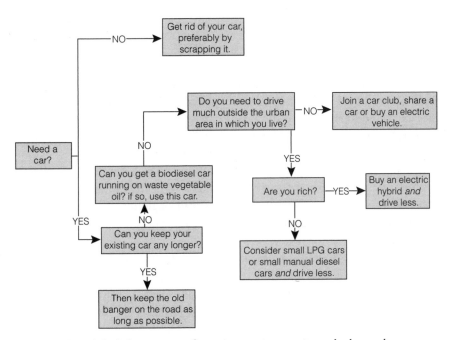

Figure 7.1 *Simplified decision tree for assistance in assessing whether to buy a new car and, if so, what type*

- Try to drive at the speed that is optimal for fuel efficiency (generally around 55–60mph). A car driven at 85 mph is typically using 25 per cent more fuel than one driven at 70mph. Keep to the speed limit.
- Air-conditioning use increases fuel consumption, perhaps by about 5–8 per cent, on average.[2] Try not to use it.

Taken together, these behavioural adjustments might save 10–15 per cent of all fuel consumption, or perhaps reduce emissions by 150kg per person per year. This is valuable; but more radical options need to be explored, as well.

Car travel: The major trends

Influenced, perhaps, by the increasing levels of congestion, our perception is that car travel is growing rapidly. Actually, the underlying picture is more complex. Although private car travel is an important source of greenhouse gases, it has not been rising at a particularly speedy rate:

- The number of private cars in the UK is about 28 million, or just over 1.1 cars per household. About 9 per cent of these vehicles are registered to businesses and therefore may be considered company cars.
- The number of households without a car is still falling slowly – 25 per cent now, it was 33 per cent in 1990.
- Households with two or more cars have increased in number significantly in recent years to about 32 per cent today. About 7 per cent of households have three cars.
- Although the number of cars is increasing, the amount of car travel per person appears to be gently declining, although commuting distances are rising. Typical personal car mileage seems to be a couple of percentage points lower than in 1999.
- The distance travelled in typical individual car trips is also flat or falling slightly.
- Therefore, the simple picture that we should have in our minds is of an increasing number of cars, but a very gradually diminishing amount of use of these vehicles, resulting in almost flat total amounts of car travel.[3]

These trends will probably continue. More and more people will own cars, particularly as the average life of vehicles seems likely to increase; but they won't necessarily use them for a much greater number of miles. The number of roads won't increase much – they already occupy an area the size of Leicestershire – and so congestion from private cars will increase slowly. Lorries and vans make the problem worse.

What is the impact of these trends on greenhouse gases? More fuel-efficient engines, advances in aerodynamics and weight reductions in some vehicles mean that the very best cars from the major car manufacturers have very much lower emissions than even a few years ago. But the improvement in the average emissions of the cars newly registered in the UK is a consistent 1–1.5 per cent a year. Taken together, all of these forces – more cars but slightly fewer miles per car and slow improvements in fuel efficiency – mean that total UK emissions from private motoring have probably peaked and may fall gently over the next few years. The prognosis for goods vehicle traffic is far less favourable.

Most organizations working in the field think that the average car travels about 10,000 miles a year, or about 16,000 kilometres. This number looks slightly high to me. Table 7.2 provides another estimate, based on calculations from UK government emissions figures.

As a compromise between the industry wisdom and my guesswork, the rest of this chapter uses an average figure of 14,500km per year, or about 9000 miles. It doesn't matter much if this number is slightly inaccurate since I am only using it as a number upon which to base estimates of improvements in carbon dioxide emissions levels. I also use an assumption that the average car on UK roads emits 170g of carbon dioxide per kilometre driven (the typical new car is slightly more efficient than this). Put another way, this means that a car generates over 1kg of extra carbon dioxide for every 4 miles (6.5km) on the road. For the purpose of calculations of lifetime savings, this chapter will assume that new cars last 16 years before retiring to the scrap heap.

Table 7.2 *Estimate of average distance travelled per year by UK private cars*

Data	Source
68.7 million tonnes of CO_2 from private cars	Society of Motor Manufacturers and Traders, 2009
28.2 million private cars = 2.44 tonnes CO_2 per car	Transport Trends, 2008
Average CO_2 output = 170g per kilometre	Department for Transport*
Total kilometres driven = circa 14,000–14,500km	

Note: *Department for Transport, Factsheets, UK Transport and Climate Change data.

BOX 7.1 – CAR TRAVEL: DATA FROM OTHER COUNTRIES

In the UK, there are just over two people per car. Per person, therefore, car travel amounts to about 6000–7000km per year (around 4000 miles). This figure is about the same as most European countries – Finland and Italy are a little higher, and Norway and the Netherlands somewhat lower. France and Sweden are about the same. The US is about 13,000km (8000 miles); but in Japan, car travel amounts to less than 4000km (2500 miles).[4]

This chapter will always use estimates of the direct carbon dioxide emissions arising from car use. In fact, a full analysis would include many other consequences of operating a car. Probably the most important of these is the carbon cost of producing the petrol that goes into the car. All of the figures for fuel consumption need to be inflated by about 15 per cent just to account for the energy cost of turning oil into refined products. And what about the costs of running the forecourts, the repair shops and the car dealerships? Some analysts have even allocated carbon costs arising from the insurance and licensing activities necessary to keep private cars on the road. To keep it simple, I do none of this and refer only to fuel burned in the engine of the motor vehicle.

Hybrid cars

I will try to demonstrate later in this chapter that trading in your old car and replacing it with a new, more efficient vehicle makes no sense if the old vehicle still remains on the road. In replacing your old motor, you have added one car to the stock of cars on the road, and although it can be argued that the incremental car adds little to the total number of miles driven by UK residents, it will certainly have some effect.

So let's assume, instead, that your old car sits smoking in the drive, having driven its last mile. Its only function now is to be broken down and recycled back into the steel and plastics from which it came. Does it make sense to buy a Toyota Prius – by far the bestselling hybrid electric car – to replace it, or not?

First of all, we need to ask why hybrid cars save any carbon emissions. After all, they are still fuelled by petrol and contain internal combustion engines like any other vehicle. In the case of the Prius, the energy saving comes from capturing the kinetic energy lost by braking and turning it into electric power in an internal battery. As a car brakes from 70mph on a motorway to 30mph on the slip road, it loses energy. In fact, the energy of the vehicle has declined by a factor of five as it makes this transition. Where does it all go? As we all know from the laws of thermodynamics, energy does not disappear. Most of the car's energy of

BOX 7.2 – ALTERNATIVES IN BUYING CARS: SOME COMPLICATIONS

When weighing up alternatives for buying cars, some complexities need to be borne in mind:

- Different fuels have different energy contents. So, 1 litre of LPG is not the same as 1 litre of petrol: it contains a lot less energy. Saying that LPG is half the price of petrol does not mean that the LPG owner's fuel bills will be halved. LPG will deliver fewer miles per litre than petrol. LPG advertisements tend not to talk about this.
- Advertised fuel economy figures are probably slightly lower than are actually achieved in practice. Perhaps paradoxically, this means that the advantages of new technologies such as hybrid petrol/electric cars tend to be understated when compared to alternative vehicles. If both hybrid and petrol cars use 10 per cent more fuel than the advertisements say, the savings from the hybrid will actually be greater than they appear (to be conservative, I've always used the published figure for low-emissions cars).

motion becomes heat as the brakes capture kinetic energy and turn it into increased temperature. The Prius works by turning the energy transformation during deceleration into potential energy in an electric battery. This electricity is then used to power the car at low speeds, replacing the requirement for the engine to be working. Importantly, this means that the car no longer needs to idle when it is stationary in traffic – instant battery power is always available to move the car. In addition, hybrid cars have smaller engines than equivalent saloons: the battery helps the car accelerate, reducing the need for a large engine.

Since this also reduces the need for fuel, the question we need to ask is whether the Prius's innovative technology offers a significant improvement over conventional petrol or diesel cars. The standard fuel economy tests show that the new Prius generates just 89g of carbon dioxide per kilometre compared to the UK average of 165g for the average new car, or 124g for a broadly equivalent Toyota model, a conventional Auris. What is the likely saving in emissions from choosing the Prius?

For the driver of the average number of miles, the Prius will save about 1.1 tonnes of carbon dioxide a year compared to a typical new UK car. Compared to the Toyota Auris in terms of size and power, the saving is only about 0.5 tonnes. Compared to the best conventional cars on the market, such as the VW Polo Blue Motion, the savings are tiny.

Does this make it a good purchase? It does offer the lowest emissions of any petrol-using car. This means the owner pays no car tax, although this benefit can also be gained by buying from a small choice of other cars.[5] The Prius owners to whom I have spoken are happy with the car's fuel economy, although they sometimes express reservations as to whether the car achieves all of the savings that it claims.

In another sense, the Prius is bad value for money. Comparing the prices of cars is always difficult; they come with very different accessories and equipment. But on the basis of the list prices, the Prius is over £5000 more expensive than the Toyota Auris. Perhaps the Prius is significantly more luxurious or commodious than the Auris but at £18,000 or so, it is a very pricey alternative. On the basis of lifetime savings of about 15 tonnes of carbon dioxide (about 0.5 tonnes a year over 16 years), the incremental cost is £500 per tonne not emitted. If you have £18,000 to spare and want to reduce carbon emissions, there are many more effective alternatives, both when considering motoring and other activities. The world is doomed to a very impoverished future if reducing carbon emissions by 1 tonne always costs £500: if the developed countries need to reduce emissions by 10 tonnes a head per year, then the total bill will be £5000, or almost one-fifth of gross national product (GNP) per capita. This would be good justification for those who claim that significant reductions on emissions are 'too expensive'. As we have already seen, emissions reduction generally costs a small fraction of the figure implied by the Prius. Indeed, the price of 1 tonne of carbon dioxide reduction, when traded on the international carbon exchanges, is currently (July 2009) about £12, or about one-fortieth of the extra price that the buyer pays for the Prius's low fuel consumption.

Later in this chapter, we will look at the impact of increased car weight on emissions. The Prius is a slightly heavier vehicle than its near equivalents – by about 100kg. Most of this extra weight is metal and metal contains what is usually called 'embodied energy'. In other words, it took fossil fuels to manufacture the components of the car, whether it is the engine or the Prius's battery. This would tend to reduce the lifetime carbon savings gained by the Prius's owner; but the effect is not large enough to outweigh the savings from the Prius's capture of braking energy.[6]

Buying a luxury car with hybrid capability will also save emissions. The Lexus hybrid SUV's CO_2 emissions are 10 per cent below the average of new cars entering the UK fleet. The manufacturer claims that Lexus cars fitted with hybrid battery systems save about 25 per cent of the emissions of a comparably sized prestige car. But it seems a strange choice to buy a luxury hybrid car. They still have emissions far higher than medium-sized efficient diesel cars.

Toyota and Lexus hybrid cars are also expensive compared to their conventional alternatives. Hybrid technology is relatively new, and manufacturers may rightly claim that the extra costs compared to other cars will tend to fall over time. So, buying a Prius does help Toyota to move down the manufacturing learning curve. Another complaint about the simple numbers contained in Table 7.3 is that high-mileage drivers, doing two or three times the UK average hacking up and down motorways, may be able to achieve much better carbon savings. This may be true, although the Prius's best performance is probably generated on a mixture of local driving, when it uses the battery, and long-distance travel, when the battery is quietly recharging. If the driver is only using the car for long journeys on higher speed roads, the average petrol consumption of a hybrid car will be worse than expected.

But in the minds of a customer, the Prius also has significant advantages over conventional cars. For example, it is exempt from the London congestion charge. It is, in fact, probably the most 'normal' of all cars that don't have to pay the charge. Some other vehicles, like the all-electric G-Wiz that I talk about later in this chapter, involve real trade-offs for the customer, such as having to plug in the battery every 40 miles (64km) in exchange for lower fuel consumption. The Prius is just like a normal car; but the regular central London motorist saves up to £2000 a year. Such a buyer will find the extra £5000 cost a small price for freedom from the congestion charge.

The exemption from congestion charging is, in effect, a government incentive to use low-emission cars. Central government also encourages the purchase of a Prius by reducing the annual road tax fees. In mid 2009, the tax disc is costs nothing compared to £150 for the average UK new car.[7] Over the course of its life, this saving will be over £2000, even before considering the likely increase in road tax bills over the next few years.

More important, perhaps, are the lower petrol bills. At a price of £1 a litre, the typical purchaser of the average new car will spend about £1040 on fuel every year. The Prius costs about £480 less, thus saving somewhat more – in excess of £7000 – over the lifetime of a car than the incremental cost compared to buying a comparable car. Of course, it might be thought that the cheaper cost of motoring might cause the Prius owner to drive more miles. With a petrol cost of about 6 pence a mile, compared to 11 pence for a conventional car of similar size, the hybrid owner may slip into a habit of greater use.

Similar behaviour is noted in Chapter 3 on central heating – better-insulated homes with lower energy bills tend to be run at a higher temperature than draughty period properties. The owners take the saving partly in increased comfort. The point? Protection from climate change isn't necessarily provided by high efficiency.

Table 7.3 *How much carbon dioxide does the Toyota Prius save?*

Car model	Kilometres per year	Emissions in standard test	Yearly CO_2 emissions (tonnes)	Extra CO_2 emissions compared to the Prius (tonnes per year)
Toyota Prius	14,500	89g CO_2 per kilometre	1.29	
Toyota Auris 1.4 litre manual	14,500	124g CO_2 per kilometre	1.80	circa 0.5
Average UK new car, 2007	14,500	165g CO_2 per kilometre	2.390	circa 1.1

In fact, I'll try to argue later – in the section on 'car clubs' – that the best way to get vehicle emissions down may be to encourage vehicle rental. Commercial car clubs offer short-term rental at high hourly rates; but users never buy the car or pay the annual fixed charges, such as insurance and duty. This addresses the problem that conventional car owners – you and me – tend to notice only the petrol costs of running a car. The purchase price, possibly paid ten years ago, is a distant memory, and our decision about how much we can afford to drive is only affected by what economists term the 'marginal' costs of driving: the extra costs of driving another mile. In most cases, this is just the petrol used; but car clubs load the full cost of driving onto the hourly rates. There's abundant evidence later in this chapter that this really does affect total car use.

Liquid petroleum gas

Liquid petroleum gas (LPG) is an alternative fuel for motor vehicles. Many LPG vehicles – and there are 120,000 or so on the road in the UK – are conversions of existing petrol (not diesel) cars to run on both LPG and petrol. The presence of the 'dual-fuel' label on the back of some conversions and the two fuel caps on the side of the car help to identify these vehicles. These cars have a petrol and a gas tank. The typical LPG driver will actually only ever use LPG, because it is cheaper, but will keep petrol in the petrol tank just in case the gas runs out.[8] Around the UK, 1400 LPG filling stations make it reasonably easy to avoid ever running out of gas.

The typical cost of converting a petrol car to LPG is about £2000, and a large number of approved installers are able to do the job, typically in the course of a working week. Generally speaking, insurance costs are no greater than a similar petrol car. The only significant disadvantages are said to be the loss of car storage capacity as a result of the installation of the gas tank, usually at the expense of the spare tyre, and some complaints about the car's performance after conversion. Neither of these concerns seems to worry many LPG users. The ones whom I have spoken to are very happy with their cars and their fuel bills.

As well as producing less carbon dioxide, LPG produces less of the other main pollutants from vehicle use. Compared to diesel engines, for example, LPG reduces particulate emissions by 90 per cent. There is also a potentially significant impact on nitrogen oxide and carbon monoxide emissions. LPG cars are definitely cleaner.

In other countries, a large fraction of all high-mileage cars and light vehicles have been converted to LPG, and users such as taxi drivers would benefit most from using gas in the UK. The tax regime has, however, not always been sufficiently advantageous to justify conversion, rather than, say, the saving on fuel bills by buying a diesel car instead.

LPG is a mixture of two chemically simple gases – propane and butane. In the UK, LPG is largely propane, but the mix is nearer to 50:50 in other European countries. The fuel is rich in energy and is slightly more powerful than petrol per kilogram. But even in liquid form, it is much lighter than petrol and so the energy content per litre is not as high. One litre of LPG is not equivalent to 1 litre of petrol. Nevertheless, advertisements for conversion often simply advertise the headline price of LPG without mentioning the shorter distance that 1 litre of the fuel will take the car. Figure 7.2 gives a simple example of what this means in practice.

These figures suggest that the carbon dioxide savings from converting a car to LPG are about 15 per cent. Proponents of LPG sometimes claim higher figures of 20 per cent or more; but these estimates do not seem to be consistent with the energy content of the fuel and its carbon dioxide production when burned in an engine. To me, 15 per cent or so seems the right percentage saving, and in the Vectra example given in Figure 7.2, the CO_2 saved would be about 350kg per year for a typical driver.

The reduction in the cost of motoring is more significant. For the average car driver, the savings will be about 35 per cent of the cost of a petrol equivalent. This assumes that the current relationship between the price of petrol and the price of LPG remains the same; lower taxation of LPG means that the forecourt price of gas is about half the price of petrol at the moment. This difference is partly an artefact of taxation because the government is using the lower tax on LPG as a means of increasing its appeal. It would therefore be an entirely reasonable view that LPG's price advantage could fall as a result of government losing enthusiasm for LPG at some stage in the future.

Currently, for the average car driver doing 14,500 kilometres (approximately 9000 miles) a year, the savings will be, perhaps, £300 to £400, depending upon the size of the car. The incremental cost of purchasing the car will be somewhere around £2000, meaning that the payback will be about six years. For a heavy driver, the return could be much quicker, which is why many taxis and other high-usage vehicles have moved to gas.

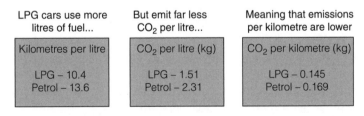

LPG cars use more litres of fuel...	But emit far less CO_2 per litre...	Meaning that emissions per kilometre are lower
Kilometres per litre	CO_2 per litre (kg)	CO_2 per kilometre (kg)
LPG – 10.4 Petrol – 13.6	LPG – 1.51 Petrol – 2.31	LPG – 0.145 Petrol – 0.169

Figure 7.2 *What are the carbon dioxide savings from using a liquid petroleum gas-powered car? An example of a manual 2005 Vauxhall Vectra 1.8i*

Source: Various, including the LPG Association (data from the LPGA website, www.boostlpg.co.uk). Some of these numbers are slightly different from the ones on the www.vauxhall.co.uk site. For example, Vauxhall says that the carbon dioxide emissions for the petrol car are 175g per kilometre.

Most LPG cars – but not all – get beneath the carbon dioxide emissions levels set for exemption from the London congestion charge. Vehicle licence taxes are also lower than for the equivalent petrol-only car. The 2005 Vauxhall Vectra owner would save £45 a year at current rates, paying £130 and not £175 and we can expect this difference to increase.

What about the carbon dioxide benefits? In the Vectra example, we estimated the savings at around 350kg a year, or about 5.6 tonnes over the 16-year life of a car. If the cost of an LPG conversion is £2000, the price per tonne saved is about £360 (Figure 7.3). This is less than the equivalent figure for the Toyota Prius.

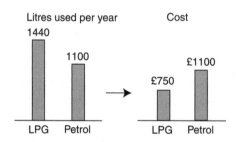

Figure 7.3 *The savings from switching to liquid petroleum gas*

BUYING A NEW CAR

Does it make sense in environmental terms to sell your old vehicle and replace it with a new and more fuel-efficient car? Of course, the answer to this depends upon a number of different questions:

- Does the old car get scrapped or does it remain on the road?
- How fuel inefficient was the old car in relation to the new one?
- How much energy was consumed building the new vehicle?

If a very old car that consumes a huge amount of petrol is scrapped and replaced by a light and low-emission vehicle, it may be that the net impact of the change is beneficial to the progress of global warming. But in most circumstances, the purchase of a new car results in a net addition to the atmospheric stock of carbon, largely because the old car also remains on the road. (Many governments introduced 'scrappage' schemes in the aftermath of the 2008/2009 recession. These schemes – meant to be temporary – resulted in the scrapping of older cars, thus removing them from the road.)

What is the correct way to show that, in normal economic times, changing your car for a new vehicle doesn't make good sense from a CO_2 point of view? We need to do our calculation in three parts:

1 First, we need to calculate the remaining emissions of the older car.

2 Second, we must calculate the savings from the lower level of emissions of a new car.

3 And, finally, we should estimate the energy cost of building a car and allocate it pro rata to the remaining life of the *old* car, or the number of years of useful life that we could have used it for.

As an example, let's examine the trading-in of an eight-year-old car during 2009. When new, this car was typical of its year of manufacture and generated, as can be seen in Table 7.4, just under 177g of carbon dioxide per kilometre.

As an aside, we might note that the EU had a target to reduce emissions to below 140g per kilometre by 2008. This objective wasn't reached, but the rate of progress in 2008 was the quickest since data were first recorded in the UK. Driven by the high price of fuel in 2008, increases in car taxes, both for business and private owners and the greater availability of very efficient models, the UK saw an unprecedented improvement in fuel economy. To meet the revised EU target of 130 grams per kilometre by 2015, progress needs to continue to be very rapid.

To get back to the eight-year-old car; when sold, it will stay on the road for probably another eight years. It will typically become the second or third car of a nearby household (it always used to be said that cars in the UK typically move northward at about 4 miles, or 6.5km, a year, as prosperous southerners sell their cars to buyers typically from slightly further north).

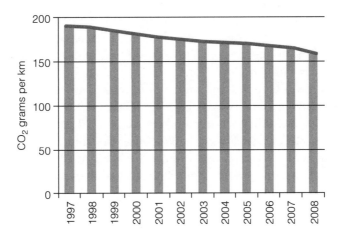

Figure 7.4 *Average new car emissions by year of manufacture*

Source: Society of Motor Manufacturers and Traders

The discarded car will probably travel relatively few miles a year for the remainder of its life. Four thousand miles (6500km) seems an appropriate average figure, although this estimate is no more than a guess.

In the eight remaining years of its life, the car will therefore produce a total of 9.2 tonnes of carbon dioxide. How does this compare to the savings generated in this time by the use of the lower-emissions new car bought to replace it? A typical new car in 2009 will generate emissions of about 158g per kilometre. The better fuel efficiency of the average new car will mean a saving of about 2.2 tonnes of carbon dioxide in its first eight years. Therefore, the replacement of an old car with a new car will typically result in a net increase in emissions of about 7.0 tonnes of carbon dioxide, or the best part of 1 tonne a year in the period before the old car is retired from the fleet. This figure is before calculating the effect of actually making the new car.

Studies of the energy taken to manufacture or process new goods are often controversial. For example, the two sides of the acrimonious British debate on the merits of wind farms are locked in an intricate argument about whether the energy used to make the turbines, their masts, the concrete approach roads and the electricity transmission plant are greater than the electricity generated during the useful life of the farm. At one extreme, the proponents of wind suggest that the energy balance swings positive over about 18 months, while, at the other, some suggest that onshore wind farms never reach energy neutrality. With such huge divergence in opinion, we need to approach the energy cost of any manufactured item with extreme caution. With all these caveats, later in this book I estimate that the carbon footprint of a very small new car is approximately two and a half tonnes. The average car will be three tonnes or more.

That was the third step in the chain; the total environmental cost of swapping an eight-year-old car for a more efficient model is over 12 tonnes, or more than the total yearly emissions of the average person. The lesson? Don't replace your car – drive the old jalopy until it retires from the road. Take pride in the age of your car and boost your credentials even as you fill up the tank for the third time in a week.

Perhaps it is obvious, but switching your car also makes no financial sense. The maximum saving in fuel efficiency is probably worth £200 for the mainstream driver. Buying a low-emissions car can also cut £100–150 a year from your vehicle taxation bill, although this number is certain to rise. Perhaps the lower maintenance charges will save £500 a year. Bluntly put, the total savings will little more than pay the interest charges on the purchase of a new motor.

Drive less

Most people need a car. Some families need two. But many of us can adjust our behaviour so as to use the automobile less. I will ignore the appalling possibility that, by reducing congestion, using your car less will encourage others to use theirs more, thus wiping out any benefit from your actions. This kind of economist's logic creates inertia and despair.

In a more optimistic frame of mind, what happens to carbon dioxide when one decides never to take the car on journeys of less than 2 miles (3km) and replaces these trips with a walk?

Table 7.4 shows that replacing all car trips of less than 2 miles does not result in a substantial reduction in car travel. Although these trips account for a total of about one quarter of all journeys, they represent only about 3.5 per cent of the 5000 or so miles that each person typically drives every year. (But note, however, that the National Travel Survey data seem to underestimate the actual amount of car travel by as much as half. The actual mileage of car travel per person should certainly be over 8000 miles. Perhaps the survey results contain a phenomenon well known to market researchers – 'virtuous' rather than accurate answers.)

If we were to assume that the survey respondents did accurately report the number of car trips of less than 2 miles, how much carbon dioxide would be saved by shifting to walking?

Short trips will typically be fuel-inefficient trips because engines take time to warm up and deliver their best fuel economy. But at average fuel economy, the saving might be no more than about 50kg of carbon dioxide a year. And even if the respondents had underestimated their journeys by a half, the benefit is unlikely to average more than 80kg.

This demonstrates an uncomfortable fact – it may be the short, needless car trips that most enrage environmentalists; but cutting out the guilty dash to the corner shop will not substantially reduce emissions. To reduce carbon dioxide, we would need to attack commuting journeys and visits to friends. Commuting journeys are responsible for about 18 per cent of all personal trips and visiting friends, 19 per cent. Neither of these activities is increasing much; but the typical distance travelled on these trips is drifting slowly upwards. Ten years ago, the typical commuting car trip was 6 miles (just under 10km); it is now almost 9 miles (14km).

Table 7.4 *Impact of always walking rather than taking the car on trips of up to 2 miles*

Distance	Driver or passenger?	Estimated average distance (miles)	Number of trips per year	Distance travelled (miles per year)
0 to 1 mile	Driver	0.5	27	13.5
	Passenger	0.5	17	8.5
1 to 2 miles	Driver	1.5	67	100.5
	Passenger	1.5	42	63
Total				185.5

Source: National Travel Survey, Department for Transport, London, 25 July 2005.

We need to further explore the question of whether reducing the number of short car trips and replacing them by walking actually saves carbon dioxide. Walking is not zero emission because we need food energy to move ourselves from place to place. Food production creates carbon emissions. Does the energy used when walking a mile, rather than driving, result in a net rise in carbon dioxide because this energy needs to be replaced by extra food?

This is an unconventional question, of course. Most people see walking as a means of using up food calories that would otherwise become extra body weight. To put it another way, most people consume very slightly more calories than they use, so, little by little, body weight increases. Figure 7.5 demonstrates this for a cohort of English men, showing that the typical weight of a person in this group rose from 81.5kg in 1993 to 86.5kg in 2004. During this 11-year period, the average weight rose by 5kg (about 11 pounds), or about 0.4kg a year (1 pound).

However, the striking fact is that a tiny amount of extra walking would work off this extra 0.4kg (see Table 7.5).

Table 7.5 shows that weight gain occurring in the UK population could be completely avoided if the typical person walked an extra 31 miles (50km) a year, or about 150m a day – provided that he or she didn't compensate for the extra exercise by eating a jam sandwich or two. The National Travel Survey (disparaged for its possible inaccuracy above in Table 7.4) says that the typical individual walks about 200 miles (320km) a year, and so the exercise necessary to restrain any weight gain would only add about 16 per cent to the distance walked.

Why is this digression relevant to the calculation of the environmental impact of switching from car to foot? My argument is this: avoiding weight gain in the UK

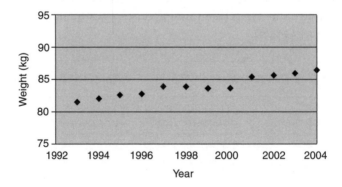

Figure 7.5 *Average weight of English men aged 45 to 54 (1992–2004)*

Source: Health Survey for England, UK Department of Health, London, 2005. Later editions of this survey focus on Body Mass Index rather than just weight. Continued increases in BMI suggest that the weight of the typical UK citizen has continued to rise.

Table 7.5 *How many miles of walking does it take to reduce weight by 0.4kg a year?*

Typical energy intake	1,050,000 kilocalories per year
Approximate surplus required to add 0.4kg a year*	2734 kilocalories
Rate of energy expenditure walking at 3 miles per hour	264 kilocalories per hour
Number of hours of extra walking required to balance energy input and output	10 hours, 20 minutes
Number of miles of extra walking	31 miles

Note: *I have used a crucial figure from lecture notes provided online by Dr J. A. Illingworth of the University of Leeds, UK. Dr Illingworth says that a person who typically consumes 1.3 per cent more energy than he or she requires will put on 2kg a year.
Sources: Various.

population requires 31 miles (50km) extra walking a year; but switching to foot for all car journeys under 2 miles would require 185 pedestrian miles. So, the typical person would lose weight if he or she stopped using a car for short journeys. In fact, they would lose more than 2kg a year (4.5 pounds). This is assuming that they didn't eat more as a result of the extra exercise. Instead, if they chose to hold their weight constant each year (31 miles' walking), they would have to eat enough to replace the energy burned by walking 154 miles (185 miles less 31 miles).

Producing food takes energy. In fact, most assessments show that Western industrial food manufacture – I include the processes on the farm – absorbs more than nine times as much energy as the food itself contains (see Chapter 10). So 1 calorie of lettuce or bread or beef takes at least 9 calories of fossil fuel to make. The question is this: does the high 'embedded' energy content of Western food mean that walking rather than driving is necessarily good for the global climate?

At one extreme, the answer is almost certainly no. The calculations in Table 7.6 show that drinking a glass of milk to replace the energy lost during a walk probably produces more greenhouse gases than the car would have done. Home-grown food, cultivated without fertilizers, would have different consequences, of course.

Even though I have tried to simplify it, where possible, Table 7.6 is complex and confusing. It has four stages:

Table 7.6 *Energy balance from walking rather than driving if the energy replacement is from dairy products*

Distance walked		1.5 miles
Kilocalories used		132 kilocalories
Milk needed to replace this energy[a] (165 kilocalories)		154ml (about 1 cup)
Methane	Typical methane production from intensively farmed cows per 154ml[b]	3.79g
	Methane to CO_2 multiplier[c]	21
	CO_2 equivalence	80g
Carbon dioxide	Energy (kWh) equivalence to kilocalories	0.00116kWh per kilocalorie
	Energy multiplier to convert fossil fuel energy into food energy	9
	Kilowatt hours of fossil fuel energy to produce 165 kilocalories	1.73kWh
	CO_2 output per kWh (e.g. from natural gas)	0.20kg
	Total CO_2 produced in the food chain to deliver 154ml of milk	345g
Total CO_2 equivalent		80g + 345g = 0.425kg
Equivalent CO_2 cost for a typical car for a 1.5 mile (2.5km) journey		0.45kg
Saving		0.025kg
But CO_2 cost of walking if two people travel by car instead of walking	0.40kg	

Notes: [a] Assumes that food energy is converted by the body at 80 per cent efficiency.

[b] This figure would be even higher if the milk was organic because organic cows produce less milk per unit of food they eat. So methane output per litre of milk is higher.

[c] Methane's impact on global warming is generally assessed as between 21 and 25 times that of carbon dioxide. I have used the lower number here.

1   First, it establishes the energy needed to replace the calories in a short walk. Then it looks at how much milk is needed to provide that energy.

2   It goes on to calculate the methane output from the cow that provides that milk and multiplies this by 21 to reflect the disproportionate impact of methane on global warming.

3   It then works out the carbon dioxide cost of the fossil fuels needed to get the milk to the home.

4   And, finally, it compares the carbon dioxide equivalent cost of drinking milk compared to travelling by car.

Table 7.6 shows that if one person walks rather than drives, she saves some emissions – but the difference is marginal. But if the car carried two people, the short journey would be better done by car.

These numbers refer to milk. If we did the same calculations for the impact of replacing energy by eating meat, we'd find the numbers were even clearer. Most assessments of the impact of intensive cattle farming suggest that 1kg of beef produces greenhouse gases equivalent to about 30–50kg of CO_2.[9] The 50g of meat eaten to replenish the energy cost of walking 1.5 miles would generate approximately 2kg of global warming gases, four or five times the amount arising from driving the average car the same distance.

In July 2007, I wrote up a small piece of research suggesting that in certain circumstances walking was more carbon-intensive than driving and the content was carried by *The Times*. Most readers assumed that I was advocating driving a car rather than going by foot and my inbox was deluged with thousands of angry responses. However, the real purpose of the work was to help to illustrate the substantial environmental impact of food production, particularly of beef and other meats.

Switching to a smaller car

When the time comes to retire your old car, you will save money and carbon by switching to a smaller, less powerful vehicle. Smaller car engines produce less carbon dioxide than big ones. This is not quite as trivial a statement as it sounds; some of the most efficient engines in the world, such as those that move huge ships, are highly efficient at turning fossil fuels into kinetic energy. What makes large car engines relatively fuel inefficient is that they are engineered to produce higher power and to move larger, heavier vehicles with faster acceleration.

An examination of the cars in the current Citroen portfolio is shown in Figure 7.6. The C5 is a very different car to the tiny C1 and has nearly double the emissions at just under 200g per kilometre.

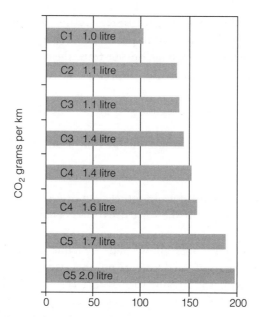

Figure 7.6 *Carbon dioxide emissions of some Citroen petrol cars, mid 2009*

Source: www.citroen.co.uk, accessed July 2009

For the household using the car for an average distance a year, the saving in carbon dioxide arising from using a 1.0 litre engine rather than a 2.0 litre version is as much as 1.4 tonnes of carbon dioxide. This is almost half of the average car's emissions, so is a more than worthwhile contribution. Of course, the emissions reduction also springs from the lower weight of the smaller cars, but this chart shows the surprising benefits of buying a car with a tiny engine.

Nevertheless, it is worth mentioning that there isn't a perfect correlation between engine size, car body weight and emissions. One car leasing company pointed out to me that very similar cars can have fuel consumptions that are up to 30 per cent different. There's no substitute for careful comparison of manufacturers' websites. But with well over 200 cars on sale in the UK with emissions of less than 130g per kilometre, the choice is certainly there.

CHANGE TO DIESEL OR MANUAL TRANSMISSION

Manual versus automatic

The car industry has done a good job of ensuring that few people recognize the fuel-efficiency deterioration from moving to automatic transmission. On the Toyota range, the equivalent automatics have emissions that are typically 12 per cent higher than the manual model. In the case of automatics, the process of transmitting engine power to the wheels through the transmission system turns a larger percentage of engine power into heat, rather than kinetic energy.

With a typical car and an average mileage, a manual transmission saves about 0.3 tonnes of carbon dioxide.

Diesel versus petrol

Diesel is much heavier than petrol and although its energy content per kilogram is lower, the greater density more than makes up for this deficiency. So, although diesel is more expensive at the pumps than petrol, it delivers more energy per litre. Better fuel economy in the diesel engine also improves carbon dioxide emissions.

I have seen a wide range of estimates for the characteristic improvement in comparably powered engines of switching from petrol to diesel. Some are as high as 40 per cent; but comparisons of similar petrol and diesel models suggest an average figure of about 15 per cent. Many examples suggest that a saving of 20g per kilometre is possible for cars with similar performance.

If the average carbon dioxide output is 2.3 tonnes per year, then switching to a diesel car of similar size will save perhaps 400kg per year (note that the average figure for all UK cars mixes petrol and diesel vehicles and would be higher if it only included the petrol cars on the road). Over a 16-year life, the savings will be over 6 tonnes of CO_2.

Diesel cars are, however, more expensive. The typical vehicle seems to be about £1000 more costly than a similar petrol motor car. So, the cost per tonne of carbon dioxide saved is about £150 – much better than for an LPG or a hybrid electric car. Each year, the fuel savings might average £160, giving a 7-year payback. There will be a small saving in excise duty as well.

Some strict environmentalists frown on diesels because of the higher levels of particulates and some other pollutants emitted. Cleaner diesel engines will reduce these problems over time and today's cars are already far better than those of even 10 years ago. Or you could use an LPG car instead, which reduces particulate emissions to very low levels.

And, as usual, there's the possibility that the cheaper costs of running a diesel acts as an incentive to the driver to travel more. One study in France showed that drivers who moved from petrol to diesel cars increased their travel by an average of 17 per cent.[10] We need to absorb this lesson – make something cheaper and people will consume more of it.

Small diesel manuals compared to average petrol automatics

A small diesel car with a manual transmission offers the best carbon dioxide performance of current conventional cars. The Toyota Yaris in its 1.4 litre diesel form, manages emissions of 109g per kilometre, compared to 118g for a smaller petrol engine. The diesel Yaris would save about 0.8 tonnes of carbon dioxide a year compared to the characteristic

UK petrol car. The Yaris is, of course, far cheaper than the Toyota Prius, one of the few cars that beats it for emissions.

ELECTRIC CARS

Decent electric cars have been promised for years; but true equivalents to internal combustion cars are still not quite here. My guess is that it will be about 2012 before we really see battery-powered cars that are a real alternative to those powered by an internal combustion engine. At the moment batteries are too large, performance is poor and none of the factors that enthuses car buyers – speed, acceleration, comfort and looks – can be found in the current range of products. There are exceptions, of course, such as the Tesla, the US sports car that was largely designed by Lotus in the UK, but these tend to be extremely expensive.

A number of electric cars for urban areas are gradually coming into widespread use in the UK. The most obvious current example in the UK is the Bangalore-made, but California-designed, G-Wiz car. It seats two people in reasonable comfort; but you wouldn't want to drive it on a motorway. It claims to have space to put a couple of children in the back, as well. They would have to be quite small children.

The car currently comes in two versions – one with lead acid batteries and the other more advanced lithium ion batteries. The lead acid version is much cheaper but only has a range of about 40 miles (about 64km). It needs roughly 9kWh of electricity to charge the battery. How does this compare in terms of carbon emissions? Using an estimate of the average UK carbon emissions from electricity generation, this car puts out about 78g per kilometre. This figure is about three-quarters the CO_2 level of the lowest emission diesel. What about the cost of running it? If a charge of 9kWh (at about 12 pence per kWh) takes the car 40 miles (64km), the cost is about 2.5 pence per mile (1.5 pence per kilometre). The lowest figure for a small diesel driving in the city is likely to be around 8 pence per mile, or more than three times as much.

Of course, such a car would never drive 14,500km (9000 miles) a year; but if it did it would (indirectly) emit about 0.9 tonnes of carbon dioxide, compared to the UK average of 2.3 tonnes. For the typical urban-only user doing perhaps 8000km (5000 miles) a year, the saving over the smallest conventional cars would be about 0.3 tonnes. The benefit over a Prius would be as little as 0.1 tonnes, although at about £8500, the G-Wiz is less than the price of the hybrid. (Unfortunately the lithium ion version is almost as expensive as the Prius.) In addition, the low weight of the G-Wiz means that far less energy is used in its manufacture.

The vehicle escapes congestion charge and vehicle taxation. The exemption from vehicle duty seems to be based on the car being classed as a powered bicycle, or, more precisely, a quadracycle. Its 1000 or so London owners also escape some car parking charges and some municipal car parks offer free charging.

Small electric city cars are clearly a useful addition to the range of emissions-reducing technologies in use in cars. They are not, however, a real replacement for conventional saloon cars yet. But rapid advances in battery technology should raise our hopes that cheap, light electric cars will replace most liquid fuel cars. In addition, increasing numbers of manufacturers are openly backing the eventual switch to electric cars and governments around the world are begin to invest in putting large numbers of charging points alongside city streets.

The advertising for electric vehicles often refers to the cars as 'zero emission'. They are not. They use electricity, generated by fossil fuel combustion. And if power generation becomes more carbon-intensive as a result of a swing towards coal-fired generation, the relatively small advantages of electric cars over diesel will decrease. This raises a thought: the best way to power an electric domestic car is by installing a small wind turbine in your garden in order to charge the battery. This way, we can be sure that the electricity is genuinely emissions free. Combining a small wind turbine and a car battery would be an exceptionally effective way of using a turbine. It would also mean that the turbine owner would not have to buy the expensive equipment necessary to plug it into the grid. The power could go straight into the car battery.

This would make an electric car truly emission neutral, but would be dependent upon the wind blowing. I suppose that if the wind wasn't turning the blades, the next best alternative would be to only charge the car in the middle of the night, when the emissions from electricity are low because the (relatively) carbon-free nuclear plant is the dominant source of electricity.

Car clubs

Finding methods of sharing cars looks a very productive way of reducing total car use. This can be done informally, with neighbours jointly owning and maintaining a car. Or it can be done through commercially operated car clubs. These clubs buy cars and place them in on-street locations, often granted free by the local authority. Local people join as members, usually by paying an annual fee of £50 or so. Upon joining, members can use the internet to book the cars close to them, or indeed anywhere else in the country. Access is via an electronic key. Use of the car is paid for by an hourly rate and a mileage charge, with the car automatically transmitting details of use back to the owner via a data-only mobile phone. Members pay for petrol when needed through a company fuel card – that is, they don't themselves pay directly because the fuel cost is included in the mileage charge.

Table 7.7 gives some details of the pricing of two UK firms operating in this market. Car clubs seem to work best in London, with its high parking charges, astronomical insurance rates and – I suspect – relatively low-mileage users. As of July 2009 Streetcar says that it has 850 cars and 50,000 members. Its coverage of central London and the immediate suburbs is good, including (to pick one example out of the air) 27 locations in Clapham. It now has cars in five cities outside London but coverage is patchy in these places.

Table 7.7 *Some pricing details of two UK car clubs*

Club	Yearly fee	Minimum hourly rate	Minimum 24 hour rate	Mileage charge
Streetcar	£59.50	£3.95	£49.50	Free 30 miles a day, then 23 pence a mile
CityCarClub	£50	£4.95	£49.50	No free miles, 16p a mile

Source: www.streetcar.co.uk and www.citycarclub.co.uk, accessed 5 January 2010

Many other countries such as Switzerland now have active car-sharing businesses. Zipcar in the US has 300,000 members and 6500 cars. It focuses on large cities on the eastern seaboard and on areas near major university campuses. Perhaps surprisingly, the prices are higher than in the UK. The minimum hourly charge in Boston is $9.25 (about £6) although this does come with free mileage up to 180 miles a day, rather than 30 miles as is the case with the UK's Streetcar.

The operators of car clubs claim major environmental benefits. Streetcar says that its members drive 71 per cent fewer miles than they did before joining (this is a major saving in carbon dioxide – perhaps 0.8 tonnes). Slightly implausibly, Streetcar says that each car that it rents takes at least 20 other vehicles off the road.[11] The car club says that an Automobile Association (AA) study showed a typical cost of £2749 a year for two trips a week in a car you own, compared to a Streetcar cost of £707 for the same journeys.

Are the cost savings advertised by the car clubs reasonable? It depends how much you drive your car. If you need it to drive to work every morning, a shared car is going to cost you a fortune. But for a driver doing two or three trips a week, a car club will make excellent financial sense. And it rids you of the need to spend time keeping your insurance current, taking the car for its annual maintenance and buying the tax disc. However for people with very old cars, car clubs may not look good financially. These cars usually have no second-hand value and the annual cost of ownership may be well below £1000.

Why do car club users tend to drive fewer miles? If you own your own car, the only cost that you think about when deciding whether or not to take a trip is the price of petrol. Even in a large old car this is unlikely to be more than 15p a mile. But Streetcar users face a £3.95 bill every time that they start the engine. The high charge causes them to ration their use to a fraction of their usual mileage. Therefore, car clubs are good for vehicle emissions and good for the wallets of their members.

Why are they not taking off faster? Why have they actually failed in some UK cities? There are a number of obvious reasons:

- The possession of a private car in the driveway gives total convenience. The user can drive off in a few seconds. The car clubs claim very high levels of availability – more than 95 per cent; but they can never guarantee a vehicle immediately.
- A car is an important symbol of status.
- The economic advantages are perhaps not important enough, or are perhaps difficult to observe and measure.
- Last, and possibly most importantly, people may resist car clubs because of the 'ticking meter'. We all instinctively realize that we are prepared to pay more for the feeling of not paying by the minute. British Telecom (BT), for example, found out before it launched its unmetered telephone calling plans that customers would happily pay 20 per cent more than was strictly rational if they knew that all calls were free once the monthly fixed charge had been paid. Imagine going to pick up a friend at the station in a car club vehicle. In your own car, a train delay would be irritating; but in the club car, the burden might double as a result. To many people, the psychological cost of this would be too great for comfort.

So, car clubs may or may not work in UK urban centres (they are never likely to appeal to those who have to drive to work every day from rural homes with no bus service). Nevertheless, the environmental benefits seem high and the cost savings real. What could policy makers do to encourage their growth? Their aim might be to:

- Increase the variable ('marginal') cost of running a private car. This means increasing the price of petrol in relation to the capital and fixed costs of car ownership. This will make the use of a private car appear to have a cost that is more similar to the car clubs. The problem? It will severely penalize those in rural areas who have to use a car for travel to work.
- Provide explicit encouragement to car clubs, perhaps by providing free parking spaces in urban areas or by letting users utilize priority lanes.

In the case of increasing the variable costs of private cars, the best way for governments to encourage car clubs is probably to introduce congestion charging – or 'road pricing' in the current parlance – as a means of discouraging private car use at busy times. The most important feature of these schemes is that rural users escape most of the charge; but the urban middle class carting their children to and from school will get hammered. If these latter people could escape road pricing by using car club cars, then the economic incentives for the schemes would increase.

The second economic incentive – encouraging car clubs, rather than discouraging private cars – will probably work best in areas where parking represents a genuine and persistent problem. Obliging developers of new housing to provide no parking except for car club vehicles would be a radical means of encouraging the move away from the two-car household.

BIOFUELS

In theory, almost all vehicles can run on oils made from plants (biodiesel) or ethanol made from grains and roots (bioethanol, or bio-petrol). Using vegetable oils as the fuel for an engine is not as eccentric as it sounds; Rudolf Diesel's first engine ran on peanut oil when it was exhibited at the Paris World's Fair in 1900.

Biofuels look as though they are 'renewable' in the same sense that electricity can be, offering substantial energy without increasing greenhouse gas emissions. But, as is unfortunately often the case in climate change debates, the reality is more complex than the proponents claim. If we substantially increase the volume of biofuel use, we will run into two major problems:

1   Biofuels may use as much fossil fuel in their production as they replace in vehicles.
2   Agricultural land is not particularly good at generating energy for use in fuels. If we were to produce a substantial fraction of our vehicle fuels from crops, most of the land area of the UK would have to be given over to this use. In terms of carbon reduction, we would be far better advised to plant this land with trees.

Before delving into the reasons for scepticism about biofuels made directly from crops, we should acknowledge the efforts of the pioneers of today's biodiesel. Many of these people are not using new agricultural products for fuel, about which there are such fundamental reservations, but are recycling waste products, such as used cooking oil. In such cases, the carbon consequences are exceptionally favourable; but the volume of used vegetable oil is tiny compared to the demand for petrol. Nevertheless, if you ever see a car powered by cooking oil, you know you are watching one of the most nearly carbon neutral vehicles on the planet. The only complaint from their enthusiastic owners is that their exhaust fumes betray the origin of the fuel, whether it is a chip shop or a school kitchen.

Made in tiny factories – a garage would be big enough to house a small plant – biodiesel from waste oil is a product we could use a lot more of. But the supplies of used oil are highly restricted and could only power just over 100,000 cars even if all of the UK's supply of waste oil was used.[12] Nevertheless, there are already 250 small factories churning out diesel that smells ever so slightly like a mobile chip van.

In theory, almost all diesel cars can use processed vegetable oils collected from chip shops, at least as part of their fuel mix. More conventionally, crops such as oilseed rape can be refined to provide oil to power cars and commercial vehicles. Petrol cars can be modified to accept ethanol – usually made from wheat or sugar beet in temperate countries – as part of a petrol mix, much as biodiesel can be added to fossil diesel. Some vehicles, such as the Saab 9-5 Biopower, can use a much richer mixture of 85 per cent ethanol/15 per cent petrol. However, very few filling stations in the UK carry bioethanol at the present time. So the Saab can also be fuelled with conventional petrol. As with LPG, the first customers will probably be fleets of vehicles that all return regularly to one location, such as delivery vans, where they can fill up with biofuel at a central point.

These fuels, biodiesel from oilseed rape or ethanol from wheat or sugar beet, are probably not competitive on cost with petrol using today's technologies. Production costs for agricultural products are greater than for petrol, even at crude oil prices of $70 a barrel. As a result, biofuels can only be a comparable price at the pumps if they are taxed at a lower level or if fuel retailers are legally obliged to mix fuels made from agricultural sources with conventional petrol or diesel. After several years of implicit subsidy, the regulatory regime has now switched to insisting that all transport fuels contain 5 per cent biomass-sourced ethanol or biodiesel.

Biodiesel and ethanol are made from agricultural products that can be grown on any arable land in the UK or overseas. Properly looked after, this land can produce fuel energy forever. However, this doesn't make the biofuels truly carbon neutral. The agricultural products use substantial volumes of fossil fuels in the forms of oil-based fertilizers, processing energy and road transport. How much fossil fuel energy is used to make a unit of biodiesel or bioethanol energy? The debate on this question is not always completely even tempered. Some sources suggest that biodiesel and, particularly, bioethanol will generally use more fossil fuel energy than they provide in the car. In other words, there is no net benefit in greenhouse gas emissions from switching a car to biofuels. The leading proponent of the view that biofuels are energy inefficient has been Professor David Pimentel of Cornell University in the US. His work suggests that neither diesel nor ethanol produced from agricultural crops actually reduces the net amount of fossil fuel used.

This is a similar conclusion to the depressing analysis in Table 7.6 that suggested that walking may actually add to climate change if we replace the energy we use by eating foods grown by the Western system of industrial agriculture. Agricultural is, in general, hugely energy inefficient, so it makes little sense to see food products as themselves a source of power. Pimentel wrote: 'the United States desperately needs a liquid fuel replacement for oil in the near future; but producing ethanol or biodiesel from plant biomass is going down the wrong road because you use more energy to produce these fuels than you get out from the combustion of these products'.[13] Perhaps with justice, Pimentel sees ethanol production in the US as simply the outcome of the distortion caused by the subsidization of uneconomic agriculture.

At the optimistic end of the opinion spectrum, biodiesel's proponents see the fuel as being four times as efficient as diesel, in terms of fossil fuel use. Numbers for ethanol are lower, seemingly because of the greater processing necessary to turn wheat, maize or sugar into the end product.

This debate will continue for years. And the future of biofuels is probably tied more to the support system for agriculture than to fundamental economics. As long as biofuels remain much more expensive than fossil fuels, their use is only going to expand significantly because of government support. This support is certainly there today, but may be more to do with the need to maintain agricultural industries than resulting from a concern over global warming. It may not be a coincidence that the UK's first bioethanol plant to use beet sugar as its agricultural input was finally approved soon after the agreement to end the repugnant EU export subsidy that has done so much to harm the sugar farmers of the tropics. The government needed to find an alternative market for beet to replace the lost markets elsewhere, and support for bioethanol does the job. This doesn't make it good for climate change, or even good for the taxpayer. The latest thinking is actually not to make biodiesel from conventional agricultural crops at all. Algae certainly offer a better ratio of the conversion of input energy to the output of fuel. The major oil companies, including Shell and Exxon are now beginning investment programmes that seek to create large-scale algae production plants that can compete with the price of conventional oil. Algae grow quickly, extracting CO_2 from the air in the process, and when dried can contain up to 50 per cent oil that can be relatively easily converted to a diesel substitute.

In Table 7.8 I look at the impact of the requirement that all fuels contain 5 per cent biomass-based material on the emissions of a medium-sized diesel car. I assume, perhaps very optimistically, that biodiesel will offer a 50 per cent saving in greenhouse gas emissions.

This is a naive analysis and needs to be made more complex. We need to include the impact of land-use change on carbon dioxide emissions. Put simply, if 1 acre (0.4ha) of land is used for crops to produce a biofuel, that land cannot be cropped for food. So if we are to make significant quantities of biodiesel or ethanol, we will need to add to the area under arable cultivation. The amounts of land needed are surprisingly large. To replace the current UK demand for diesel with its biological equivalent would require about 12–13 million hectares of arable land if the crop grown was oilseed rape.

Table 7.8 *The carbon dioxide impact of switching to 5 per cent biodiesel*

	Typical CO_2 emissions per kilometre	Average emissions per year, assuming 14,500km (9000 miles) driven
Conventional diesel car	0.150kg	2.18 tonnes
5 per cent biodiesel car	0.146kg	2.12 tonnes
Saving		2.5 per cent

At the moment, only about 4.5 million hectares are cultivated in the UK. So, to replace fossil diesel, we would need to roughly quadruple the land area under crops. Since this would entail moving onto land that is of marginal fertility, yields would suffer greatly. Since a large fraction of all UK land that can be productively used for arable cultivation is currently already being worked for food, there is little prospect of ever growing enough oilseed rape. Even if biodiesel is sold only in the 5 per cent form, we would still require about 0.6 million hectares. In itself, this seems too much and would more than double the acreage of rape. Seen from the air in May, most of lowland England would glow a bright yellow from the flowers of this impressively bright brassica.

Even if we could convert some extra land to arable cultivation, would this be good for climate change? The answer is almost certainly no because the land would be better used for forests that sequestered carbon. One hectare of English oak (*Quercus robur*) captures about 275 tonnes of carbon dioxide over 100 years.[14] At 50 per cent energy efficiency, oilseed rape grown on the same land probably replaces about 225 tonnes of fossil fuel diesel emissions over the same period. In other words, it is slightly better to convert 1ha to the growing of a slowly maturing tree than it is to convert it to oilseed rape for biofuels. Using the land for fast-growing willow, and then coppicing the trees for fuel and burning it for electricity would be even better – although this depends upon the percentage efficiency in the power plant burning the wood chippings from the willow.

George Monbiot has made similar arguments about the conversion of tropical forests to palm oil plantations that are intended to produce the feedstock for biodiesel.[15] He points out that the furious rate of planting of tropical plants was largely driven by the EU's imposition of a target for the biological content of vehicle fuels by 2010. Perversely, this apparently benign aim is inflicting huge damage on areas that should be kept as slow-growing forest.

All cars currently on the road can run on petrol and diesel that contains a small percentage of biofuels. Some vehicles have been specially engineered to use fuel that is mostly biodiesel or ethanol. In some other countries, such as Sweden, considerable numbers of vehicles can run on E85, made from 85 per cent ethanol and 15 per cent petrol. This fuel is widely available at the pumps. Saab, the Swedish car manufacturer, makes a range of cars that run on E85 and it makes very aggressive statements about the emissions savings that result:

> The Saab 9-5 BioPower is a flex-fuel car whose fossil CO_2 emission level can be reduced by as much as 70 per cent compared to a standard petrol-engined car.

This statement is, to say the least, highly controversial. Almost all assessments of ethanol suggest that it saves 40 per cent, at the very most, of the emissions from conventional petrol. It is true that the footprint of ethanol made from tropical sugar cane may achieve better results, but very little of the fuel available in Europe comes from this source, being primarily made from wheat or beet sugar. Although the BioPower range is marketed with standard green symbols, such as falling leaves, the manufacturer also emphasizes the improved acceleration in cars engineered to burn ethanol or E85. One review stated

> For the 9-5 BioPower Saloon, for example, the zero to 62mph dash can be accomplished in 8.5 seconds, compared to 9.8 seconds when running only on petrol.[16]

The extra fuel used to accelerate faster will, of course, add to the total emissions of the car, meaning that the actual fuel consumption is likely to be greater than the standard tests might suggest. The environmental credentials of the Saab BioPower are thin.

BOX 7.3 – CARBON EMISSIONS FROM CARS: DATA FROM OTHER COUNTRIES

The pattern in the rest of Europe is similar to that in the UK. New cars are becoming more efficient but vehicle fleets are increasing in number, meaning that total emissions from cars are falling slowly, if at all. Technology is improving the emissions performance of Europe's cars quite rapidly, and the gains are far from exhausted, but these gains are being eaten up by increased car ownership and a slow swing away from public transport in many countries.

Private cars are responsible for about 12 per cent of all European emissions, approximately the same figure as the UK. Britain has slightly fewer cars per head of population than the EU average (469 per thousand population in the UK compared to 559 in Germany and 500 in France) but the vehicle is typically used for slightly more miles. The average age of cars in Britain is the lowest in the EU (6.7 years compared to 8.5 years). Rapid economic growth in the early part of this century means a larger number of cars under 5 years old than elsewhere.

Nevertheless, average new car emissions are slightly higher than the rest of Europe (2007 figures). In 2008, only 11 per cent of cars sold in the UK were less than 121g per kilometre compared to 16 per cent in the rest of Europe.[17]

FASHION AND FAD

The complicated economic analysis necessary to work out how best to reduce emissions from private cars should not disguise the important requirement to reduce car use in all Western societies. New technologies, such as hybrid cars or oilseed rape for biodiesel, may or may not assist us in cutting vehicle emissions. What will definitely work is getting drivers to cut their annual mileage. Technology, such as the recurrent dream of creating hydrogen cars, may actually impede the search to understand the social levers we might use to cut car mileage. Fantasizing about a hydrogen car may reinforce our optimism that science, rather than behavioural change, will solve our problems. To restate the point made at the beginning of this chapter: moving 1 tonne of metal from standstill to 60mph is an inherently energy-intensive activity. Nothing can gainsay this. And because car travel requires reliably available liquid fuels – gases not being dense enough to store in a conventionally shaped vehicle – the scope for replacing hydrocarbons with renewable energy is limited. Cars are vital to most people's lifestyle and until we find a way of changing this, we are going to struggle to reduce transport emissions fast enough to meet our goals for emissions reductions.

8

· ·

public transport

All motorized travel is carbon-intensive, but bus and rail are generally far better than cars. Actual carbon emission figures vary according to the type of vehicle and the number of people using it. Intercity coaches are best – as low as 20g of CO_2 per passenger kilometre. These coaches travel long distances and often carry large numbers of passengers. This makes them the best form of travel if one wants to avoid carbon dioxide. On the other hand, empty rural buses are sometimes as bad as cars in terms of emissions per passenger.

The average UK citizen travels about 700km on railways each year. The average emissions per kilometre of travel are about 60g – about half the emissions of a very fuel-efficient car if only one person is travelling. Some commuter lines will be much better than this, but powerful and heavy long-distance trains may be worse than the average, especially if they are powered by electricity. Total emissions per year average just less than 35kg.

People travel shorter distances by bus – only 400km a year – but the average emissions per year are probably slightly higher than rail at an average of about 70g per kilometre. Long-distance coaches are much better than buses because they generally are quite full and don't have to stop and start like a city bus.

The conventional view is that all public transport has relatively low emissions. This belief has considerable truth, but is not a wholly reliable guide to action. A decision today to take the coach rather than drive to London from Birmingham has undeniably positive effects; but across all buses and trains, carbon emissions are more substantial than one imagines. Nevertheless, most people travel very little on public transport. The typical individual accounts for about 35kg of carbon dioxide emissions from rail services, and about the same from bus and coach travel compared to over 1 tonne from car travel.

RAIL

The UK government uses a figure of just under 60g of carbon dioxide per passenger kilometre, or less than 40 per cent of the typical car.[1] Of course this implies that having just three people in a car means that the car is actually more efficient than the train. Individual railway operators produce their own estimates of carbon dioxide per passenger kilometre. National Express says that its rail services average 41–44g of CO_2 per passenger kilometre.[2] First Group suggested a figure of 50g.[3]

Whether one takes the government figures or those from the industry, rail is about half the figure for British Airways' carbon dioxide emissions per passenger kilometre (or one-quarter if one takes into account the other pollutants created by air travel). So, on average, train travel is far better than cars or flying. This conclusion is sometimes questioned, but researchers who note the particularly high emissions of some long-distance trains can still find good reasons to question whether high-speed diesel lines are really much better than car travel. And for long-distance commuters, travelling perhaps a hundred miles a day, emissions can be as high as a family car. For example, the hundreds of people travelling every day from Oxford to London are probably sharing total emissions of about 10kg a working day, or about 2 tonnes a year per person.

The more typical UK resident travels on a train only 17 times a year, for an average of 40km a time. Total journeys over the year amount to about 700km per person, slightly below the European average.[4] This implies carbon dioxide emissions per person of about 35kg, or less than a quarter of one per cent of the sum of all emissions. But until the 2008/2009 economic recession, train travel had been rising fast. The UK rail industry is responsible for 2 million tonnes of carbon dioxide, and increases in travel are likely to push this number up to over 3 million tonnes by early in the next decade. If this is as a result of substitution for car or air travel, then we can be happy. If the travel is, instead, incremental and will arise from further growth of longer-distance commuting into London and other cities, then it illustrates the effect on emissions of having the population living slightly further away from their place of work every year.

The relatively small current emissions of about 2 million tonnes of carbon dioxide for the rail industry disguise two important trends. First, the total amount of rail travel has been rising, particularly within the London commuting area. This makes for greater efficiency in fuel consumption. But, second, many of the new long-distance trains are heavier and more aggressively powered than the older diesel commuter trains. The Pendolino train, running at high speed between Manchester and London, weighs as much per passenger seat as half a Landrover Discovery. The exciting new trains can go faster, accelerate more rapidly and weigh far more per passenger seat than old stock. But they use far more fuel. In these respects, they are like modern cars compared to the older generations of automobiles, or big liquid crystal display (LCD) TVs compared to the televisions of five years ago. Improvements in rail locomotive efficiency have been swallowed up by faster speeds and heavier carriages. This is, of course, a recurring theme across this book.

One example makes this clear. Elderly Class 168 diesels, carrying 278 seats on the regional rail network, are powered by engines with a total output of 1260kW. New 'Adelante' trains, which were added to the Oxford to London route a few years ago before being withdrawn because of maintenance problems, have engines of 2800kW output but only carry 265 passengers. Therefore these new trains had well over twice the engine power per seat. Unsurprisingly, Adelante emissions are one-third higher per passenger kilometre than the average diesel train in the UK.[5] Trains are losing their advantages, particularly on the less crowded routes.

One interesting study tried to show how car travel from London to Edinburgh can be less polluting than high-speed rail.[6] It relied on some assumptions that can be criticized, such as assuming low thermal efficiency in power stations; but it did demonstrate that long-distance rail travel does not solve the carbon dioxide problem. More particularly, it shows that trying to help rail to compete with air travel by improving track speeds always has a significant penalty in terms of fuel consumption. Faster speeds require heavier, more powerful trains, which significantly reduce the fuel use advantage over air travel particularly since wind resistance for surface vehicles rises far more than proportionally to increased speed.

Electric trains are probably more energy efficient than their diesel equivalents. Electric trains are lighter, partly because they don't have to carry fuel. Diesel locomotives, like diesel cars, lose much of the energy in their fuel as heat. Further electrification of the rail network, such as the proposed move to electric trains between London and South Wales almost certainly makes good sense. It would be even better if the electricity were generated from low-carbon sources. The electric line between London and Paris is partly powered by French nuclear electricity and, as a result, has carbon emissions of about 18g per passenger kilometre, less than a third of the average UK train.

Those interested in accurately calculating their carbon 'footprint' from rail travel need to make an adjustment if they sit in the bigger seats in first class. First-class carriages have much lower capacity than the crowded standard service. So, as with executive class air travel, we need to apply a premium. Carbon dioxide output from first-class travel will be approximately 50 per cent more than travel in standard seats.

BUS AND COACH

Outside London, bus travel is still falling in most parts of the country. This fact, and the huge differences between empty rural buses and fully occupied intercity coaches, makes data on bus emissions particularly uncertain. The government's estimate is that bus travel outside London is almost as carbon intensive as a small car at 110g per kilometre.[7] This high level arises partly because the average bus is carrying less than 10 people. In London the figure is lower at 83g, a figure that is nevertheless higher than train journeys.[8] Energy efficiency gains in recent years have been difficult as bus operators are obliged to switch to buses with low emissions of pollutants other than carbon dioxide. Buses and coaches are a major contributor to low air quality around city centres but less polluting vehicles unfortunately tend to use more fuel. Coaches between cities are much more efficient. National Express, which operates both buses and coaches, gives figures showing a threefold difference in emissions between its buses and its coaches. Coaches – usually run over long distances – have half the emissions of rail (30g of carbon dioxide per passenger kilometre compared to 60g); but their buses are 50 per cent less efficient than rail (99g per passenger per kilometre, about the same as the best hybrid electric car with one person in it).

BOX 8.1 – BUS AND RAIL TRAVEL: DATA FROM OTHER COUNTRIES

Bus travel in other countries is sometimes substantially higher than in the UK. Denmark and Greece have a typical bus mileage of over 5km a day, compared to little more than 1km in the UK. The UK share of bus and coach travel in total surface transport is 6.5 per cent compared to nearly 9 per cent in the 15 pre-expansion European Union (EU) member states as a whole; but France and the Netherlands, for example, are substantially lower than in the UK.

UK rail travel is also a slightly smaller share of total surface travel than in the EU15 as a whole (5.5 per cent versus 6.5 per cent). Unlike the UK, countries such as France and the Netherlands, with low bus travel figures, have substantially higher rail travel at 8.6 per cent and 9.3 per cent, respectively.[9] Emissions from rail vary significantly between countries, depending upon, first, whether the system uses electricity or diesel, and, second, whether the electricity is generated by nuclear power or coal, at the other extreme. The French fast trains (trains à grande vitesse, or TGVs) use electricity for power; but most of this is generated by nuclear power.

The average number of bus or coach trips per year is about 60, with the distance travelled about 400km, compared to 700km on the railways. For someone travelling in a mixture of bus and coach, the total emissions from this average number of journeys would be about 30kg.

Despite the immediate appearance to the contrary, urban buses are nevertheless probably very much better for the atmosphere than private cars. The data suggests that two people travelling in a car would have lower emissions levels than travelling on a bus.[10] This would probably be mistaken because the car's fuel consumption as it jerked along between endless traffic lights getting in or out of a city will probably be little better than half that of the same car travelling at 60mph on a motorway. A like-for-like comparison of urban bus and car travel would probably show that bus travel was substantially better than cars.

The typical bus produces about 1.3kg of carbon dioxide for each kilometre travelled.[11] The average car, over the mixed cycle used for the standard emissions test, has an output of about 170g per kilometre, or about one-seventh of the bus. So, it's very likely that buses are more efficient than cars in all circumstances when they have at least seven times as many occupants as the typical car (1.59 occupants). And since the average bus has about ten passengers, bus travel is usually better than a car. Many buses, of course, do not achieve this occupancy level, particularly in rural areas; so the assumption that buses are invariably less polluting is a contentious one.

Coach travel definitely offers very substantial savings over the car. National Express believes that its London to Birmingham coach reduces emissions by over 90 per cent compared to the same trip by a car with a single occupant – if the coach is full.[12] Many coaches do, indeed, operate at near capacity, and for city-to-city travel, they represent a very low-emission type of transport, easily beating rail. At the time of writing, First Group is just about to introduce a new intercity service, modelled on US Greyhound buses between London and the south coast. It claims that the emissions will be less than a quarter of the comparable car journeys, even though its big new coaches are fitted with relatively few seats. Attempts by governments to increase coach use – as long as it is diverting customers from rail, car and air – are particularly to be valued. Comfortable and spacious coaches should be less polluting, and cheaper, than rail travel.

Of course, it is always better not to travel using fossil fuel energy at all. After the first edition of this book was published I got several letters from people complaining about the lack of attention paid to cycling. Cycling enables a person to get around a town or city faster than in a car or a bus, and almost as fast as a train in some circumstances. A well-maintained cycle needs only about a third as much energy as a person walking for every mile covered. So even though a cycling commuter will generally need to eat more to replace the energy lost when on the bike, it still makes excellent sense to ride everywhere you can. Of course, cycling is great for improving basic fitness and, I suspect, helps make people more mentally alert when at work. I've never met a lazy cyclist.

For the sake of completeness it might be worth recording the typical emissions of Tube trains and passenger ferries. The London underground works out at about 65g per kilometre, slightly better than most light rail or tram systems.[13] Ferries are much higher at 115g and this number assumes that most of the fuel cost of the ship are borne by the freight lorries also being carried. Pure passenger ferries, particularly the very fast ones, are very bad indeed for emissions for each kilometre travelled.[14] Black cabs are also very heavy fuel users – much more than the equivalently sized car.

9

air travel

Travelling by air, in contrast to the bus, is a disaster for the environment. Although an efficient aircraft, travelling fully loaded, can cover miles with less fuel per person than the average car, aircraft travel covers vastly greater distances than cars. The average car goes 9000 miles (14,500km) a year, with an average of about 1.5 people in it at any time. One return flight to the US will probably exceed the per-person emissions of a year's car use.

The only really significant change to our lifestyle that we need to make to get our carbon emissions substantially lower is to cease to travel by air. With this single choice, we can make the most important step to meeting the long-term requirement to cut our contribution to climate change.

To a surprising extent, air transport use drives individual greenhouse gas emissions. Of course, variations in car use are important. But air travel really determines how much carbon dioxide a person generates. Air travel is inherently more polluting than car journeys. As well as carbon dioxide, jet engines emit oxides of nitrogen, which are powerful warming agents. In addition, aircraft put out huge quantities of water vapour at high altitude in the form of condensation trails. These contrails are now thought to worsen global warming, although the science is not yet completely clear. As a result of these two extra sources of emissions, most experts now think that air travel emissions are about twice as bad as the simple carbon dioxide output might suggest. The precise value of the multiplier we should use remains uncertain: the IPCC continues to use a figure of 2 to 4 but the prevailing scientific opinion is tending towards the lower figure.[1] But whatever figure we use for estimating the full impact, a few flights to remote locations, and we have been responsible for tens of tonnes of global warming gases.

Across the world as a whole, air travel is probably responsible for about 2.5 per cent of carbon emissions. Multiply this by 2 to account for the nitrogen oxides and water vapour, and we are up to about 5 per cent. In the UK, the figure is already nearly 6 per cent for carbon dioxide alone and 12 per cent after the multiplication. Until the recent recession, air travel had been growing by 5 per cent a year, and although engines are becoming more efficient, carbon emissions are certainly increasing by around 2.5 per cent a year. No one sees an end to this growth – cheap air travel is immensely popular and many governments are willing to build airports to accommodate the extra travel. The consequence of unconstrained growth of aircraft emissions, even at the relatively modest rate of 2.5 per cent compounded a year, is to double aircraft emissions in the next 30 years. In the UK, that will mean average emissions per person of 3 tonnes just for air travel. This is inconsistent with any aspirations to reduce national emissions by 80 per cent by 2050.

Table 9.1 *Carbon dioxide emissions of a typical UK individual taking no flights*

Source of carbon dioxide emissions	UK yearly average
Electricity in the home	0.8 tonnes
Gas in the home	1.6 tonnes
Car use	1.2 tonnes
Other ground transport	0.1 tonnes
Total	3.6 tonnes

However much an individual does to minimize his or her impact on the environment, any measures are dwarfed by the impact of taking a few air flights a year. No single step that we could take as individuals to take responsibility for global warming comes close to deciding to stop flying.

What is the impact of flying compared to these totals? Table 9.2 gives examples of particular trips that have approximately the same impact as each of the major categories of emissions from home activities and personal transport. The figures include the two times multiplier applied to properly weight the other greenhouse impacts of flying.

About half the people in the UK don't take any flights at all during the course of a year. Those that do fly, fly an average of twice a year. For many of these people, the impact will be greater than everything else combined.

The total number of flights taken by UK individuals from UK airports is currently about 55 million a year. With 60 million people in the country, the average person takes less than one air trip a year. So, on average, people's greenhouse gas emissions from air travel are significant, but not overwhelming. For the increasing number of individuals frequently travelling by air, both for business and leisure, aircraft emissions are their most important contribution to global warming.

Table 9.2 *The impact on personal carbon dioxide emissions of a small number of flights*

Source of carbon dioxide emissions	UK yearly average	Air travel equivalent
Electricity in the home	0.8 tonnes	One return flight London/ Athens
Gas in the home	1.6 tonnes	One way to New York
Car use	1.2 tonnes	Two return flights to Athens
Other ground transport	0.1 tonnes	Barely enough to get up to cruise altitude

THE SCIENCE

No one pretends to be sure about the precise impact of aircraft emissions on the air above us. The complex cocktail of chemicals being added to the atmosphere several kilometres above our heads has effects that are very difficult to accurately assess. The environmental effects of flying also vary dramatically depending on the altitude of the aircraft.

The primary emissions from aircraft engines are carbon dioxide, oxides of nitrogen and water in the form of vapour. The effect of carbon dioxide added to the thin air 10km up is well known. Oxides of nitrogen almost certainly add to global warming because they react with the oxygen in the high atmosphere to form ozone, also a greenhouse gas. The net effect of the ozone is reduced because it scavenges methane, helping to *reduce* the concentration of this gas in the upper atmosphere.

The most important uncertainty, about which debate rages fiercely, concerns the precise consequences of the emissions of water vapour in the form of condensation trails ('contrails'). If, as is looking reasonably likely, contrails are both warming agents in themselves and significant contributors to the development of high-level cirrus clouds, the net impact of air travel could be several times greater than the impact of carbon dioxide alone. The UK's Royal Commission on Environmental Pollution wrote in 2002:

> *Contrails and cirrus clouds reflect some solar radiation and therefore act to cool the surface. They also absorb some upwelling thermal radiation, re-emitting it both downwards, which acts to warm the surface, and upwards. On average, the latter warming effect is thought to dominate.*[2]

Probably the most important single piece of empirical evidence for the effect of cirrus cloud came in the days immediately after the 11 September 2001 attacks. Civilian aircraft travel ceased for several days. The difference between day and night temperatures in the US increased significantly because, it is thought, some of the effect of the cirrus cloud 'blanket' had been removed. The daytime temperature increased (as more solar radiation got through to the surface), but the night-time temperature fell more. Today, as more and more aircraft criss-cross the skies, they may be weaving what is, in effect, a denser blanket of cirrus cloud, increasing average temperatures over the day, particularly in regions of dense airline traffic. However, it has to be admitted that the arguments about cirrus clouds are far from settled.

Nevertheless, the consensus assumption across the world is that the Royal Commission is right, and contrails and the consequent cirrus cloud do help to retain the sun's heat in the atmosphere. But few scientists are prepared to guess at the exact impact of these phenomena. So, instead, most people accept the rough estimate that the global warming impact of air travel is roughly between 2 and 3 times that which would be suggested by carbon dioxide alone. It will take several years at least before there is an agreed assessment. In the meantime, most commentators and scientists tend to assess the emissions of an aircraft by working out how much aviation kerosene is burned, calculating how much carbon dioxide results, and then multiplying this number by two and dividing by the typical number of people on the plane. A piece of simple arithmetic then gives us a figure for the global warming emissions for each passenger.

As a very general rule, CO_2 emissions from aviation average about 150g per passenger kilometre. It is lower for 1 hour hops inside Europe in planes run by efficient operators with new planes and high seat occupancy. In these cases, the figure can be as low as 100g. Conversely, long-distance flights in older aircraft can be at least 200g per passenger kilometre. (The figures are just for CO_2 and exclude the other global warming effects.)

The scientific uncertainty allows some institutions to underestimate the impact of flights. In particular, it allows the airline industry to avoid using any multiplier at all and only calculate the volume of carbon dioxide. I am afraid to say that I think that this is deeply dishonest and reflects badly on the airlines concerned. It also acts further to confuse the public, who are then less likely to take action to reduce their emissions from air travel.

CARBON DIOXIDE EMISSIONS

Internet sites that offer estimates of the global warming impact of air travel are proliferating. Many of them have grown up as institutions working to offset the effect of air travel by 'offsetting' the environmental impact. For example, they run programmes to reforest arable land or to invest in fuel-efficient cooking stoves in developing countries. These sites have little calculators on them that work out the carbon dioxide generated from an individual person's flight – for example, from London to Rome.

These amounts vary from site to site – sometimes by as much as 30 per cent. Three UK sites produced estimates ranging from 1.2 tonnes to 1.54 tonnes of CO_2 for the carbon dioxide output arising from a flight from London to New York and back.[3] These variations arise because we can all make different assessments of the likely distance actually travelled after air traffic re-routings and because different aircraft have varying fuel economy. But all of the ones I have seen only include the carbon dioxide and not the emissions of nitrogen oxides or contrails. So, according to the scientific consensus, the sites offering offset are ignoring the impact of other pollutants and are certainly not taking into account the blanketing effect of high-level cirrus. A far more appropriate measure – and certainly one that is properly cautious – would clearly be to increase these figures by a factor of two or three.

With this multiplier, the full effect of flying becomes clear. A return flight to New York 'costs' between 2.4 and 4.62 tonnes of carbon dioxide. Put another way, this trip is responsible for 25 per cent or so of the yearly carbon emissions of the typical UK citizen. If we are to reduce average carbon output by 80 per cent, which is stated government policy, then a single trip to the US would use up the whole yearly allowance.

Of course, most flights from the UK are to destinations within Europe. Journeys to the US are relatively unusual. Approximately 65 per cent of all flights from the UK are to European destinations, with 13 per cent to other UK airports, 11 per cent to North America and 12 per cent to the rest of the world.[4] According to the carbon calculator of www.climatecare.org, a round-trip flight from Glasgow to Paris creates 0.22 tonnes of carbon dioxide. Other sites have higher figures. After multiplying by two, the real number is probably somewhat over half a tonne carbon dioxide equivalent. Heathrow to Naples and back would be 50 per cent more. Even these short-hop flights are difficult to reconcile with low-carbon lifestyles.

Individuals seeking to estimate the carbon impact of an individual flight can look at one of these calculators and get an estimate of the implications of travel, and then make their own decision as to whether to apply a multiplier to reflect the other pollutants. The airline industry, beginning to step up its public relations campaign as it sees looming problems ahead, stresses the ability of modern airliners to match the emissions of cars (but a saloon car carrying four passengers is still far more efficient than the most modern of aircraft). The most important difference, however, is the distances travelled by air. A flight to New York and back is not far short of the average distance driven by a car in the UK each year.[5]

Very approximately, UK citizens are now responsible for over 35 million tonnes of carbon dioxide pollution through aircraft travel each year. (Why is the figure 'very approximate'? We cannot be sure about the number of non-UK citizens travelling to and from the UK, and UK citizens travelling between other countries.) Multiplied by two and the number becomes almost 1.2 tonnes per head, or 10 per cent of the total.

Fuel efficiency is improving as engines become better and aeroplanes lighter. Until the recession of 2008/2009, planes were flying fuller, with fewer wasted seats, and small improvements in routing and in air traffic control means less wasted kerosene. But, taken together, these improvements are probably reducing fuel costs per passenger kilometre by no more than 1.5 per cent per year.[6] On the other hand, traffic growth was about 7 per cent per year in the period of 1993–2004.[7] Slowly improving fuel efficiency does not compensate for rapid increases in the numbers of flights. Over the last few decades, the UK airline industry has increased its consumption of kerosene at about 6 per cent per year although this growth was slackening even before the financial crisis of 2008 struck the world economy.

An early 2008 study from the UK's Civil Aviation Authority looked at the reasons why flying had not been growing so rapidly in the years leading up to the economic downturn. It pointed to several factors: increases in Air Passenger Duty, improved long-distance rail services and travellers' knowledge of the long waits and delays at some airports. But, as might be expected from the regulator of the aviation industry, it chirpily concluded that the underlying social forces still seem to point in the direction of more and more flying. 'Analysis of the passenger characteristics associated with increased air travel show that, if anything, the trends in UK demographics (increased ownership of property abroad and couples having children later in life) point towards lifestyles with higher rather than lower propensities to fly.'[8]

What about the effect of slower economic growth in the last few years? Recent data show a rapid slowdown in aviation, with summer 2009 showing year-on-year reductions of over 5 per cent in air travel. Some people see this as the beginnings of a permanent slowdown in aviation but it seems to me more likely that it is simply a magnified effect of the reductions in household income caused by the recession. As economic growth returns, aviation is likely to be the principal beneficiary.

The policy failures

The UK government's 2003 White Paper on air travel saw passenger volumes through UK airports rising to between 400 million and 600 million people a year by 2030.[9] As the White Paper put it, this means that total numbers of travellers will be between two and three times what they were in 2003. The government's policy has largely been to accommodate this growth by planning to build new runways. It plans no attempt to restrict demand.

Despite its relatively small importance in the national carbon account, air travel represents a hugely significant part of our emissions inventory. It is the only source of emissions that is growing rapidly. Even the optimistic forecasts from government see it increasing, and at a disturbingly rapid rate, until 2040. Independent researchers, such as the scientists at the Tyndall Centre, project that emissions will be as high as 47 million tonnes of carbon dioxide by 2010, or well over 2 tonnes per head after including the tripling effect of including other pollutants.[10] As the Tyndall Centre has appropriately put it, the growth of air travel is likely to mean that total emissions from other sources will have to fall almost to zero if we are to meet our long-run goal of cutting UK greenhouse gas output to less than 3 tonnes a head. This is clearly an unbelievably challenging task.

This is why we see a tone of unadulterated panic in the writings of many of the scientific experts in the field. Alice Bows of the Tyndall Centre wrote: 'if we are serious about climate change we must act now to curb aviation growth'.[11] The growth of aviation is so clearly incompatible with temperature stability that scientists working in this area simply cannot understand why the government is failing to act to hold back the growth. It could, for example, refuse to allow new runways to be built; but its policy seems to be to 'predict and provide' the new capacity at airports to meet the growth in UK demand. The lack of interest from governments, both in the UK and elsewhere, in holding down the rate of growth of aviation is deeply frightening and provides the clearest example of the need for individual citizens to exercise self-restraint. Although Air Passenger Duty is likely to get more expensive, flying is now probably going to remain cheap and easily affordable for the richest quarter or so of the UK population. So if the government is happy to expand airports and travel prices remain low, someone interested in reducing her footprint has to rely on self-discipline when deciding to reduce flying, even though it may mean fewer winter holidays in the sun, enjoyable city breaks in foreign capitals or trips to far-off island paradises. Unsurprisingly, most surveys of public opinion suggest that only a tiny percentage of UK individuals have taken that choice.

What would happen if the same rate of tax were applied to kerosene as it is to petrol? Using British Airways' fuel consumption figures, a flight from London to Rome and back would incur fuel taxes of about £60. This would be significant, I agree, but by itself is unlikely to hold air travel volumes at or below current levels, even if the tax were applied across the world. And since a vast network of bilateral treaties ban the taxation of aviation fuel, the chances of even this happening are negligible. Taxation, unless at unprecedented levels, is unlikely to be sufficient to deal with the enormous problem of aviation's impact on the atmosphere. From 2012, aviation will be included in the European emissions trading scheme but even if the price of permits rises surprisingly fast from 2009 levels, the price of air travel will barely be affected.

Putative technological fixes

The last refuge of those wanting us all to keep flying is a blind faith in technology. Speaking to a committee of the House of Commons in early 2006, Prime Minister Tony Blair said:

> *I just think it is unrealistic to think that you will get some restriction on air travel at an international level, and therefore I think necessarily the best way to go is to recognize that that is just the reality and instead see how you can develop the technology that is able to reduce the harmful emissions as a result of aviation travel.*[12]

The government's reluctance to intervene in the largely untaxed world of international aviation is not shared by many of its own constituent parts. Government agencies and individual scientists have often taken a far more robust stance.

The Royal Commission on Environmental Pollution, for example, in response to the last major government pronouncement on aviation, said that the document:

> ... *fails to take account of the serious impacts that the projected increase in air travel will have on the environment. Earlier this year the government published an Energy White Paper setting out its strategy for tackling global climate change, and set challenging but necessary targets for greenhouse gas emissions. Today's Aviation White Paper undermines those targets and continues to favour commerce over vital carbon dioxide reduction measures.*[13]

Sir David King, the government's chief scientific adviser earlier in this decade, was reported as saying that the impact of aviation on global climate change was 'an issue of enormous concern'.[14] Even Labour party backbenchers – a group usually reluctant to criticize its leaders – have joined in the criticism. Paul Flynn, the MP for Newport West, wrote in his blog that 'we cannot tax aircraft fuel; but we can and must tax their emissions as the greatest single source of pollution'.[15] Later in the comment, he says: 'Our donkey-brained leaders could take us over the precipice. We need a paradigm shift to change our fundamental assumption on the way we live and how we run our economies. Action should be massive and swift.'

The government's independent adviser, the Sustainable Development Commission, was almost as forthright about the issue of aviation. In a June 2004 report, it wrote: 'Governments around the world have failed completely to confront this problem so far. On the contrary, they have done everything they can to encourage further growth in order to promote short-term economic growth and development.'[16]

Think-tanks have weighed in to the issue. The Institute for Public Policy Research, often described as close to the Labour party, published a volume on aviation and climate change in which it concluded 'that unfettered growth would not comply with the objectives of sustainable development'.[17] In fact, it is rare to find anyone, other than people who dissent from all the concerns over climate change, who thinks that air travel can continue growing as fast as it is. This is depressing: we have a high degree of consensus on the problem; but political leaders are frightened of taking any action that might shave emissions by more than a few percentage points of growth.

The unfortunate fact is that there are no technological fixes that will solve the aviation problem within the next 30 years. Aeroplanes will get lighter, airframes slightly more aerodynamic and engines will get more efficient; but there are no thrilling breakthroughs on the horizon. This is not just because technological progress is relatively slow; it is also because today's stock of aircraft will continue circling the globe for decades to come. These jets are simply not going to disappear. British Airways keeps its aeroplanes for approximately 20 years. The low-cost airlines tend to use newer aeroplanes and buy them fresh from the factory. These aircraft are still going to be in use in 2030. Better technology will not reduce the emissions from these planes.

New concept aircraft, such as the blended wing design that merges the wing with the fuselage, will eventually come to reduce the carbon effect of new aircraft. It may be possible to introduce new types of engines ('open rotor') that will use less fuel – but make much more noise. But just as today's electric hybrid cars are not reducing total emissions, these new aeroplanes will simply add slightly less to global emissions than a plane of the current generation. Other madcap suggestions, such as replacing the entire world aircraft fleet with planes that burn hydrogen, fall down because nobody has yet worked out how to store the gas in a dense enough form to transport in a civil airliner. Hydrogen simply does not carry enough energy for each unit of volume, meaning that the fuel tanks need to be four times the size of those for kerosene. As one might imagine, the illustrative drawings make the resulting aircraft look strange and ungainly. But looks apart, a project to build a hydrogen airliner is decades away.

The industry itself is laying great store on the possibility of using biofuels made from oil seeds as a substitute for aviation kerosene. Several commercial airlines have made trial flights using modified jatropha oil in the fuel tank for one engine. Jatropha oil comes from the berries of an otherwise unattractive tropical shrub that can be grown on land of low fertility and without irrigation. So the air travel industry has begun to push for widespread cultivation of this crop, saying that it will not crowd out food production. My simple calculations suggest that to replace today's volume of jet fuel with jatropha oil will probably require over 2 per cent of the world's land area to be devoted to this crop. This may be possible, but the likely impact of a switch to biofuels is to force further deforestation and the eviction of small-scale farmers from arable land so that jatropha shrubs can be grown instead.

The amount of air travel in which a person engages is the primary determinant of how much carbon he or she is responsible for. Frequent flyers can generate hundreds of tonnes of damaging emissions per year. In a study carried out by Oxford's Transport Studies Unit, the 10 per cent of the population with the highest output of greenhouse gases had a carbon burden of 19.2 tonnes a year from flying, or not far from twice the average UK emissions from all sources.[18] These people had emissions over ten times the UK average from flying.[19]

The Oxford study demonstrates the very high percentage of all transport emissions that come from the top 10 per cent of travellers. This group was responsible for about 42 per cent of all transport-related emissions. Most of their carbon came from flying. Amazingly, the lowest 20 per cent of people emitted only 1 per cent of the total transport carbon in the survey. People in the top 10 per cent were responsible for 100 times more carbon than the people in the lowest 20 per cent.

These numbers are extraordinary. Although over half the UK population now travels by air at least once a year – though almost half do not – a very small percentage of people travel many times as often. The pollution from aircraft is overwhelmingly the responsibility of a small number of people. And the Oxford study points to the disproportionate impact of those on high income. Cheap air travel may seem to be a great leveller, making long-distance travel available to all; but its most important impact has probably been to allow the richest few per cent of the population almost unlimited freedom to pollute as much as they want, barely thinking about the financial impact.

Air travel poses the greatest threat to the climate of any single source of carbon. The rich and the powerful are those most tied – sometimes against their will – to the use of the rapid movement between remote cities. It is difficult to think of a high-income occupation that does not push its practitioners towards the frequent use of aeroplanes.

Those most sensitive to the threat from aviation to the long-term prospects for the world's poorest billion people have begun, albeit only in very small numbers, to 'offset' their emissions by paying companies to plant trees or engage in other carbon-reducing actions to compensate for their flights. Is this enough? I suggest not: it may salve the guilt, but it does not assist in changing society's behaviour or attitudes. Offsetting has serious problems: the promised carbon reduction is less certain than many of its proponents claim. But, more important, buying a few pounds of carbon offset for a trip to New York is sending a signal to governments and companies that the expansion of air travel is compatible with a stable climate. This proposition needs to be attacked wherever it is found. This means that the only morally responsible course of action is to avoid flying except in emergencies. People need to accept that this action may reduce chances of promotion and opportunities to see new parts of the world. The unhappy truth is that the arrival of rapid climate change is going to curtail human freedom – we cannot do everything that we want. The particular virulence of aviation's impact on eventual global temperatures means that severe and uncompromising self-restraint is an obligation. Those of us who seek to change the behaviour of others must stop flying. If we do not, we are fatally undermining our own campaign. Perhaps like many others, I am appalled by the international conferences on climate change that involve thousands of delegates travelling many miles by air.

For many people, giving up flying is simply a step too far. Attendees at the talks that I give on climate change often say that they can adjust all the main aspects of their lifestyle except this one. Avoiding all air travel is an uncrossable bridge: at a rational level, they know that their air miles are a part of the world's most important problem; but they do not want to change their own behaviour. Of course, this is in some ways an intelligent response – their own actions are not going to reduce the pace of temperature change one iota. But I sometimes sense that behind the 'skiing holiday' is a different sort of calculation. People are discounting the future. Some smokers are the same – they are happy to shorten their life expectancy in return for the immediate pleasures of nicotine. Those who admit the impact of flying, but continue to argue for their own freedom to fly, are similar. The benefits now are greater than the future costs. Governments instinctively recognize this – hence, the lack of any substantive action on aviation growth rates.

The free-market idealists are an even more difficult group to deal with. In their view, the problems of climate change can all be addressed by proper pricing of carbon dioxide emissions. Once what economists call 'externalities' have been priced into air travel, we should travel as much as we want to – there can be no moral difficulties if we simply follow the signals provided by the price of air travel. So, in the free-market economist's view, as long as the true cost of carbon dioxide pollution has been incorporated into the price, it is perfectly OK to fly or to drive a sports utility vehicle (SUV).

BOX 9.1 – INTERNATIONAL AIR TRAVEL: DATA FROM OTHER COUNTRIES

Information on international travel is not reliable because of the difficulty of dealing with flights by passengers coming from abroad and transferring to other aeroplanes. Eurostat data suggest that the number of passenger journeys to or from UK airports was about 143 million in 2001, compared to 97 million in Germany and 66 million in France. UK journeys were almost one-quarter of all 15 European Union (EU) member state journeys, though per inhabitant, the figures for Ireland and the Netherlands are at least as high.

Many of the most intelligent economists know that this is not a tenable position. For example, they realize that market pricing is not going to work sufficiently fast to protect the glaciers feeding the water supplies of much of Asia and Latin America. So, instead, they deny the reality of climate change, but then gradually shift into saying that even if it does exist, we should simply get used to higher temperatures. Ruth Lea, a very effective free-market apologist, typically suggested in a letter to the *Financial Times* that international bodies should focus on helping poorer countries adapt to higher temperatures rather than trying to control the causes of climate change.[20] Other reputable bodies say similar things.[21] These people think that it is acceptable to continue to fly many times a year.

I don't want to live in a world in which mankind seeks to manage its relationship with the planet in this way. Rather than being constantly at war with nature, contesting its authority over the planet, I would prefer to live at peace. If this means taking less of the world's beneficence, and adjusting my style of life to avoid borrowing from future generations, I am content. For me, this means no air travel unless absolutely necessary. I haven't flown for six years and I hope I can continue with this abstinence. Other people won't be able to do this but nevertheless I think it vital that people claiming to be environmentalists make the strongest possible effort to avoid flying because of its incompatibility with the 1 or 2 tonnes per person per year emissions target that the world needs to adopt.

part II

---

indirect emissions

10

food

The food industry, one of the most carbon-intensive in the world, is by far the largest indirect contributor to UK emissions. The figures in this chapter suggest that producing and distributing food creates over five times the volume of the most energy-intensive manufacturing industry: iron and steel.[1] This isn't just about the carbon costs of transporting foodstuffs. The issue of 'food miles' is now becoming well understood; but it is only a very small portion of the problem. The whole chain of supply is a huge user of fossil fuel from fertilizer on the fields to customers' cars going to supermarkets.

This chapter suggests that the food industry adds over 2 tonnes of greenhouse gases to the individual's total emissions every year, or about one-sixth of the total. This figure may actually be too low, since it excludes the carbon dioxide and the methane emitted by the soil in intensive agricultural systems. The energy used to provide the food on our tables is about nine times greater than the calorific value of the food itself. In addition, the food chain is responsible for a large fraction of the emissions of methane and nitrous oxide, other greenhouse gases with a much greater impact on global warming for each tonne emitted.

Changing food purchase habits can dramatically alter the climate change impact of our lifestyle. In its implications, it is comparable to the decision to abandon air travel. The four most important rules are these: buy organic where possible, local when available, keep away from processed and packaged food and, most important of all, buy less meat and fewer dairy products.

revious chapters have concentrated on how our actions directly cause emissions, whether by travelling, heating our own homes or running electric appliances. The rest of this book looks at indirect emissions and, lastly, at how we can counteract the carbon dioxide that we cannot otherwise eliminate from our lives.

The food supply chain is by far the most important source of indirect carbon emissions. Unlike many other indirect emissions, our choices of what to purchase can significantly affect the greenhouse gases for which we are responsible. So this chapter has two purposes: to provide an estimate of the greenhouse gas emissions resulting from the major steps in the UK food supply chain; and to identify how changes in the purchasing habits of a household might affect the food industry's carbon emissions. What do people need to do to reduce the impact of their food consumption on climate change?

I show that by changing eating habits, an individual could – at least in theory – reduce greenhouse gas emissions resulting from food consumption by 85 per cent. This would require very substantial changes in diet for all but those who already eat organic, unpackaged whole foods and who are completely, or almost, vegan. On the other hand, an individual pursuing a more limited programme to reduce carbon emissions from the food chain could still cut his or her emissions by over two-thirds. I think that many households would find the necessary changes in food consumption acceptable.

The central role of the food system in world greenhouse gas emissions is becoming increasingly well understood. Rising population, greater amounts of livestock cultivation and an understandable predilection for a greater variety of foods on the plate are conspiring to increase the pressure on the world's limited amount of good quality land. The need for food is forcing the world to cut down forests, to degrade the world's productive farmlands and to factory-farm livestock, causing immense problems of waste disposal. All of these things are increasing the flow of greenhouse gases from the soil and from plant matter into the atmosphere.

THE FOOD SUPPLY CHAIN

Various commentators have given estimates of the impact of the food supply industry on greenhouse gas emissions. Lawrence Woodward of the Elm Farm Research Centre, for example, reported in 2002:

> *It has been estimated that the CO_2 emissions attributable to producing, processing, packaging and distributing the food consumed by a family of four is about 8 tonnes a year.*[2]

I have found it impossible to find a source which provides a justification for this figure or – even more helpfully – which breaks down the estimate into its constituent parts in order to identify the impact of each part of the food supply chain. This is my aim here; but I am aware that the lack of published research may mean that some of my estimates are inaccurate. With this caveat, my conclusion is that the figure of 2 tonnes per person is likely to be a slight underestimate. Food production and distribution is, indeed, the single most significant source of greenhouse gases in the UK.

Getting food to the home is a complicated task:

- In an advanced economy using intensive agriculture, the process starts with the manufacture of fertilizer from fossil fuels. The fertilizer, alongside other agrochemicals, is shipped to the farm.
- The farmer uses fossil fuels to carry out activities on the farm, such as ploughing, sowing and harvesting. Farm animals produce methane, a significant greenhouse gas. Nitrogen-based fertilizer breaks down in the soil and gives off nitrous oxide, which contributes even more (per kilogram) than methane to global warming.
- The supply chain takes the food, both animal products and plant materials (for example, grain and vegetables) to processing companies. Such companies include heavy energy users, such as sugar beet processors. Primary processors turn farm products into materials that can be further processed by food manufacturing companies. For example, millers grind wheat, which is then sent to factories for the manufacture of biscuits.
- Most food in the UK is sold in a packaged form. It has been cooked or otherwise prepared and is then encased in materials to protect and preserve it, and to allow it to be displayed attractively in shops. Once packaged, it is sent to the huge distribution warehouses of the supermarket chains and thence to individual shops.
- The food shop – usually now a large supermarket – uses energy to run its operations. The store is heated, lit and uses electricity to run its food chillers and freezers. The fridges all use fluorine-based refrigerant gases which has global warming effects many

thousands of times more powerful than CO_2. Small amounts leak from each supermarket chiller system every day.

- Most food purchases are made by customers who drive to the retailer. They bring home their food, prepare and eat it, and dispose of the packaging and kitchen waste. Some studies suggest that a third of all food bought in the shops is disposed of uneaten. Only a small proportion of this waste is composted; instead, it is put into landfill where it produces greenhouse gases as it rots in the ground. Some of this gas will escape to the atmosphere and add to global warming.

The greenhouse gas consequences of each of these stages can be calculated. There is a degree of imprecision, sometimes substantial, in each of the calculations. Nevertheless, I believe that the numbers in this chapter are reasonably robust and are usually supported by two or more different sources or calculations.

TOTAL GREENHOUSE GAS EMISSIONS

Emissions are calculated using the standard yardstick of carbon dioxide equivalence. The food supply chain emits large quantities of methane – generally assessed as 21 times as powerful a warming gas as carbon dioxide – and nitrous oxide, thought to be about 310 times as powerful as CO_2. In the UK about a third of all methane and two-thirds of nitrous oxide come from agriculture.[3]

Table 10.1 summarizes the emissions from each of the main activities in the supply chain. It does not deal adequately with three additional important sources of climate changing gases:

1 The first is the gradual loss of soil carbon as a result of intensive agriculture.
2 Second is the greenhouse gas emissions incurred in other countries as a result of growing food for UK tables. The UK is a net food importer: if we took into account the carbon costs entailed by other countries in growing our food, our own figures for carbon consumption would look a great deal higher. But calculating or, indeed, reliably estimating this figure is extremely difficult (I do, however, assess the costs of transporting food from other countries to the UK).
3 Neither do I look at the impact of global food demand on world deforestation, which causes at least 20 per cent of all greenhouse gas emissions. Unless we change what we eat the world's growing population and taste for meat is going to further increase the loss of vital forests.

The estimates in Table 10.1 are provided for the UK, rather than per person as I have tried to do in the rest of the book. This is because many of the numbers are individually quite

Table 10.1 *The main sources of greenhouse gas emissions in the UK food chain*

Activity	Million tonnes per year (CO_2 equivalent)
Fertilizer manufacture and transport	9
Methane from animals and slurry	19
Methane from tilling and soil management practices	4
CO_2 from farm operations	6
Fertilizer use generating nitrous oxide	27
Road transport in the UK	7
Road/sea transport outside the UK	7
Air freight	2
Food and drink manufacturing and processing	11
Manufacture of packaging	10
Operation of retail stores	8
Consumers driving to shops	3
Landfill gas from rotting food: methane + CO_2	13
Landfill gas from rotting packaging: methane + CO_2	4
Approximate total	130 (or about 2.1 tonnes per person per year)

Source: Various sources as cited in main chapter text (see notes 4–32 on pages 285–286).

small and it seems better to provide the UK total. At the foot of the table, I give the figure for the typical individual.

Fertilizer manufacture

Fertilizer manufacture uses natural gas as a raw material and results in substantial emissions of carbon dioxide from the manufacturing process.

Fertilizer use is shrinking slowly in the UK. The gradual and painful reform of the Common Agricultural Policy (CAP) is tending to slowly decrease the acreage of land under intensive cultivation in the UK. The growth in the acreage under organic cultivation, albeit from a very low base, also tends to reduce fertilizer use.[4]

The UK imports substantial quantities of nitrogenous fertilizer, and the carbon implications of the use of imported material is included in the estimate of about 9 million tonnes of carbon dioxide. I have calculated this figure from data provided by the Soil Association.[5]

I have not included an emissions figure for the production and transportation cost of agricultural liming products necessary to reduce the acidity to the soil after application of nitrogen fertilizer. Lime will eventually add carbon dioxide to the atmosphere as it breaks down in the soil (the percentage of all liming materials added to UK soils as a direct result of the need to reduce the acidity arising from the previous use of nitrogen fertilizer does not appear to be known).

Ruminant animals and slurry

As coal mining has declined, agricultural animals are now the main source of methane (CH_4) in the UK. Ruminant animals, such as cows and sheep, produce methane as a result of the digestive process (the breaking down of organic compounds in the stomachs of these animals creates methane, which is then largely emitted from the animal's mouth and nose). Dairy cows are particularly important sources of methane because of the volume of food, both grass and processed material, that they eat. Animals kept in organic systems actually produce more methane per litre of milk because organic cows give less milk per unit of food eaten. Other, non-ruminant animals also produce methane, but in much smaller quantities. Don't forget that the emissions of methane additionally contribute to the impact of clothing purchases on a person's carbon footprint.

In intensive farming systems, particularly those in which cows are kept indoors for most, or all, of the year, additional methane is created by the anaerobic breaking down of manures in slurry heaps. When animal wastes rot in the presence of air, they largely produce carbon dioxide as a waste product. Without air, manure rots to give off methane and some carbon dioxide. In intensive animal husbandry, manures are collected and stored without air, thereby emitting methane. Methane is also emitted to the atmosphere from soil disturbance, the drying out of peaty wetlands and other agricultural practices.[6] Some, perhaps most, methane from farms could be collected and combusted in a small electricity generating plant or it could be purified and added to the gas mains. (Natural gas is primarily methane.) But, at the moment, the UK is well behind countries like China and Germany in using agricultural methane for power rather than simply letting it escape. Figures for the amount of methane from UK agriculture come from the *UK Climate Change Programme 2006*, which estimated that the carbon dioxide equivalent UK output of methane from agriculture was 19.1 million tonnes in 2004.[7]

I have checked this number by multiplying the number of methane-producing farm animals by the average methane output per head. This produces a figure of 18.9 million tonnes of carbon dioxide equivalent, excluding the contribution of goats and hens, which would increase the figures slightly. Animals and slurry are thus responsible for about a third of a tonne of greenhouse gases per person per year.

Carbon dioxide from farm operations

Farms use significant quantities of fossil fuels to keep animal sheds at the right temperature and with the appropriate amount of light. Farm machinery needs diesel fuel to carry out tasks such as ploughing, sowing and fertilizer application.

The UK government estimated the carbon output from farm operations at about 5.5 million tonnes of carbon dioxide for 2004.[8] The UK Environmental Accounts give a figure of 5.6 million tonnes of carbon dioxide for 2004.[9]

Methane from tilling and soil management practices

The soil contains methane as a result of the breakdown of organic matter, such as roots, in the absence of air. Tilling the soil allows this gas to escape. In pasture, much of the methane would be captured by organisms able to digest the gas. In fact, properly managed grasslands will generally mean that all methane emissions, including that from roving herbivores, will be absorbed by plant-living microbes. We need to be clear that not all livestock add to the methane problem – it is livestock in intensive systems or on overstressed grasslands.

Intensive agriculture seems to result in a major loss of carbon from the soil. The volume of carbon in world soils is far greater than in the atmosphere and the growth of industrial agriculture is probably resulting in a substantial flow from the earth to the air.[10] However, the estimates of the volume of carbon dioxide being emitted from UK soils differ greatly from source to source, so I have included a low figure for this loss. Recent work seems to suggest that the carbon losses from UK soils are more significant, which may be a result of higher temperatures arising from climate change or from changes in agricultural methods.[11] In contrast, organic agriculture probably improves the carbon content of the soil, acting as a net extractor of CO_2 from the air.

Fertilizer use generating nitrous oxide

When nitrogenous fertilizer is applied to the soil, it breaks down and some nitrous oxide (N_2O) is emitted to the atmosphere. Nitrous oxide is a particularly powerful global warming gas. In terms of its effect on climate change, this source is the single most important element of the food chain. Organic agriculture largely avoids artificial fertilizers, of course, and this is the prime reason why this form of agriculture is much less harmful to the global atmosphere. This fact is not well recognized and needs to be better understood. Buying organic food is probably good for the global atmosphere but because organic farms need to stock animals to provide manure for fields, and these animals give off methane, this assertion is difficult to prove.

Road transport in the UK

Food produced in this country is shipped long and increasing distances.[12] Food manufacturing plants are becoming larger, taking raw materials from wider catchment areas. Processors are shipping to the regional distribution centres of the supermarket chains. The supermarkets are hauling huge volumes to their stores.

Studies now say that 25 per cent of all UK heavy lorries on the roads carry foodstuffs and raw materials for the food processing industries.[13] I have used the calculations of the direct carbon dioxide cost of this traffic in Table 10.1; but a full costing should probably also include the increased congestion (and therefore higher carbon dioxide emissions) of all other road users as a result of the food-related traffic. In Table 10.1 I have used figures taken from an extremely detailed 2005 study carried out for the UK Department for Environment, Food and Rural Affairs (Defra) for all transport emissions, including air freight, which estimated that all of these processes caused emissions of about 7 million tonnes.[14]

The movement of food includes the transportation of raw materials, semi-finished goods and final products to the supermarket distribution centres, as well as food retailers' distribution from their warehouses to shops. This figure does not include the emissions costs from private cars travelling to and from shops.

Road and sea transport abroad

Food shipped from abroad generally comes by road or sea. Increasing volumes of imported foods means a larger carbon dioxide cost. The UK is gradually getting less self-sufficient in food, so we can expect the 'food miles' that we generate as a nation to increase.[15] Table 10.1 shows that the food miles in foreign countries, excluding air freight, already amount to the same as the total for UK transport.

Air freight

The shipment of fresh foods into the UK by air is growing rapidly.[16] The consequences are made more severe because of the greater global warming impact of air travel compared to carbon emissions from surface transportation, and the 2005 Defra study includes an estimate of this effect.

Food and drink manufacturing and processing

Food is increasingly processed. According to the figures from their environmental reports, the big manufacturers of packaged foods, such as Nestlé and Unilever, appear to be making substantial strides in reducing the emissions resulting from manufacturing processes.[17] Nevertheless, overall food manufacturing energy requirements are not decreasing rapidly, possibly because of compensating increases in the energy needed for manufacturing the increasing amounts of chilled food sold to UK supermarkets.[18] Chilled food manufacture involves a large number of energy-intensive processes compared to the production of the 'ambient' foods that are typically produced by the largest global food conglomerates. Visiting a bottled sauce factory a few months ago, I was struck by the energy efficiency and simplicity of the process. This would not be the case in a ready-meals factory, a fact that the industry itself increasingly recognizes and seeks to correct.

The Food and Drink Federation estimates that the carbon dioxide emissions of the food production sector were about 11.5 million tonnes in 2003.[19] Per household, this is about 0.45 tonnes, compared to no more than 0.15 tonnes for all the cooking done in a home using a gas cooker. This is a surprising comparison for most people assume that cooking would be done more efficiently in large volumes. Unfortunately, this gain is more than counterbalanced by the energy costs during food processing, such as the quick chilling of cooked food.

The manufacture of packaging

Almost all food is now heavily packaged. Although customers often complain about the excessive packaging protecting many foods, they still seem to show a preference for buying wrapped rather than loose foodstuffs.[20] One of the packaging industry trade associations did detailed work in 1996 on the energy contained in food packaging.[21] It estimated that each UK individual was responsible for 1.9GJ/year of energy used to make food packaging. This equates to about 526kWh/year. If 50 per cent of the industrial use of energy was electricity and 50 per cent gas, this would produce emissions of about 10 million tonnes of carbon dioxide, which is the figure that I have used.

The energy costs to make the packaging used for food are about two-thirds of the energy value of the food itself.

Operation of retail stores

Large supermarkets are major users of energy. Tesco reports that its emissions are over 50kg a year of greenhouse gases per square foot of retail space.[22] This number is going down but because the chain is expanding total emissions are still going up. UK supermarkets have poor (but improving) records when it comes to energy use, possibly because of the greater emphasis on chilled and frozen products in Britain, which require prodigious refrigeration costs. Tesco's energy use is approximately three times the energy cost to run the same area of the average UK home.

For its financial year 2008/2009 Tesco reported that its global emissions were about 5 million tonnes.[23] About half its turnover is in the UK, so I have assumed that its UK footprint was about 2.5 million tonnes. Tesco is responsible for approximately 30 per cent of all food sales in the UK. Therefore I have estimated that total emissions from grocery retailing are about 8m tonnes.

Consumers driving to shops

As grocery retailing becomes more and more concentrated in larger out-of-town shops, the distances travelled by customers have risen and the use of the car has increased. The average householder drives almost 600km a year for food shopping.[24] This is consistent with the government's figure of 3 million tonnes of carbon dioxide arising from shopping for food by car and bus.[25]

Landfill gas from rotting food

Waste food from the home and from catering establishments is still mostly taken to landfill sites. Once incarcerated, it produces methane and carbon dioxide. The methane is now largely captured and burned; but some still escapes to the atmosphere.

The average person throws away about 500kg of waste a year. 17 per cent is kitchen waste, or about 85kg a person.[26] In addition, people are responsible for catering waste, but this figure is not included. About 88 per cent of all food waste goes to landfill; but the small percentage that is composted almost all comes from catering establishments.

85kg of food waste (plus some water) will turn into about 27kg of methane and 71kg of carbon dioxide.[27] Landfill operators in the UK now capture almost 75 per cent of the methane from their sites.[28] So each person's food waste will produce about 8kg of methane a year, or about 144kg of carbon dioxide equivalent. The methane and carbon dioxide will therefore equal about 215kg of greenhouse gas (144kg + 71kg). Multiplied by the 60 million people in the UK, the figure is about 13 million tonnes of carbon dioxide equivalent.

Landfill gas from rotting packaging

The same issue arises from the disposal of putrescible packaging, such as paper and cardboard. Cardboard and paper packaging will rot away to methane, water and carbon dioxide in landfill. The UK produces about 9.3 million tonnes of packaging waste a year.[29] About 4 million tonnes are paper and board, of which about 2.2 million tonnes are recycled. A total of 1.8 million tonnes go to landfill. This will produce about 145,000 tonnes of uncombusted methane and 1.5 million tonnes of carbon dioxide, with a total impact of well over 4 million tonnes after taking into account the greater global warming effect of methane. In fact, the strong preference that many people express for cardboard and paper packaging, rather than plastic, is not strictly rational. Plastic is light, embodies relatively little energy and, most importantly, doesn't rot. The honourable souls who press for the use of biodegradable for packaging are helping to add to carbon emissions, not to reduce them.

OTHER SOURCES OF CARBON FROM THE UK FOOD CHAIN

I haven't been able to include estimates of the carbon implications of:

- food cultivation overseas;
- food manufacture and packaging overseas.

The UK is a net importer of food with the trade deficit in agricultural products recently hitting about 1 per cent of GDP.[30] We are only about 55–60 per cent self-sufficient in food in the typical year and this is tending to fall. There is, therefore, good reason to suppose that the foreign portion of our food chain is increasing in size. So its emissions of greenhouse gases as a result of goods supplied to the UK market are probably rising as well. I have found no estimates of how much the UK's declining self-sufficiency is increasing carbon emissions elsewhere in the world; but the inclusion of these figures would increase the per-person figure for carbon dioxide to well over the figure of 2.1 tonnes used in this chapter.

What these figures mean

A figure of 2.1 tonnes per year for the food production chain is larger than the typical individual's emissions from car use (1.2 tonnes), home heating (1.2 tonnes) or home electricity use (0.7 tonnes). Therefore, an individual can productively focus on food purchasing as a means of decreasing personal responsibility for carbon emissions.

The typical UK adult consumes about 1900 kilocalories a day. Over the course of the year, this means that the individual needs about 800kWh of energy in the form of food.[31]

It is illuminating to compare this figure with the global warming cost of the whole food chain. Natural gas that generated 800kWh of energy would result in the emission of about 0.15 tonnes of carbon dioxide, or less than 7 per cent of the global warming cost per person of the UK food chain. It doesn't have to be this way. The UK food chain is very carbon-intensive; it requires massive inputs of fossil fuel to sustain itself. But individuals could choose to consume their daily foods in ways that avoid most of this carbon. The main options for those seeking to reduce their impact on the planet's atmosphere are:

- Eat organic food. Organic food doesn't require fossil fuel-based fertilizer, saving the energy needed to produce the fertilizer and the greenhouse gases that result from its application to the field. It may also help rebuild the levels of carbon-based matter in the soil.
- Buy local food. Locally produced foodstuffs, bought directly from the producer or via a local shop, save transport. It will also probably save in packaging and manufacturing.
- Eat less meat and dairy. Farm animals, particularly dairy cows, produce methane. But organic dairy products probably don't save any carbon emissions and may actually increase methane production. Eating a vegan diet is a reliable way of reducing carbon, supplemented, perhaps, by (non-vegan, of course) local eggs, honey and other wonderful foods.
- Buying minimally packaged foods makes a difference both to the amount of energy used in the packaging and in the methane resulting from packaging materials sent to landfill.
- Avoid processed food and cook the raw ingredients at home. The gas used per person for cooking in UK homes generates one-third of the amount of carbon dioxide used in food manufacturing. Large industrial cooking processes may be efficient; but the manufactured foods need chilling and storing after cooking.
- Compost all organic materials, including food packaging.
- Where possible, buy simple foods, sold at ambient temperature, rather than chilled. Avoid supermarkets for their obvious wastes of energy.
- Does being a vegetarian help? By itself, probably not much. All other things being equal, simply stopping eating meat will not reduce emissions very much, particularly if consumption of dairy products rises to compensate for eating less meat. Dairy cows produce over twice as much methane as beef cattle. Becoming a vegan would very definitely help.

BY HOW MUCH CAN THESE MEASURES CUT GREENHOUSE GAS EMISSIONS?

Each of the preceding steps reduces emissions by cutting one or more of the sources of greenhouse gases given in Table 10.1. Table 10.2 shows the ways in which these actions could reduce the greenhouse gas emissions from the food chain.

Table 10.2 *Ways of reducing greenhouse gas emissions from the food chain*

Action	Completely, or almost completely, removes the following	Partly removes the following
Switch to organic food	Fertilizer manufacture Fertilizer use generating nitrous oxide	
Buy local food	Air freight	Road transport in the UK and abroad (only a small percentage of UK residents can buy all food locally). May also result in a reduction in the carbon costs of operating retail stores
Eat less meat and dairy		Methane from ruminant animals Carbon dioxide from farm operations since arable farming will be less energy-intensive
Buy minimally packaged foods	Manufacture of packaging Landfill gas from rotting of packaging	
Avoid processed food		Food manufacturing Road transport in the UK Packaging
Compost all organic materials	Landfill gas from rotting food Landfill gas from rotting of packaging	
Avoid supermarkets		Operation of retail stores

The only portion of the food chain not directly affected by at least one of these actions would be the methane impact of tilling and soil management. And it is certainly possible that good organic agriculture cuts methane emissions from the topsoil, so the benefit of switching to organic agriculture is even greater.

If farmers used renewable electricity, then the emissions from the operation of farms would be reduced. An individual growing some of his or her own food could also expect to reduce these carbon costs as well.

To reduce the carbon costs from food purchasing to as close to zero as possible would oblige the consumer to switch to an entirely organic, vegan diet, bought locally from a small shop selling unprocessed and unpackaged goods at ambient temperatures (perhaps 50 per cent of the energy cost of operating supermarkets seems to come from operating freezers and chillers).

This would mean largely buying whole foods, such as nuts, grains, seeds, dried legumes and fruit, sold at room temperature. Fresh fruit and vegetables and preserves should be bought from local sources. Items such as bread should be made at home if they cannot be bought locally. Of course, it would be even better if the fresh foods were produced on an allotment close to home (for those unable to be vegan, meat, eggs, milk and honey would be best bought locally).

What carbon dioxide costs would remain if everybody adopted a vegan, organic diet, bought their food locally as far as possible, and largely used unprocessed and unpackaged food? Table 10.3 provides an estimate. Of course, the numbers are necessarily extremely approximate, but give a good indication of how much emissions could be cut by radical changes in food purchasing habits.

These changes would reduce national emissions from 126 million tonnes to about 19.75 million tonnes or, seen at the level of the individual, from about 2.1 tonnes to below 0.35 tonnes per person. This result is supported by Swedish research that compared the total greenhouse gas emissions from four different meals with the same energy and protein content. The paper showed a range from 190g of carbon dioxide equivalent for a vegetarian meal with local ingredients to 1800g for a meal containing meat, with most ingredients imported – a ratio of almost ten to one.[32]

This mixture of unprocessed and local organic vegan foods is clearly unacceptable to a very large fraction of the people in the UK. So, what is a reasonably attainable target that at least some people might accept? Table 10.4 estimates the saving if all UK residents changed their food procurement habits in order to minimize greenhouse gas emissions, but did not radically diverge from their current pattern of consumption. Once again, these are estimates that seek to show the extent of the carbon reductions that might be possible if we changed our food consumption habits. They can only be illustrations because each different type of food is grown and processed in a different way. We cannot accurately estimate the gains in lower emissions from changing our consumption patterns but we can make reasonable estimates.

The reductions in Table 10.4 require us to switch almost entirely to organic cultivation, reduce methane output by buying less milk and meat, and move to a largely whole food diet with minimal packaging, bought and produced locally, and not sold through the supermarket system. This is a long way from the way in which most families today buy and consume their food; nevertheless, it is within the capacity of many of us to alter our behaviour to achieve this result.

Table 10.3 *Remaining greenhouse gas emissions after major switches in purchasing behaviour*

Remaining sources of greenhouse gases after changes to purchasing behaviour	Comments	Greenhouse gas emissions remaining (million tonnes of CO_2 equivalent per year)
CO_2 costs from farm operations		3
Methane from tilling and soil management practice		4
Food transport in the UK and abroad	Cut by three-quarters as a result of purchasing mostly local food	3.5
Food manufacturing	Cut by three-quarters as a result of the move away from packaged food	2.75
Operation of retail stores	Cut by half as a result of a switch to ambient food sold in small shops	2
Consumers driving to shops	Cut by half	1.5
Landfill gas from food and packaging	Cut by almost 90% as a result of lower waste, smaller amounts of packaging and composting (note that rotting food will produce CO_2 in a compost bin, so there are still some greenhouse gas impacts from composting)	2
Packaging costs	Cut by 90% to cover the costs of simple polythene or other containers, reused where possible	1
Total		Approximately 19.75 million tones

These figures suggest that substantial but manageable changes to food purchase behaviour could result in a two-thirds reduction in emissions, with total UK output of greenhouse gases falling from 126 million to 41 million tonnes. This reduces the individual's emissions to less than 0.7 tonnes, down from 2.1 tonnes.

Table 10.4 *Remaining greenhouse gas emissions after moderate switches in purchasing behaviour*

Action	Main exceptions	Reduction opportunity	Greenhouse gas emissions remaining*
Purchase organic food for all meat, dairy, vegetables and most packaged goods	Imported fruit and some types of packaged goods	Perhaps three-quarters of emissions from fertilizer manufacture and use	9
Buy local food (sold by local retailers) Possible for vegetables, some fruit, eggs, meat, honey, bread and some packaged goods in large areas of the UK	Almost everything not bought locally has gone long distances via the supermarket distribution system	If all food were bought locally (and without using freight transport), the saving would be 16 million tonnes a year Perhaps 50% of this is possible	8
Eat less meat and dairy products		Perhaps possible to cut methane emissions from cows and sheep in half by reducing meat purchases and dairy consumption	9
Buy minimally packaged foods (probably by concentrating on whole foods)	Difficult to buy some staples without packaging	Probably possible to avoid at least half the carbon costs of packaging	5
Avoid processed foods More home cooking and more purchase of ingredients, rather than prepared foods		Almost certainly possible to reduce carbon costs of food manufacturing by 75%	3
Avoid supermarkets		May be possible to avoid half the cost of operating shops by shopping in small stores and buying ambient goods	2
Compost		Possible to avoid the methane costs of rotting food and packaging by composting (combined with less waste and less use of packaging)	5
Total			41 million tonnes

Note: *Million tonnes of CO_2 equivalent

THE CARBON COST OF SPINACH

Increasing interest in eating a healthy range of fruits and vegetables means a larger number of aircraft lumbering across the oceans carrying fresh produce in the hold. We can argue about the nutritional benefits of eating exotic foods all year; some say that the availability of these foods has helped to improve healthy eating habits, while others point to easy access to substitutes from the UK. A stalk of broccoli from Lincolnshire in February may not be as appetizing as South African grapes, but it does have many of the same beneficial effects.

However, whether we worry about 'food miles' or not, an increasing amount of freight is shipped into the UK by air. About 1.2 million tonnes of cargo comes into the UK this way each year. Much of this is perishable foodstuffs, and the percentage will probably grow. It varies from South African grapes to Asian prawns and Kenyan cut flowers. Anything quickly perishable from outside Europe brought to your supermarket probably came by air. The key exceptions are likely to be long-lived fruit, such as bananas, which are sent by ship. The energy cost of sea transport is very much lower than air freight, although not as insignificant as some people claim.

Some time before writing this section of the book, I looked at a bag of anaemic-looking fresh spinach that had just been delivered as part of our weekly shop. The country of origin was the US. This ordinary leafy vegetable, grown in Northern Europe for at least seven months of the year – and reasonably hardy in the cold frame on my allotment – was being shipped from somewhere in the southern states of the US to Heathrow to feed the customers of UK supermarkets.

The energy cost of getting the spinach from (perhaps) southern California was not recorded on the packet. We shouldn't be surprised, for the figures are truly extraordinary. The food value of this 225g bag of spinach was about 60 kilocalories. The carbon dioxide created in order to get it here weighed about 1kg, or four times the weight of the food. The typical UK power station would have generated almost 2.5 units (kilowatt hours) of electricity for this amount of carbon dioxide. This makes shipping the calories contained in the spinach about 35 times less efficient than generating electricity.

This figure is before taking into account the especially destructive effects of carbon dioxide and other emissions when released high in the atmosphere. Include this in the calculation, and a bag of spinach weighing less than 0.25kg is responsible for a global warming effect equivalent to over 3kg of carbon dioxide. It only takes 15 of these bags for the purchaser to exceed the total fossil fuel use of a typical Afghani. And until I looked at the packet, I wasn't aware that the food came by air.

Another way of thinking about this is to compare the spinach to the effect of an energy-saving light bulb. One of these light bulbs in your house might typically save enough electricity to avoid 6 or 7kg of carbon dioxide a year. Two bags of midwinter spinach, bought casually off a supermarket website, completely wipe out the virtuous effect of another energy-efficient bulb.

AN APPENDIX ON PETS

Dogs and cats eat large amounts of meat and cereals. Unfortunately for those of us who keep animals for companionship, this means that they have large carbon footprints. One recent study suggests that a medium-sized dog eats over 3kg of meat a week and almost 2kg of cereals[33] – more meat, therefore, than the typical person in the UK. Giving a precise figure is difficult because some of the food used for animals would not be of a sufficient quality or palatability for human use and would have been thrown away. It can be reasonably contended that this wasted food therefore didn't add to carbon emissions. Nevertheless, the total impact of the dog's diet is probably several tonnes of greenhouse gases a year. Let's guess at about 3 tonnes and multiply this by the 7 million dogs in the UK. This alone equates to perhaps 3 per cent of total UK emissions. Cats and other animals would add substantially to the figure. The unpalatable fact is that domestic pets are a significant element in the UK's national footprint.

11

other indirect sources
of greenhouse gas emissions

T his chapter looks at the other main sources of emissions that occur in everyday life. It covers the energy used in your workplace and the greenhouse gases associated with what you buy.

THE WORKPLACE

The air-conditioned modern office is a particularly energy-intensive place. Reliable averages aren't available, but I have done a survey of the annual reports of large companies. This survey suggested the following approximate figures for energy use per employee (Table 11.1).

These are high figures: 3 tonnes of emissions for a place in which the employee spends less than a quarter of his or her time is a frighteningly large number. It is driven by the need for electricity-guzzling air-conditioning and the presence of large numbers of electric appliances such as computers and printers. But, whatever the justification, the emissions from new office buildings are greater than the sustainable level of total emissions of 1 or 2 tonnes per person. These figures are for office staff but, for example, media companies and High Street retailers have even higher figures. Some companies have a level as high as 15,000kWh of electricity per employee (over 8 tonnes of emissions just from this source).

There are many exceptions to this rule, but energy use in newer buildings is typically greater than in old offices. The principal reason is the arrival of widespread air-conditioning, which might typically double the average electricity used in the building. Until very recently, architects and developers assumed that the energy costs of running a large building were financially irrelevant and did not trouble to design offices with limited needs for cooling. Energy costs in office-based businesses are usually less than 0.1 per cent of turnover, so this attitude made sense. (Even some manufacturing companies, such as pharmaceutical firms, have energy costs of no more than half a per cent of their total revenue.)

Table 11.1 *Typical gas and electricity consumption per employee
in large office-based companies*

Gas	About 1500 kWh	About 0.3 tonnes CO_2
Electricity	About 5000 kWh	About 2.7 tonnes CO_2
Total direct use of energy	About 6500 kWh	About 3 tonnes per employee

The figure of 3 tonnes quoted in Table 11.1 is derived from looking at the published records of a variety of large companies. Very different data come from a survey of companies of all sizes. According to the Carbon Trust, the average office creates about 131kg of carbon dioxide per square metre each year. Typically, offices allocate 10–12 square metres of space per person, meaning the Carbon Trust's figure is about 1.3–1.5 tonnes for each employee, far lower than the figures I calculated for the largest companies. The difference probably arises because (i) big companies generally occupy big buildings and these generally have higher energy costs per square metre than smaller offices, (ii) larger companies are more likely to use modern air-conditioned offices and (iii) big businesses generally have more computers and large corporate data centres, which are also particularly greedy users of electricity.

After energy use, the most important sources of emissions from office work are paper consumption and the purchase of office equipment. My survey suggests that the average office worker uses about 25kg of paper a year, probably adding another 100kg of emissions to the footprint. The purchase of office equipment might add as much as half a tonne per person, largely from the replacement of computers. As we show later in this chapter, a new desktop computer and screen has a large carbon footprint.

Office emissions are important, but for most people there is no choice about where to work and we often have very little influence over building design or even minor things such as when the lights are turned off. For those who have the opportunity, working at home is preferable. The extra emissions might seem high, and the cost of keeping the heating on all day in the winter may be a couple of hundred UK pounds; but almost all homes are better than an air-conditioned office. If you are obliged to work in a glassy office building with high heating and air-conditioning bills, it makes the best sense to put pressure on the employer to commit to buying electricity that comes from new renewable sources (see 'Green electricity' in Chapter 13) or thoughtfully to offset the emissions by planting trees. Or, perhaps even more productively, it might be possible to get your employer to do an audit of electricity consumption and then take measures to control it. The Carbon Trust's figure for the average UK office of 226kWh/year per square metre is nearly twice their 'good practice' target of 128kWh/year. Today's electricity prices may mean it makes sense for an employer to work on reducing the most egregious source of waste. Simple steps can include:

- heating the building to a lower temperature in winter and air-conditioning it to a higher temperature in summer;
- buying energy-efficient computers and peripherals (this will reduce air-conditioning needs in summer, as well);
- turning off lights and office equipment at night and on weekends; and
- ensuring that light levels are high in the right areas, but reducing them elsewhere.

It is, of course, not just offices that need to be managed in this way. Many public buildings need to work on cutting their emissions. One busy church that I know has energy costs of almost £8000 and emissions from gas and electricity of perhaps 50 tonnes a year. When I did an audit, total standby energy consumption was about 1.5kW, or the equivalent of 15 large conventional light bulbs on all the time. This costs the parish about £500 and adds over 2 tonnes of carbon dioxide to the atmosphere every year.

The buildings in which we work and engage in our social activities are important users of energy. In most workplaces, I suspect that massive amounts could be done to reduce consumption with absolutely minimal effort. Generally, employers have simply never concerned themselves with this issue, and active work from a few concerned employees can have a huge impact with minimum inconvenience. In fact sensible businesses now encourage groups of motivated employees to drive forward the company's efforts to reduce energy costs.

OTHER SOURCES OF EMISSIONS

So far, we have focused on cutting indirect emissions from altering food consumption habits and from better energy use in offices. The third and final recommendation is, unfortunately, the most general and unspecific: it is simply to consume less of the material things of life. Even a small new car might embody 3 tonnes of carbon dioxide. A total of 120 beverage cans – the average UK consumption – produce 20kg of emissions if not recycled. One tonne of cement forming the base of a patio gives off nearly one tonne of CO_2 when it is being manufactured. Supplying water to the average home creates about 80kg of carbon dioxide per person per year at the pumping stations.[1]

Embedded CO_2 in purchases

In this chapter I look at some of the everyday things we buy and try to estimate how much their embedded greenhouse gas emissions add to our personal carbon footprint. By 'embedded' I mean the climate-changing gases that were generated in the process of growing or mining raw materials and then turning these things into a usable product. The primary conclusion from the next few pages is somewhat disturbing. Some of the things that we buy most often have a very substantial carbon cost. The last chapter showed how the food that we eat generates substantial – but far from obvious – emissions. The same is true for clothing and paper use, which probably follow food as the most important of our personal purchases in terms of their climate change impact. To complete the picture, I'll also look briefly at some of the other goods that have an important impact on world emissions: consumer electronics, cars, cement and precious metals. All told, the items I look at represent about 2 tonnes of the average person's carbon footprint. Much of this total is created abroad and so tends to be disregarded in UK policy-making.

Three main themes recur throughout the next few pages:

1   The best way to cut emissions is to reduce the quantity of what you buy and use. Make things last longer. Buy better quality goods that will do their job for twice as long. Use previously used goods where possible.
2   The environmental cost of making something will often dwarf the emissions it generates in use. This isn't always true. Cars, for example, use far more energy being driven than in their manufacturing process. But for many items of clothing, for example, the embedded emissions are far more important than the energy used in washing and drying. And a mobile phone that is replaced every year adds more emissions when it is made than when it is in use.
3   The weight of something is a very poor guide to the emissions created during its manufacture. Gold jewellery has a carbon footprint about 30,000 times its weight, whereas emissions from steel manufacture are probably less than 2 tonnes per tonne of metal.

Clothing

After food, the most important source of indirect personal CO_2 emissions is probably clothing. The typical Briton is responsible for almost a tonne of greenhouse gases from the purchase of new clothes. Most of the CO_2 arises in the countries where the fabrics are made and the clothes are manufactured, so we cannot see many of the emissions in our national carbon accounts.

These emissions arise in a bewilderingly complex series of ways. For natural fibres such as wool, cotton and cellulose-based viscose, there's the growing of the crop and its harvesting. Then the raw fibre has to be turned into a usable textile. Cotton, for example, needs to go through many different processes to make it into a roll of fabric. The textile then needs to be cut and sewn so it becomes a useful piece of clothing. Artifical fabrics, such as polyester or acrylic, are made from oil. First, the oil is processed under heat and pressure to make sturdy polymer filaments and then a fabric is woven before it is made into a fleece or a blouse.

This part of the chapter identifies a number of surprising conclusions. First, it isn't obvious that natural fibres are less energy-intensive than oil-based fabrics. In fact, wool is probably substantially worse than polyester. Second, some clothes, particularly those made from cotton, use more energy in the later stages of making the garment than in the cultivation of the crop itself. Third, the use of a tumble dryer to dry clothes that have been washed may be a more important source of emissions over the lifetime of a piece of clothing than the CO_2 embedded in the garment itself. Perhaps also surprisingly, the emissions from transport are relatively unimportant, even when the cotton is grown in Uzbekistan, spun in Thailand, and then made into a shirt in China before being shipped to a British supermarket.

The key recommendations are clear:

• Avoid wool clothing – the methane emissions from sheep make wool a very climate-unfriendly material.
• People buy a lot of clothes that they don't wear very frequently before throwing them away. Buying fewer clothes of a more durable quality is a good way of cutting emissions.
• Organic cottons, or replacements for cotton such as hemp and bamboo may only make a marginal difference to emissions. This is because most of the energy cost of a fabric is incurred in the manufacturing phase, not in the growing of the crop itself. Cutting and sewing a shirt uses the same amount of energy whether the cotton is organic or not. (But, please note, organic cotton is infinitely better for the environment in other respects.)
• Don't worry too much about where a garment comes from. Transport emissions are actually quite small.
• Don't tumble dry clothes, or iron them when not necessary. This may make more of a difference than choosing the right fabric.
• Dry cleaning is not an important source of emissions for most types of clothes.

Where clothes are made and how this affects emissions

The textile industries of Europe have largely disappeared. Clothes are made from cotton grown in the US, wool from Australia and man-made fibres from Asia. Garments are then manufactured in low-wage countries in Latin America and parts of Asia. Patagonia, the leading outdoor clothing company, has calculated the distance some of its products travel. A typical example is a polyester jacket for cold weather trekking which travels about 18,000km before it arrives at the Patagonia warehouse.

Most of the carbon emissions from the creation of clothes occur a long way from the places where the clothes are bought and worn. This means that the CO_2 impact is even less visible than for something made in the UK. We have, in effect, got other countries to do our pollution for us. Don't assume that this means that the international movement of goods between the producing and consuming nations is a major part of the climate change problem. The climate impact of shipping a T-shirt between China and Britain is small: one estimate is 24g, or about as much as driving a car two hundred metres.[2] We want China and other countries to continue making many of our clothes. The clothing industry there is an extremely important provider of jobs and exports. One United Nations agency estimated that Cambodia, for example, generated more than 80 per cent of its total export earnings from clothing and other textiles.[3] There's no clear reason to start making clothes in Europe just to reduce transport emissions. The big problem is a different one – we can't easily monitor our progress on climate change if a large proportion of the things we buy are made far away in multiple countries, many of which are not covered by the existing agreements on reducing emissions.

In Britain we sometimes congratulate ourselves on our relatively successful record on greenhouse gases. But sadly the truth is that as we have imported more and more of our goods from Asia and elsewhere the picture is much less flattering than we might think. If we make a crude assumption that 80 per cent of the footprint of our new clothes is generated abroad and not recorded in UK figures, our clothing purchases should add about three-quarters of a tonne of CO_2 to individual emissions. This alone is about 6 per cent of our total emissions per person.

The pattern of our clothing purchases

People differ. Some wear little else but woollen suits, cashmere socks and silk ties. Others spend their days in man-made fibres or T-shirts and jeans. The carbon footprint varies enormously. But, to generalize, a person in the UK buys about 50 items of clothing a year, weighing something like 20kg. The typical piece of clothing is kept for about three years and is then thrown away or given to a charity shop – almost half of all clothes are put into second-hand use. Detailed estimates are difficult to find but the material used in these new clothes is estimated in Table 11.2. Please don't rely on these figures because the sources for the information are quite poor.

It may help if I also give some estimates of how much an item of clothing weighs. A lightweight men's suit is about 1.5kg, a T-shirt about 250g, and a chunky sweater about 1kg. Just to give two examples of our purchase patterns: we each buy about seven T-shirts and the average female buys one viscose blouse each year.

What is the carbon footprint of each type of fabric? Once again, the data is far from robust. There have been several studies of greenhouse gas emissions from clothes, but they

Table 11.2 *Average UK clothes purchases per person per year*

Cotton	6kg
Polyester	6kg
Wool	3kg
Viscose	3kg
Other (acrylic, silk, etc)	2kg

tend to differ substantially from each other. I have taken all the studies that I can find and averaged the numbers. So we can only rely on these results for the most general of conclusions (Table 11.3).

The numbers may seem very high to you. Can it really be true that 1kg of clothing (four T-shirts or one heavy cotton sweater, for example) is responsible for more than 30kg of CO_2? We should see these numbers as rough and ready, but the evidence does point strongly to carbon footprints of approximately these levels.[4] One study did produce a much smaller figure. Stormberg, a Norwegian clothing retailer, commissioned work that suggested that cotton has a footprint nearer to 6 times the weight of the clothing rather than 30 or 40. But most of the other reports that are now publicly available give very high figures.

Table 11.3 *CO_2 equivalent greenhouse gas emissions in kilograms*

Fabric	Footprint of raw material per kg (approximate)	Footprint of all manufacturing processes per kg*	Total footprint in kg per kg of clothing
Cotton	10	20–30	30–40
Wool	60	20–30	80–90
Polyester	20	15–30	35–50
Viscose	10	20–30	30–40
Other	20	15–30	35–50

Note: *This includes all the processes to turn raw fibre into finished clothing. In the case of natural fibres, this includes cleaning the wool or cotton, then turning the short fibres into threads and weaving into a fabric. For polyester, this figure includes all the processes after the making of the filament.

In general, it is the process of turning the raw material into a finished garment, rather than growing the cotton or making the viscose, which produces the most greenhouse gases. In the case of cotton, for example, turning a cotton boll into a thread requires a long sequence of processes that all use electricity, starting with the cleaning and combing of the material. To a lesser extent this is also true for oil-based fibres, such as polyester. By the way, one of the advantages of polyester or acrylic clothing is that although the fabric does derive from

BOX 11.1 – WHY DOES WOOL PRODUCE SUCH HIGH EMISSIONS?

Goats produce the light soft wool known as cashmere and the coats of other animals can be shorn to produce other unusual wools such as alpaca or vicuna. But wool is usually made from the fleece of sheep. Like cows, sheep produce methane as part of their digestive process. The effect on the carbon footprint of wool is striking.

Table 11.4 *How much methane is produced per kilogram of wool?*

Typical methane output per sheep per day	About 20g
Weight of methane per sheep per year	7kg
Global warming impact of methane	21 times that of CO_2
Total global warming impact per sheep per year	175kg
Average weight of a sheep's fleece	About 3kg
Global warming impact per kg of wool	Almost 60kg

This makes sheep wool by far the worst fabric from a climate change point of view with the footprint of each piece of clothing being 60 times its weight. Furthermore, this figure is calculated before taking into account the processing of the fleece. It also assumes that all the weight of the wool is turned into clothing. In reality there are losses down the chain of the manufacturing processes, such as cleaning and spinning the wool.

We can look at the impact of wool clothing in another way. In the UK the average person acquires 3kg of new wool clothing each year – perhaps a new suit, a sweater and a few pairs of woollen socks. This is approximately the weight of one sheep's fleece. Somewhere on a Welsh hill or an Australian sheep farm there is an animal providing the wool clothes for me or for you. This animal belches methane, adding the equivalent of about 175kg of CO_2 to the atmosphere each year. In New Zealand, the country with the highest ratio of sheep to people in the world, the methane from the animals generates about half the total national emissions. There are urgent research programmes seeking to find way of altering animal diets to reduce the amount of methane that is belched, but it is unlikely that we will see much rapid improvement. Although there's an economic incentive to cutting methane production because the production of the gas in the animal's stomachs wastes energy that would otherwise provide nutrition, dietary changes haven't yet reduced methane emissions to a significant extent.

If we all bought polyester products instead of wool, the number of sheep in New Zealand and elsewhere would fall, and this would reduce the total emissions of climate-changing gases. This is an easy conclusion to state, but the impact on many sheep farmers would be severe. In Wales and elsewhere, hill sheep farmers are often grindingly poor and only survive because of agricultural subsidies. A global warming-driven campaign to reduce the consumption of woollen clothes and other textiles would make their position worse. In some hilly and infertile areas, this might mean the end of any form of commercial farming and the land would be unused, probably gradually reverting to heathland and forest. Many people will resist this because sheep farming is vital to the economic survival of many remote areas. But, nevertheless, the conclusion is undeniable; encouraging the keeping of sheep to provide wool for clothes is adding to the world's emissions of greenhouse gases. Those of us who can afford to buy cashmere clothes face the same dilemma as if we bought wool; goats also belch methane.

A major part of the problem could be avoided if old woollen clothes could be properly recycled, with the yarn being reclaimed for further productive use. Older garments are handed to charities or put into council recycling bins from where the clothes may be sent to poorer countries for resale. However, very little recycling of the wool from clothes takes place in the UK or elsewhere. The UK businesses that used to reuse wool (usually by turning it into 'shoddy' prior to its reuse in coarser textiles) have almost entirely disappeared and I could find none actively seeking old sweaters to turn into new wool for garments.

oil, a fleece is generally kept for a long time and then finally put into landfill, where it permanently sequesters the carbon contained in the original oil.

The impact of our yearly purchases

In the last few pages we have looked at the typical pattern of clothing purchases and the approximate emissions connected with each type of fabric. How does the overall picture turn out? The figures in Table 11.5 may be wrong by 50 per cent in either direction. But even if they overstate the size of emissions from new clothing by a factor of 2, it points to the troubling significance of clothing manufacture in world emissions.

The logical suggestion is that we should all buy fewer, higher-quality clothes and wear them for longer. There is something in this, but it is not as simple as we might hope. Most people – perhaps 70 per cent of the current world population – buy second-hand clothes, not new garments, for all or part of their needs. Almost half of the weight of new clothes

Table 11.5 *The emissions associated with different fabrics*

Fabric	Kilograms bought per year	Global warming emissions per kg	Total impact kg CO_2 equivalent
Cotton	6	30–40	210
Wool	3	80–90	255
Polyester	6	35–50	255
Viscose	3	30–40	105
Other	2	35–50	85
Total	20		910

bought in Britain end up being reused, either in the UK itself or in poorer countries to which the clothes have been shipped. If Britons buy fewer clothes because they are seeking to reduce costs or decrease their contribution to global warning, the amount of clothing flowing second-hand to poorer countries is reduced.

BOX 11.2 – THE WIDER ENVIRONMENTAL ISSUES FROM COTTON FARMING

The simple T-shirt symbolizes the issues facing us as we try to work out how to deal with the world's overuse of natural resources. T-shirts are generally made from cotton, a fibre that needs huge volumes of water, pesticides and fertilizer to grow successfully. Some estimates suggest that 20,000 people die every year from pesticide poisoning on cotton farms around the world. The cotton plant requires unimaginably large amounts of irrigation. It typically takes almost 4000kg of water to produce just 1kg of cotton.[5] To give the most obvious example of this effect, the water abstracted to irrigate cotton in Uzbekistan has helped drain the Aral Sea to the point where it is now a small fraction of its former size. Soil quality has been affected by excess salt in irrigation water, reducing its productivity for decades or centuries to come.

Countries in which cotton can be grown without huge environmental damage, such as parts of Africa, are pushed out of the world market by aggressive agricultural support from other producers. Cotton exports from the US are heavily supported, distorting the world market and making it difficult for small farmers to compete successfully. It's getting worse. The production of cotton has approximately doubled in the last 30 years, multiplying the destructive environmental impacts of cotton growing.

The making of cotton clothing also has a relatively large climate change impact. Most analysis shows that emissions of greenhouse gases are about seven times the weight of the cloth. World production of cotton fibre is about 4kg per year for every person in the world, implying an average human footprint of over 30kg of greenhouse gases, about three-quarters of 1 per cent of all emissions.

Britons buy seven T-shirts a year, typically wearing them less than 25 times before disposal. Can this wastefulness continue? Probably not. If everybody in the world copied UK patterns of consumption of cotton, the environmental impacts of cotton farming would be massively extended, ruining large areas of the world's fragile soils. Although this book is about climate change, we should not forget the wider effects of the abuse of the world's soils and other ecosystems.

The greenhouse gas impacts of using the clothing

Most studies of clothing suggest that the greenhouse gas impacts of the use of clothing are far greater than the initial production of the clothing. These reports generate this conclusion because they assume that all clothes are washed at high temperatures and then tumble dried and finally ironed. We can actually be pretty confident that this result is not correct – the electricity used in a typical house to power washing machines, dryers and irons is simply not enough to outweigh the figures for the creation of new clothes.

Table 11.6 contains some figures I have extracted from earlier in this book. They show that the total amount of CO_2 generated by cleaning the clothes is less than half the amount emitted by the manufacture of the garments.

If a new shirt was washed 50 times in a high temperature wash and was then always dried and ironed, it's true that the total climate change impact would be greater from its use than its manufacture. Let's look at the figures in more detail.

Rough calculations to show that the carbon footprint of washing, drying and ironing a shirt can conceivably be larger than the emissions from making the shirt:

Table 11.6 *CO_2 generated by the average household laundering clothes*

Appliance	Electricity use in average household per year, kWh
Tumble dryer	400
Washing machine	270
Iron	100
Total	770
CO_2 produced to generate this electricity	432kg (assumes grid electricity at 0.56kg per kWh)

- **Washing** – 1 shirt of 300g is one-tenth of a 3kg load in a washing machine at 60°C using 1kWh per wash: 0.1kWh per wash. 50 washes = 5kWh.
- **Drying** – amount of water left in a 300g shirt: 0.135kg of water. Electricity needed to evaporate this: 0.275kWh. 50 washes = 13.75kWh.
- **Ironing** – 5 minutes, during which the iron element is actually heating for 3 minutes. Usage = 2kW. So the iron uses 0.1kWh per ironing or 5kWh hours in total.
- **Total electricity use:** 5 + 13.75 + 5 = 23.75kWh, equivalent to 13.34kg CO_2.
- Total usage per kg is 44.47kg CO_2 compared to 30–40kg CO_2 for the shirt itself.

So if you do use the washing machine at a high temperature, and employ the iron and the tumble dryer, then usage could be more important. But for the large majority of clothes, this is unlikely to be the case.

Recycling and reuse

Recycling of textile fabrics is difficult. According to UK government statistics, most clothes end up in domestic rubbish that is collected and usually put into landfill.[6] Very few fabrics are genuinely recycled and reappear as 'new' clothes.

The only company I can find that is making a substantial effort to recycle its fabrics is the US outdoor garments company Patagonia. This company can now recycle some, though not all, of its polyester and cotton products. Polyester fabrics are chopped into small pieces and zips and buttons are removed. The material is then turned into tiny granules and broken down into the original monomer. It is then re-plasticized and made back into a filament, from which it can be woven into a fabric. The aim of all recycling is to operate a closed loop, with everything being made from reprocessed old worn-out clothes and with minimal use of virgin fibre. The Patagonia system is as near as possible to this aim. The savings are likely to be well over half of the energy used in the original manufacture. But – and it is an important 'but' – recycling does not reduce the energy used after the fibre has been made. The manufacturer still has to weave the fabric and then cut and sew it into a finished garment. Full recycling is good, but creating clothes that last longer – and that their owners still enjoy wearing – is at least as important.

Cotton and wool are difficult to recycle into new clothes, partly because the original fibres will tend to become shorter and less strong when reprocessed. It is much the same with paper: after being recycled three or four times, the fibre length in the material becomes too short. Indeed centuries ago old clothes were sometimes turned into paper when they could no longer be worn.

I haven't found any UK companies that even attempt to reprocess cellulose-based fabrics, such as viscose, that are originally made from grass or trees. In general, man-made fibres like polyester should be easier to recycle but, with the exception of Patagonia, recycling is rare. The highest priority should be given to recycling wool, because of the global warming impact of sheep, but this is the fabric that is probably least likely to be fully reused.

Other textiles

We don't just use textiles for clothes. We also buy carpets, curtains and soft furnishings. The total weight bought each year is slightly less than the clothing we purchase. It's perhaps about 18kg and most of this is probably man-made fibres for furnishings. The global warming impact will also be substantial, but I haven't found a good way to estimate the impact.

World patterns

How do patterns in the UK use of textiles compare with the rest of the world? The average person in the UK buys about almost 20kg of new clothes a year compared to 11kg elsewhere around the globe. The global figure is made up approximately as follows:

- 4kg cotton
- 0.2kg wool
- 6.4kg synthetic
- 0.5kg cellulose-based fibres.

Comparing these figures with the UK averages shows that Britons are about average in polyester clothing purchase, a bit high on cotton and very high both on wool and cellulose fabrics like viscose. People in the UK need more clothes because the temperature is colder than average and, unsurprisingly, use disproportionately more wool.

Mobile phones

At various times newspaper commentators have picked on mobile phone chargers as symbols of the wastefulness of Britons. But the surprising thing is that it isn't using a mobile phone, or leaving the charger in the socket, that matters. It's making the phone in the first place and operating the mobile phone network. What you do with your phone once you have bought it isn't that important.

Inside a mobile phone are a host of printed circuit boards, full of hundreds of tiny components. These circuit boards contain minute quantities of rare metals and chemical compounds. The metals use large amounts of energy to extract, refine and manufacture. The components and the complete phone are then flown all around the world during the manufacturing and sales process. In fact, phones and other small electronic devices are one of the few products other than fresh food for which transport emissions really make a difference. As a result, it is not whether you leave your mobile phone charger in the wall socket or how much you use your phone that matters, the frequency of replacement is all that really counts from a carbon footprint point of view.

Of course phones vary hugely and accurate numbers are difficult to find. The best information I have come across suggests that a mobile phone typically contains about 25kg of embedded CO_2 and other greenhouse gases – about half of this arises from the electronics and half from other sources.[7] This is over a hundred times the weight of the phone itself.

If you replace it every year or so, the manufacture of the phone dwarfs the other emissions from the use of mobiles. The next most important source of emissions is from the mobile network itself. The companies running phone systems use large amounts of electricity to power their base stations and the computers that move the digital data around their networks. Orange provides some figures suggesting that its annual energy use is about 20kWh per mobile subscriber, meaning about 11kg of emissions. This is slightly less than half the figure for the carbon cost of making the phone.

Then there's the electricity used in the home when the charger is in the wall socket but not actually charging the phone. (Large numbers of people keep the little wall transformer plugged in all the time.) The manufacturers are reducing the energy used when the transformer isn't working but a typical older model might use half a watt. Over a year this is over 4kWh and about 2.4kg of emissions.

Mobile phones are usually kept on the whole time. They are in communication with the base station, saying where they are. If they didn't do this, the network wouldn't be able to find your phone when an incoming call or text message arrived. The power employed to do this is tiny – usually much less than a watt. Charging the battery to replace this energy is not a major use of energy. For a typical mobile, I suspect this is less than a kilowatt hour per year.

What about the cost of using the phone? The typical mobile is used for calls of about 200 minutes per month in Britain. (This includes taking calls from other phones, not just outgoing chats.) The energy used by a mobile phone varies according to how close your phone is to a base station – further away and the phone ramps up its power to maintain the quality of the call. But on average the phone is using less than one watt. So over a year, the total energy used in taking and receiving calls is less than a twentieth of a kilowatt hour. That's less than the equivalent of boiling a full kettle just once in that year. Very roughly, this means annual emissions of less than a thousandth of the carbon cost of making the phone in the first place. Figure 11.1 illustrates how the hierarchy of emissions involved in a mobile phone runs.

So the recommendation is crystal clear. If you want to reduce your emissions from mobile use, keep your phone for as long as possible. If you change phones every year, your

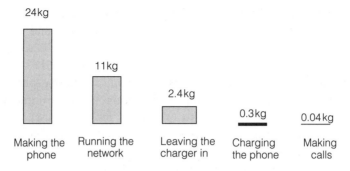

Figure 11.1 *Greenhouse gas emissions from mobile phone use*

Note: All figures per year, except for making the phone.

footprint is 38kg. Keep the device for another year, and your annual footprint is 26kg. Three years and the figure is 22kg, or not much more than half the cost if you only keep your phone for a year. Nothing else you can do makes much difference: the mobile phone manufacturers have done well to drive down electricity use in the phones, but the increasing complexity of the devices has meant that the carbon cost of making them remains high.

About 30 million phones are sold in the UK each year. Multiply this number by 25kg for the emissions generated in making each one, and the total impact is about three-quarters of a million tonnes. This is important, but no more than about 0.1 per cent of the UK's total greenhouse gas output. Almost all the carbon cost of making a phone is created outside the UK, so it doesn't appear in our national emissions accounts.

The other important issue is how to recycle phones once they have been used. Most mobile phones around the world are simply kept in drawers when they cease to be used. A 2008 Nokia survey suggested that most people didn't even know that they could be recycled, though knowledge in the UK was far better than some other countries.[8] The company says that over two-thirds of a phone can be put to alternative use, but its examples suggested that the phones would be converted into much lower technology products or simply be burnt in an electricity-generating incinerator. This wastes a lot of the energy initially employed to make the completed printed circuit boards. Nokia said that the recycling of 3 billion phones – approximately the number of phones in the world today – would reduce emissions by an amount equivalent to taking 4 million cars off the road (presumably for a year). This sounds a lot, but is probably no more than 10 per cent of the original energy cost to make the mobile.

So it may actually make more sense to refurbish our phones and then sell them for reuse elsewhere in the world. This is increasingly happening in the UK. On the internet today I can apparently sell my tatty Nokia E61i for £38 and it will be reused elsewhere in the world. This is much better than having Nokia crush my phone and turn it into a part for a saxophone, which is one of the more absurd future uses that the company proposes. Reusing a phone may save 100 per cent of the carbon cost, compared to 10 per cent if the phone is scrapped and some of its elements recycled. The mobile phone maker Sony Ericsson correctly says that 'products are by definition not environmentally friendly'. They're right and we should be aiming to use as few mobile phones as possible.[9] This means trying to keep our phones for as long as we can and then having them refurbished as many times as possible. It also implies that we should be aiming to convince the manufacturers and mobile phone companies that we want durability and robustness designed into our phones rather than planned obsolescence.

Computers in the home

The manufacture of mobile phones is costly in terms of energy and natural resources. As you might expect, computers are far worse. Data from Apple suggest that making a laptop computer involves the emissions of about a quarter of a tonne of CO_2.[10] A big desktop is even worse, with emissions of over half a tonne of greenhouse gases. That's approximately 50 times the weight of the product itself.

In the case of a laptop, the emissions from manufacture are greater than the carbon emitted during the use of the machine. As discussed in Chapter 6, a laptop uses much less electricity than a desktop machine, so its lifetime emissions come from the manufacture and shipping of the computer rather than from its day-to-day use. The manufacturer assumes that the typical machine lasts four years. Apple doesn't provide estimates for the amount of daily use that it assumes in its calculations, but a quick checks suggests that Apple assumes that we have our computers on most of the working day, every day of the week. This looks like it might be an overestimate of the amount of actual use, meaning that for a laptop, the carbon costs of manufacturing are even more important in calculating the computer's total footprint. Even for the desktop, which uses far more electricity, manufacturing may actually be more important than the electricity used to power the computer for four years.

Table 11.7 *Comparison of CO_2 involved in the production and transportation of desktop and laptop computers (kg CO_2 equivalent)*

	Production	Transportation	(In use)
24 inch iMac	511	69	787
MacBook	230	46	179

As with mobile phones, the extremely complex chain of suppliers around the world and the frequent use of air freight to ship components between continents means that transport emissions are surprisingly high at ten or more times the weight of the computer (Table 11.7).

How does Apple calculate these figures? It is far from a simple task.

Apple's Environment team arrived at this estimate using a sophisticated life-cycle analysis of carbon emissions at each phase of production, starting with the mining of raw materials. We account for the manufacturing of the product as well as its packaging. Then we add the emissions related to transporting it to market, the power consumed during the product's use, and the energy required for eventual recycling. Apple also factors in the environmental impact of our offices and other business operations, which account for about 5% of total emissions.[11]

It is interesting that if one looked at Apple's own emissions one would only be observing about a 20th of the footprint of its products. Of course most electronics suppliers would be in the same position. Few consumer electronics companies make many of their own components.

The conclusions are less clear than those drawn for mobile phones, but computer users should be aware that the best way of reducing the emissions from computer use may not be to turn it off when not in use, but simply to keep it for longer. A two-year longer life for an Apple laptop is more important than a 30 per cent reduction in electricity consumption for the machine.

Most global computer companies do not encourage their customers to keep their machines for longer. This business strategy has obvious risks. But one UK manufacturer is striving to encourage longer lives for office and home computers. Very PC is a Sheffield-based company that will guarantee that its machines last for five years. Owners have to

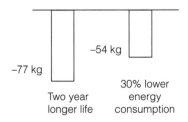

Figure 11.2 *Impact of two different choices for reducing the carbon footprint of an Apple laptop computer*

commit to having their machines serviced after three years and then Very PC will commit to replacing any machine that fails before its five year anniversary. The purpose of the three year servicing is primarily to remove dust that may have settled on internal components. Dust tends to reduce the rate of heat dissipation in a computer, increasing the stress on components. It is not an unreasonable suggestion to say that a good vacuum cleaning may do more to reduce the carbon footprint of your computing than ruthlessly powering the machine down when it is not in use. Of course I'm not trying to suggest that we shouldn't buy low-energy-consumption computers and use them intelligently, but I also want to stress that much of the carbon footprint comes from manufacture and it therefore makes good sense to keep computers as long as possible. I accept that Windows-based machines tend to get clogged with files, reducing their speed and agility over the years. But the answer may be to get someone to clean up the machine's hard drive, not to replace the computer just because its performance has declined.

Cars

The main components of a car are metal and this dominates the carbon footprint. A tonne of steel made from iron ore generates about 1.5–1.8 tonnes of CO_2 in a modern steel plant.[12] It would be less if it were made from steel scrap. The other parts and the process of assembling the car probably add another tonne of emissions for each tonne of weight.

A new small car weighs about 900kg and so will be responsible for about 2–2.5 tonnes of emissions in its manufacture. This sounds a lot but if the vehicle is driven the average amount it will emit about 20 tonnes during the course of its life. So the carbon cost of manufacturing the car is only about an eighth of its total lifetime emissions.[13] Put another way, the CO_2 emissions from the manufacture of a small car are typically less than 200kg per year of use. Please briefly consider this number: spread over its life, the manufacture of your car may have less environmental impact than the consumer electronics that you buy. The main impact from buying a car comes from using it, but for an iMac the main impact comes from the manufacture of its circuit boards and other components. In other words, physical size has very little relationship to the carbon emissions from manufacture. The refining of tiny amounts of rare metals requires more energy use, and hence emissions, than the melting of large quantities of iron ore to make the steel for a desirable new car.

Motor manufacturers are making good progress at reducing the emissions from family cars. Better aerodynamics and improved energy efficiency are reducing the average emissions per mile at a surprising rate. The improvement is being aided by a gradual reduction in the weight of the typical car. Very small cars are now well under a tonne while modern larger saloons are about a tonne and a half. These figures are well down on even a few years ago. This means not only that the running costs of cars are tending to fall, but also that the CO_2 impact of making the car in the first place is gradually diminishing.

Additionally, years of government and EU pressure are now obliging manufacturers to ensure that literally everything in a new car can be recycled and used again. But it still makes good sense to buy a smaller car. I looked at the weights of the cars in Toyota's range in July 2009. The weight of the tiny Aygo was 800kg and the mid-size Avensis saloon was almost exactly twice as much. Since the CO_2 footprint of a car is strongly correlated with its weight, this means that the emissions from the manufacture of the smaller car are probably little more than half of the Avensis. The carbon-conscious consumer should be looking for lighter cars as well as considering the impact of fuel consumption per mile. Interestingly, although the Avensis weighs twice as much as the Aygo, its most efficient variant only uses about 25 per cent more fuel per kilometre.

One of the questions I am asked most often is whether it saves emissions by buying a second-hand car or other appliance. The conventional economist would probably say that it doesn't make much difference. Buy a used car and you will help bid up the price of other second-hand models, albeit by a tiny amount. To the average buyer the price of a new car becomes very slightly more attractive compared to an older model. So if you buy an old car, this means that someone else will be just a little bit more likely to buy a new one. That's the thing with economists, they will always say that what you do will have counter-intuitive results. Depressingly, your behaviour never has any effect.

My logic is slightly different. Human beings are social creatures, usually doing what is expected of them in the society and time in which they live. So if you buy a second-hand car or, better still, keep your old pile of junk for 20 years, it sends a message to your neighbours that it isn't obligatory to change to a new turbocharged four-wheel drive monster every two years. Cars can now last a very long time – use yours sparingly, intelligently and keep it for as long as possible. Today's carbon-aware citizen maintains her car properly to make sure it lasts two decades.

Cement and concrete

Cement is an important part of many building materials. It is used in concrete floors, walling blocks and many other components of today's new buildings. Most cement is made from calcium carbonate mixed with a clay. When heated to very high temperatures, calcium carbonate splits into quicklime, usually called Portland cement, and carbon dioxide. So the making of cement creates emissions both from the large amount of heat needed to make the product and from the CO_2 that is necessarily emitted during the production process. This CO_2 will weigh about half a kilogram per kilogram of cement while the carbon dioxide from the combustion of fossil fuel for the intense heat required in a cement kiln adds another 200–600g per kilogram.

Nobody is quite sure, but most estimates suggest that the world cement industry is responsible for about 5 per cent of global emissions. This surprisingly large figure arises because the world is now producing about 2.5 billion tonnes of cement a year, almost a third of a tonne per person on the planet. Much of this arises because of the pace of construction in China and other newly industrializing countries. But, to be blunt, Westerners bear some responsibility for this because we are buying the Chinese products made in the new buildings that are using so much cement and concrete.

Cement use in countries like the UK is slightly lower than the world average. It's about a fifth of a tonne per person, creating somewhat less than 2 per cent of national emissions in the process. UK cement works are quite efficient and the heat energy needed to make cement averages about 300g of CO_2 per kilogram of production, meaning that the total carbon dioxide cost is about 800g per kilogram, or 0.8 tonnes per tonne of cement. Relatively minor further energy improvements are possible but the long-term goal is a production system that captures carbon dioxide and then stores it safely underground. Carbon capture and storage (CCS) will be needed at cement plants at least as much as it will be required at fossil fuel power stations. And, as with power stations, the implications for the cost of production are quite severe. A CCS-equipped cement plant will need far more energy to make cement and then capture the CO_2 than its conventional equivalent. So it is not going to happen fast.

Today's plants, which vent the CO_2 to the open air, produce about 0.15 tonnes of CO_2 per head of UK population. Of course, few of us actually buy a bag of cement in the typical year. Cement is used to make concrete for new buildings, sports stadiums and for such things as bridges and railway lines. Concrete is made from cement and water, combined with aggregates such as pebbles, sand or rubble. The percentage of cement in concrete isn't particularly high – usually less than 15 per cent. So the climate change impact of a tonne of concrete is much less than a tonne of cement. One estimate suggests that the CO_2 from concrete is no more than about 200kg per tonne compared to about 800kg for a tonne of UK-produced cement.

Nevertheless, 'green building' advocates say that architects and builders should avoid using any building materials made from cement. There is a problem with this: concrete is very good at absorbing heat. In the jargon it has high 'thermal mass'. This means that a house made using concrete and bricks will not heat up as fast during a summer day and internal temperatures will typically be cooler than in a conventionally built house that doesn't use concrete wall blocks and concrete floors. (A high thermal mass isn't quite the same as good insulation. Think of thermal mass as being similar to a bath of cold water. It takes a lot of energy to heat it up but it is a poor insulator.) In the summer, a house with a good thermal mass absorbs some of the energy that would otherwise heat up the interior of the building. During the night, the concrete gradually releases the heat energy it has absorbed during the day. Similarly, in the winter a house using concrete components will tend to hold its heat better overnight than a house built with lighter components, such as those with timber frames. This reduces the need for central heating.

The concrete industry fiercely defends the use of cement-based building materials, saying that houses with high thermal mass have lower emissions in the long term. Although the carbon dioxide effect of building a house using concrete materials rather than, say, a timber frame is initially higher, it will need less heating. As UK summer temperatures rise in the next few decades, many houses with low thermal mass will also need air-conditioning on the hottest days. So the emissions related to a concrete house may not be higher over the course of its lifetime than a timber-framed or panel home.

One study suggests that a new small house generates about 35 tonnes of emissions from its construction and the material used in building it. A light-framed house is about 32 tonnes compared to about 37 tonnes for a home using concrete.[14] The difference is relatively small – only about 5 tonnes. This initially higher figure is outweighed by the lower energy costs in use. The study authors say that within 25 years a new house has repaid the costs of the larger amounts of embedded energy in a house using concrete for thermal mass. A concrete house may be more comfortable and energy efficient than homes built using standard lightweight materials.

My argument is not that we should encourage the use of cement and concrete. No, we should try to avoid buildings that absorb large quantities of cement in their construction and start to use building materials that have high thermal mass – thus limiting the need for heating and for air-conditioning – but which can be made without emitting large quantities of CO_2. Green building specialists have recommended a wide variety of materials such as rammed earth walls and hemp mixed with lime (sometimes known by the brand name Hempcrete). Even a thick layer of sheep's wool insulation can provide an improved thermal mass to a lightweight building. These solutions all use well-established techniques known to builders for many centuries to provide well-insulated homes with high thermal mass that provide a buffer against temperature changes during the cycle of the day.

A well-constructed green building will have lower running costs and greater protection against swings in outside temperature. So why are these techniques not used by the major housebuilders? One reason, of course, is the natural caution of the home buyer. Asked whether they want to invest their life savings in a building made of heavily compacted rammed earth – a material with excellent thermal mass – or of reliable old-fashioned concrete, most families would stick with the sort of home they are used to even if the prices were the same. The building firms are also conservative – for very good reasons. A new construction technique that failed would very probably ruin the firm. So the experimentation that is going on in the UK to resurrect older techniques is carried out by skilled enthusiasts who find it difficult to convince conventional builders of the promise of their work, even when the results in their trial buildings are outstanding in terms of cost, thermal comfort and carbon emissions.

Another alternative is to use modern materials that can be mass produced but which don't involve large carbon emissions and have good thermal characteristics. DuPont produces a walling material called Energain that has a core that liquefies at about 22°C, absorbing significant amounts of energy as it melts. This helps buffer the temperature inside a house, ensuring that it doesn't go much above 22°C as long as the external temperature isn't too hot. As the heat of the day declines in the evening, the energy is given back as the panel returns to a solid.

Many researchers are trying to find ways of getting good thermal characteristics of concrete at a lower carbon cost. Several are trying to develop forms of concrete that are not based on calcium carbonate but on substances such as magnesium silicate. In theory, the chemistry of these compounds could mean that cement would be 'carbon positive' because they extract CO_2 from the air. We can be very hopeful that viable technical solutions can be found that appear to provide good concrete with minimal carbon emissions. The problem is then convincing construction companies that the new materials will maintain their strength for hundreds of years. Getting technical and regulatory approval will be extremely slow – even though the possible savings to global emissions could be of the order of 2–3 per cent.

As things stand, it may be that a mass-produced house made partly from concrete is no worse in the longer term than the lightweight equivalent made with a timber frame. Sadly very few of us can afford to buy our houses from the architects and construction specialists who are rapidly advancing the techniques of green building. Genuine eco-housing is still almost entirely developed by tiny firms building a few houses every year.

Gold and silver

What has the highest ratio of weight of greenhouse gases produced during the production process to weight of the final product? Gold jewellery takes a lot of beating. Gold mines vary enormously in the amount of energy they use but a 10g wedding ring made from pure gold probably has a carbon footprint 10,000 times as much as its weight. Making this simple piece of jewellery therefore contributes about 100kg of CO_2 to the atmosphere. But even at the July 2009 gold price of about $1000 an ounce, the cost of the energy used to make the ring is unlikely to be more than 10 per cent of the value of the metal. This is another illustration of the main problems the world faces in trying to reduce its use of fossil fuels – for some of the largest users of energy, the cost of fuels is a small fraction of the value of their products. The incentives to make major improvements in efficiency are comparatively minor.

The UK's total imports of gold for jewellery are about 40 tonnes a year. This may not seem much, but multiply this by the figure of 10,000 mentioned in the previous paragraph and you get almost half a million tonnes of CO_2 each year. The number seems impossibly high, but once you remember that typical gold ores contain just a few grams of the precious metal in every tonne of rock, the calculation becomes more plausible. To get the gold for a single wedding ring, huge volumes of solid ore are crushed into a powder and the gold extracted by a nasty-sounding chemical process using cyanide. And as the world runs out of its high-grade ores of precious metals, the typical energy used in refining gold is likely to rise.

Most of us only buy gold objects a few times in our lives and the annual purchases of new gold are only about two-thirds of a gram per person. This gives average emissions of slightly less than 10kg, about the same as a T-shirt. What about silver? Silver probably has an impact of less than one-fiftieth of gold for each unit of weight. We buy many more silver items than gold but, because silver is often applied as a surface to other metals ('silver plate'), it is difficult to accurately estimate the footprint of our new silver jewellery and ornaments. As with cars, I suppose it is always better to look for second-hand ('recycled') precious metals and jewellery.

Paper

Virgin paper takes huge amounts of energy to make. Once you think about it, this is intuitively obvious. A tree needs to be cut, transported and then smashed into fibres and mixed into pulp before being rolled through an enormous machine that forces the water out from the paper. The making of pulp and paper is one of the most important sources of greenhouse gas emissions in the world.

It will vary greatly from manufacturer to manufacturer, but making a tonne of virgin paper uses about 7000kWh of energy. The production process also employs prodigious amounts of water, and the chemical effluents from paper plants are a major pollution problem. Making recycled paper uses much less energy and involves less water. The pollution problems are greatly reduced and the energy needs are about half those of virgin paper.

Even today, with internet newspapers, paperless invoices and declining letter-writing, we use large amounts of paper. Almost 20 per cent of UK household waste by weight is composed of paper and cardboard which equates to about 75kgs per person each year. Very roughly, this is composed as shown in Table 11.8.

I assume that the weight of what we throw away is the same as what we bring into the house – 75kg going into the rubbish bins therefore means 75kg of paper coming into our homes in the form of newspapers, magazines, books, junk mail, bills, Christmas cards, packaging and other material. For comparison, I have also done some estimates for paper use in offices and I think office workers typically use about a third as much as they do at home. The use of paper in both the home and office is tending to fall quite rapidly.

Table 11.8 *Paper and cardboard waste from UK households*

Type of paper or card	Annual weight per person going into household waste (kg)
Newspapers	25
Magazines	15
Other paper	5
Cardboard	30
Total	75

The environmental impact of different types of paper and cardboard varies enormously. Almost all newspapers are now made from recycled material. But magazines generally use virgin coated paper because the paper is whiter and is thought to be more attractive to hold. (But some people say that recycled papers are now quite good enough for use in glossy magazines, so next time you communicate with a magazine that you read, tell the owners you'd rather they used recycled paper.) Cardboard is often made from recycled and pulped papers and card.

What are the emissions arising from our paper use? This is a much more complicated issue than you might imagine.

• First, over half our paper comes from overseas. Most newsprint is made here, but Scandinavian manufacturers produce much of the rest. The UK's national emissions accounts don't record much of the impact from our use of paper.

• Second, although recycled paper is much less harmful than the virgin equivalent, you can only recycle paper five or so times before the individual fibres get too short to use in paper-making. (The same is true of cotton clothing – you can recycle T-shirts, but not for ever.) So although you personally may only use recycled paper, we can never truly have what is called a 'closed loop' that sees paper being endlessly recycled. For as long as we use paper we will need new trees to provide pulp with longer fibres.

• Unlike most European countries, the UK is a major exporter of waste paper, mostly to China. Other places process their paper and card locally, but much of our material goes into making new paper elsewhere. It's important to recognize that the UK produces enough waste paper to make much more recycled paper than it does.

• Almost all UK households now have paper recycling bins and most businesses are making a much greater effort to recycle their waste; however, the best estimate I can come up with is that only about half of UK paper is being recycled.

Greenhouse gas impacts

I am going to have to make some crude calculations to try to assess the footprint from the use of paper and cardboard. But I think the numbers will be broadly accurate. The crucial simplification I make is to assume that paper mills use electricity that has a carbon footprint of the UK average. This is a questionable assumption because more than half of the country's paper is made abroad, where electricity may or may not be generated with fossil fuels, and because the big UK newsprint producers do use some renewable sources of power. But, as always, I say that if this electricity hadn't been used to make paper, it would have been employed elsewhere. Using renewable power doesn't make paper-making any less energy-intensive.

The implication of Table 11.9 is that the footprint of the average person's use of paper at home is about one-third of a tonne a year (365kg), of which just under half (157.5kg) is incurred in the UK. We also need to account for the methane produced when newspapers are not recycled and put in general household rubbish. These papers will generally end up in landfill where they will emit methane, some portion of which will not be captured.

One estimate from the Carbon Trust suggested that this added about 1kg of CO_2 equivalent for each 6kg of paper. The Trust looked at the Daily Mirror, a UK national newspaper, and concluded, based on an assessment of what percentage of the papers were likely to end up in landfill, that each 182g newspaper could be said to emit methane equivalent to 30g of CO_2. If this figure is replicated across all paper and cardboard it will add about 4 per cent to the footprint of paper.

Table 11.9 *Carbon footprint of paper and cardboard manufacture*

	Usage (kg)	Percentage from recycled	$kgCO_2/kg$	Total CO_2 (kg)	UK percentage	UK CO_2 accounts (kg)
Newsprint	30	80	3.5	105	50	52.5
Magazines	15	10	7	105	50	52.5
Other paper	5	40	6	30	50	15.0
Cardboard	25	60	5	125	30	37.5
Totals	75			365		157.5

A digression on forests

Some people think that we should minimize paper use because it will help maintain forests. The thought is that if making paper means we need to cut down trees, then paper-making must cause deforestation. This plausible notion is almost certainly wrong. Paper use in the UK encourages the planting of trees, mostly in Scandinavia, to meet the future demand for pulp. Paper-making encourages the productive management of forest lands that otherwise would almost certainly be left to decay.

Just to be clear – I'm not arguing that all woodland should be aggressively managed to produce as much wood as possible. Untended ancient forest has massive importance for biodiversity and no one argues that it should ever be converted to growing trees for paper. But converting low-quality pasture lands to fir trees involves little loss. After all, these areas will often have been single species boreal forest anyway before man arrived and cut all the trees down.

This isn't an argument for an increased use of paper from virgin wood. Even if all paper plants are powered by renewable energy – as they mostly are in Scandinavia – it would be better to use that electricity to run our homes and offices. Using less paper is a positive step for climate change.

Would we reduce the carbon footprint by making paper from other fibres?

Most paper was originally made from hemp, a non-narcotic plant very closely related to marijuana. Hemp grows quickly, generally doesn't need much fertilizer and can be harvested annually. I haven't found any good statistics, but it seems that it requires far less energy to make paper using hemp. Timber has to be broken apart using massive amounts of energy but hemp is less woody and has the strength of straw. To be made into usable paper, hemp also needs much less whitening than paper made from wood. Conventional paper mills use chlorine for bleaching, but hemp can be treated with hydrogen peroxide, a chemical with far fewer polluting effects.

Importantly, hemp has longer fibres and so can be recycled many more times than wood-based paper before it becomes unusable. We would need less new paper for every ream sold and each page would use less energy to make. So if the world was prepared to invest in creating a paper industry based entirely on this crop, we would significantly reduce the emissions from paper-making. Unfortunately, there are no signs whatsoever that this is likely to happen. Hemp paper is available, but often at ten times the price of paper made from wood. It remains the choice of enthusiasts – who might also use bamboo paper or even paper made from cotton rags – but no industrial manufacturing capacity has been put in place.

Paper not disposed of in household rubbish collection

People in Britain are said to be among the biggest users of toilet paper in the world. One study claimed that per capita use was about 18kg a year, equivalent to about a quarter of total other household paper use.[15] I weighed a typical roll and worked out that the average person is using one every three days. The total length of toilet paper used per year is over 3km per person.

Tesco stores have recently started to put a carbon label on some of their own-brand toilet paper. The company calculates that the emissions from one sheet of recycled paper are about two-thirds that of new paper at about 1.1g. This implies that recycled toilet paper has a footprint of about twice the weight of the product. For the average person this means that the total emissions from toilet paper use are about 36kg a year if the recycled sort is used and over 50kg if other types are purchased. Most toilet paper sold in Britain is made here, so these emissions should be added to the average UK footprint for paper of nearly 160kg (and 365kg for paper made in all parts of the world). Paper is an important source of emissions for most individuals.

What can we do?

The list is obvious. It is best to buy recycled paper and to ensure that all paper and cardboard then gets recycled in its turn. Those users not using recycled paper – such as magazines – need to face consumer pressure to change. There's no really good reason why almost all printed matter cannot use recycled material. We need to try to reduce the amount of direct mail sent but we shouldn't get too worked up about this issue. Direct mail represents about 4 per cent of total paper use in the UK and almost all of the paper is from recycled sources. We can also reduce the number of bills and statements sent to us in paper form, although the effect would also be quite trivial.

The two most important things to do would be to buy fewer magazines and newspapers and ensure that the amount of cardboard coming into the home is minimized. Remember that the issues over cardboard packaging are quite complex – a thin layer of cardboard can help protect goods that would otherwise be damaged, resulting in higher emissions from replacing the broken goods. It may be unpopular but cardboard packaging has a vital role in getting things safely from shops to home.

WHAT THIS ALL MEANS

We've thrown a lot of numbers into this chapter. Let's put them into one chart to show how a typical range of purchases add to our emissions. The main assumptions I have used are given in the endnotes at the back of the book.[16]

It is the ordinary and the unremarkable things that really stand out.

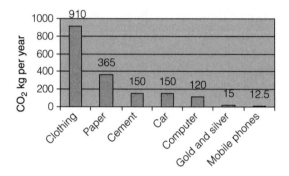

Figure 11.3 *Annual emissions from an individual's purchases*

part III

---

other
analysis

12

domestic use
of renewable energy

A household can generate its own electricity from a wind turbine or solar photovoltaic panels. Water heating can be supplemented by solar collectors on the roof and heat pumps can provide low-carbon central heating. Wood-burning stoves offer an inexpensive way of replacing the use of gas for heating. Domestic fuel cells have been a promising technology for some years and may soon offer a low-cost way to reduce carbon emissions. None of these technologies are without their problems and some are very expensive for each unit of carbon dioxide they save. Very small scale use of renewable energy – such as might be used in a domestic house – will usually be far more costly and less efficient than when the same technology is used on a commercial scale.

This chapter looks at the ways in which domestic households can currently use renewable energy to reduce carbon emissions. It addresses six types of technology:

1 solar photovoltaics;
2 wind turbines;
3 heat pumps;
4 solar hot water;
5 biomass for domestic heating;
6 fuel cells and small-scale combined heat and power (CHP).

SOLAR PHOTOVOLTAICS

Solar photovoltaic (PV) panels generate electricity through the action of the sun's rays falling upon a silicon layer and causing the passage of electrons. Now 30 or 40 years old, the technology has always slightly disappointed. Expectations of rapid improvement have come to little, and the most efficient panels still convert no more than about 20 per cent of the energy falling upon them. Typical figures are lower than this, and the average installation in the UK today will probably turn no more than 15 per cent of solar energy into electricity.

Solar PV installations on the roofs of UK homes are few in number – probably less than 8000 – although the rate of growth is certainly increasing. The cost is daunting, with an array that generates 2kW in bright sunshine possibly costing more than £10,000.[1] Grants used to reduce this figure by up to £5000 but the UK has moved to a different scheme to encourage an increased number of domestic installations: 'feed-in tariffs' pay the householder for each kilowatt hour of electricity that is generated from the solar panels even those which are used in the house and not fed into the electricity grid. In the financial analysis in this chapter, I use the numbers to illustrate the impact on the householder.[2]

Payments have also been announced for installations that produce heat from renewable sources such as wood.

First, I have to confess that although solar PV has many advantages, such as its long life, low maintenance requirements and visual unobtrusiveness, I am not quite sure why the UK government should promote this technology. In cloudy Britain, the amount of electricity generated by a typical installation will never compare with the same amount of money spent on a commercial wind turbine, for example. A £10,000 installation will generate a maximum of about 2000kWh each year in a good sunny location. If this were sold at typical prices in the wholesale electricity market it would earn about £100 – a return of 1 per cent on the investment. The same amount of money put into a large wind turbine in a good site would produce at least ten times as much electricity. But let's shelve this scepticism and look at household PV in a bit more detail.

If you are thinking of putting photovoltaics on your roof, you'll need to check that you have space that faces approximately due south and is not overshadowed by buildings or trees. For maximum output, the tilt of the roof should be about 35° to the horizontal. A roof facing due east will probably capture about 80 per cent of the energy of panels facing due south. Similar degrees of attenuation affect roofs that are either flat or very steep.

The amount of power that you will generate varies by latitude. The tip of Cornwall gets as much as 30 per cent more than northern England. As a result, a PV installation in the south-west, where electricity costs are generally higher as well, is more economically rational than in the north of England or Scotland (in June 2009, Southern Electric's electricity price is about 6 per cent higher in Devon than it is in Newcastle, so the saving from PV panels might be almost 40 per cent greater in the far south-west of England).

As with wind turbines, solar PV installations are generally connected to the grid, athough they can be used to charge batteries. The house uses the electricity first, if necessary, and any surplus spills over to the local electricity system. The panels generate direct current and this is passed through 'inverters' that convert the power into alternating current, closely synchronized to the 50 cycles per second pattern of the electricity network. Output from the roof has to go through these expensive electronics, a meter that registers how much is generated and, possibly, a meter that says how much is exported to the grid, rather than being used in the home. These all add to the cost.

The finances of domestic PV

PV installations are rated like wind turbines in terms of the amount of electricity they can generate under optimum conditions of sunshine or wind speed. In the case of PV panels, they will generally capture most at about midday during the summer months. The maximum solar radiation reaching the panels will be about 1kW per square metre at this time. At about 15 per cent efficiency, it therefore takes about 12 square metres to provide 2 'kilowatt peak', or 2kWp. This will fill most of the available space on most domestic roofs, but the largest houses may be able to accommodate as much as 5kWp.

Under typical southern England conditions, a 2kWp installation will harvest about 1600–1800kWh/year (the equivalent of about 850 hours operating at peak potential). The figure might be below 1500kWh/year for an installation facing due west, rather than directly to the south.

In financial terms, solar PV attached to the grid offers two benefits to the owner: first, a reduction in electricity bills and, second, a payment for the renewable energy generated. Most installers assume that reasonably sized domestic installations will export about a third of their output into the grid. The rest is used in the house. Table 12.1 illustrates how the economics work out at the proposed level of the feed-in tariff.

At a 41.3p feed-in tariff, the return is over 9 per cent per year on a cost of £10,000 or so. The life of photovoltaic systems is probably between 25 and 30 years, although the amount of electricity generated will slowly fall over the latter years. So, this is an acceptable investment at today's interest rates but not an overwhelmingly attractive one. If electricity prices increase substantially, the returns will improve. It seems to me that the financial benefits are good enough to make it worthwhile to consider adding PV to domestic houses. The CEO of a major German solar installer told me that any returns over 6 per cent are usually enough to unlock interest in the countries in which his company works.

The price of solar PV will come down. In fact, by the time you read this, the price of panels will probably be 20 per cent lower than it is now in summer 2009. The worldwide glut of ultra-pure silicon means that panels are plentiful and relatively cheap. But the cost

Table 12.1 *Medium-sized PV installation (2kWp) in a good location*

Total output	1800kWh
Expected usage in the house	1200kWh
Export	600kWh
Value to homeowner (at 41.3p feed-in payment):	
Reduction in electricity bill at 13p per kWh	£156
Feed-in payment at 41.3p per kWh generated	£743
Export payment at 5p per kWh	£18
Total	£917

of a PV installation is only partly determined by the price of panels. The other major element is the inverter, the box of electronics that turns the sharply varying direct current from the roof into good quality AC power suitable for the grid. And then there's the cost of scaffolding and the work necessary to fix the panels securely to the roof. This cost is unlikely to decline sharply, although it may reduce as installers get more experience in putting panels on the roofs of houses.

WIND TURBINES

As is particularly well understood by anybody living on the coastline of the British Isles, the UK is a windy place. The wind blows here on more days per year and at greater force than almost anywhere else in Europe. Across the UK, we are reckoned to have about 40 per cent of the EU's wind energy (Scotland alone has 25 per cent).[3] Against stiff opposition from local interests, large numbers of new commercial wind farms are being built in the exposed quarters of the UK. The number of large turbines – now over 2000 – may even eventually exceed the number of windmills (over 10,000) that flourished during the 18th century before the advent of steam power.

Large domestic wind turbines have been available for several decades. UK companies such as Proven Engineering supply systems on masts specially erected for the purpose. They need to be installed at least a 100 metres away from the nearest neighbours to avoid any noise problems. (Many owners are happy with the sound made by the turbines and have them much closer to their own houses.) These windmills offer a good supply of electricity to farms and other places with no connection to the power grid, but there are only a few thousand installed in the UK. Now, at today's electricity prices, and with the likely advent of feed-in tariffs, these large turbines are close to making financial sense for buildings already attached to the grid. The cost of the machines is high; Proven suggests a price of about £17,200 plus installation costs for its 6kW machine while the figure from its competitor Evance is somewhat lower, at around £12,000 for the hardware, for a slightly smaller 5kW version.[4]

Proven suggests that its 6kW turbine will generate about 12,000kWh in a good location. If 6000kWh is used on site, it saves £780. The feed-in tariff is 26.7p per kWh. At these prices the turbine is likely to pay back the investment in about six or eight years. In really windy locations it will be sooner. Remember that the power available in the wind goes up with the cube of the speed. So wind averaging 4 metres per second – a typical sheltered spot in England – will generate less than a third of the power of a turbine on a windy hilltop with speeds of 6m/sec.[5]

The grail for turbine manufacturers has been to build a much smaller turbine that can be put onto the gable of a domestic house, supplying power that supplements the existing electricity supply. The challenges have been substantial: domestic turbines must not shake the building excessively and must be nearly completely quiet. Two small Scottish companies have been producing domestic wind turbines that meet these requirements for the last three or four years. Unfortunately, it turns out that wind speeds near urban houses tend to be very low, and are accompanied by turbulence that reduces the power that the turbine can capture. The amount of electricity generated has often been far lower than initially promised by the manufacturers. So even though these little turbines have come down in price to no more than £1500 or so, a purchase would make little financial sense. As time goes on, these problems may be solved – possibly by the use of rotating vertical turbines erected on poles – but householders should currently be extremely cautious about some of the claims for small-scale domestic wind power.

Interestingly, it may actually make more sense to use even smaller turbines, such as those used on yachts, canal boats or in fixed caravan sites, to charge 12 volt batteries. For maximum effectiveness, the turbine will have to be located some way from the house, preferably with no other buildings nearby. The electricity can then be used to power phone chargers, low voltage lights or other 12 volt appliances such as small fridges. The cost of a reliable and long-lived turbine like the Rutland 913, a pole with guy ropes, a battery and the electronics to control the charging may be as little as £700. For this money, you might get as much as 400kWh a year in a very windy location. A 12 volt system powered by a wind turbine seems to be eligible for feed-in tariffs in the UK but the owner would have to prove the electricity was eventually used and electricity production would have to be metered accurately. But if these problems could be solved, the feed-in tariff payment could be worth £120 on top of £50 of electricity. It'll also be a talking point around your neighbourhood for years to come.

Heat pumps

Several manufacturers of 'ground source' heat pumps have successfully operated in the UK market for many years. For large buildings, these machines offer a good way of reducing energy costs and carbon footprints, particularly if they are installed during construction. The last year has seen a growing interest in 'air source' pumps because they are cheaper and far easier to install on a domestic building than their ground source cousins. In the next few pages, I'll take a look at the implications of buying one of the new generation of air source pumps for use at your house. It seems to me that air source pumps are likely to be heavily promoted over the next few years as a low-carbon alternative to other ways of heating rooms and hot water. This may be true, but I want to provide a note of mild scepticism. For many householders, the benefits will be as modest as a rooftop wind turbine. Don't get carried away by the general enthusiasm – many homes, particularly older ones, are simply not suitable for heat pumps. Government, manufacturers and installers need to be very much more cautious in encouraging the use of heat pumps and should use far more conservative payback assumptions.

What is a heat pump?

When a gas is compressed, it heats up. When it is uncompressed, it cools. Imagine the simplest possible compressor – a bicycle pump. Hold your finger over the exit and push the pump handle. The air inside will get very hot. Lift your finger and let the hot air out, and it cools again. Imagine that the cylinder of the bicycle pump was inside your house but the exhaust air was vented through a window. When you pumped the bicycle pump, the chamber would get hot, and this heat would heat the room. As the air left the pump and was exhausted to the outside air, it would cool, tending to reduce (to a very tiny extent of course) the external temperatures.

This is the principle of a heat pump. The heat from the compressed gas is used to increase temperatures in one place whereas the reverse – heat loss from the decompression – decreases temperatures in another place. Think of this as taking a block of air and separating it into a hot gas and cold gas in two different places. When temperatures are high, you can reverse the pump, putting the cold air into the house and the hot air outside. Most heat pumps transfer the heat or cold into water that is then circulated round the house. So a domestic heat pump can, under certain circumstances, use a house's existing network of hot water pipes and radiators for heating and for cooling. Similarly, a heat pump can provide the hot water for domestic baths and showers.

How much energy do heat pumps save?

Heat pumps look like a free source of energy and good ones are indeed very efficient. But they do need compressors and other electrically powered devices to work. (Or, in the case of the bicycle pump, the compression is provided by the person pumping. He or she will be using energy to work the pump.) So heat from heat pumps is not free. The ratio of energy used to power the pump and the useful heat output is called the coefficient of performance, usually abbreviated to CoP. This figure is critically important when you are assessing how much money or carbon you will save. The CoP will vary according to the air temperature and the demands placed on the pump. Broadly speaking, the greater the temperature difference between the interior of the house or the hot water supply and the outside temperature, the lower the CoP of the heat pump. A poor CoP means that you will use a lot of electricity for each unit of useful heat.

Today, attention is focused on heat pumps that use the outside air for their energy. These are called air source heat pumps (ASHPs) and are relatively easy to install in domestic houses. The unit can be attached to the wall or sit on the ground, taking up little space. The best ones, such as Mitsubishi's Ecodan have a CoP of about 3–3.3 in average British conditions. I've used an average figure of 3.15 in the calculations that follow. As heat pumps improve, this number will rise but please don't simply use the manufacturers' figures when you are assessing them. Be cautious, just as you would be when assessing a car maker's claims, and look for real world examples; plenty are now available on the internet.

Ground source heat pumps can achieve better CoP figures than their air source equivalents. But they are more expensive to install and get their 'fuel' from small pipes that run underneath the garden, collecting and dispersing heat energy. The garden has to be dug up to install these pipes. Although a rural house with a large area of land and no access to a gas supply might well benefit from using a ground source pump, I've focused here on the air source equivalent.

Radiators versus underfloor heating

Hot water from the heat pump can be circulated using a house's existing pipework and radiators. Unfortunately some householders will see substantial problems. The water coming out of heat pumps is usually far cooler than from conventional gas or oil boilers. Typically, the water is at 45°C compared to perhaps 75°C from an ordinary boiler. As you might imagine, this means that radiators do not get really hot, and the amount of heat that they transfer into a room is much less. The solution is either to replace all the radiators with much larger ones with a far greater surface area, or to install a dense network of hot water pipes under the floors. In a new house with a heat pump it is almost certainly best to avoid radiators and use underfloor pipes throughout the house.

Heat pumps can also heat water for showers. This water needs to be hotter, which adversely affects the efficiency (the CoP) of the heat pump. Modern air source pumps take the water up to 55 or 60°C, which is hot enough to bathe in.

How much do heat pumps cost?

Unsurprisingly, the cost varies enormously according to the complexity of the installation and the size of the pump. In an average-sized new house, the extra cost compared to a conventional boiler is probably £2000–3000. To replace an existing boiler in a house already standing will add slightly more, particularly if any radiators need to be replaced. One system I have recently seen cost about £6000 compared to perhaps £2000 for a good condensing boiler. The government is currently offering a grant of £900, which makes a real difference but still doesn't create an overwhelming incentive. This is being replaced by

Table 12.2 *Energy savings from using an air source heat pump*

(*a*)	Typical gas use for heating	15,000kWh
(*b*)	Boiler efficiency from new condensing boiler	88%
(*c*)	Total heat demand (*a* × *b*)	13,200kWh
(*d*)	Heat pump CoP	3.15
(*e*)	Electricity need to drive heat pump (*c* ÷ *d*)	4190kWh

a new subsidy scheme in April 2011. A slightly larger than average UK house on the mains gas network might use about 15,000kWh for room heating, and much smaller amounts for water heating and cooking. If an air source heat pump has a CoP of 3.15, this means that replacing a gas boiler should significantly reduce the amount of energy used to heat the home. The figures are shown in Table 12.2.

In this example, the electricity needed to heat the house is less than a third of a gas boiler. But electricity is far more expensive than gas for each kilowatt hour. In June 2009, the cheapest tariff on the British Gas website offers a price of just over 3p a kilowatt hour for gas and slightly less than 10p for electricity.[6] I've used the most up-to-date numbers to give the most accurate assessment.

Using these rates, I calculate that an air source heat pump will save the average customer on the gas network about £50 a year. This is not a good return on the investment of several thousand pounds. The government's Energy Saving Trust suggests typical savings of £300 for a home with gas but this seems unreasonably optimistic. It is probably a mistake for government bodies to exaggerate the benefits of new technologies in an effort to persuade the public to adopt them.

But if you use electricity to heat your house, the savings could be more impressive. Many of the 5 million homes off the gas network employ night storage radiators that take advantage of low overnight electricity rates. The radiators heat up at night and then give off their heat during the day. However there are two problems. First, the householder will have to put new radiators in the property, adding to the cost and disruption. Second, heat pumps usually work all the time, and not just at night. So if a householder puts in a new heat pump, she will be using both low price night electricity and very expensive daytime power. Personally I doubt whether the savings will be much greater than £200–300 a year, not the £870 estimated by the Energy Saving Trust.

The CO$_2$ savings

The CO$_2$ savings also tend to be exaggerated. A heat pump uses electricity (largely generated from burning gas or coal) to replace a boiler that typically burns gas. The CO$_2$

saving therefore depends on the relative efficiency of heat pumps and large-scale power stations. The amount of carbon dioxide produced by a power station depends on the fuel it burns and the quality of its generating equipment. An old coal-fired station produces a kilogram of CO_2 for each kilowatt hour. A new gas plant has carbon dioxide output of well under half this figure. The UK average varies from year to year depending on which power stations are working. As at June 2009, the most recently published figure by the Carbon Trust suggested an average figure of 0.54kg of CO_2 per kilowatt hour. This figure is derived from a five-year average of power stations supplying the National Grid, mixing coal generation with gas, nuclear and wind.

We can easily work out the CO_2 savings from running a heat pump to heat a typical house (Table 12.3).

This is a more substantial reduction than the financial saving, cutting emissions from heating by about a fifth. Since home heating is often the single most important source of emissions, a heat pump may be worthwhile in some houses. But you need to consider the disadvantages I list below and note that the cost of the pump for every tonne of CO_2 saved is very high.

Table 12.3 *Carbon dioxide savings from heat pump use in the average home*

(a)	Gas needed	15,000 kilowatt hours
(b)	Kilograms of CO_2 per kilowatt hour of gas burnt	0.19kg
(c)	Total CO_2 from house heating ($a \times b$)	2.85 tonnes
(d)	Electricity needed to power heat pump	4190kWh
(e)	Kilograms of CO_2 per kilowatt hour of electricity used	0.54kg
(f)	Total CO_2 from heat pump for house heating ($d \times e$)	2.26 tonnes
	Total saving ($c - f$)	0.59 tonnes

Table 12.4 *Cost of a heat pump per tonne of CO_2 saved*

(a)	Possible life of heat pump	20 years
(b)	Annual savings of CO_2	0.59 tonnes
(c)	Total savings	11.8 tonnes
(d)	Possible extra cost of buying a heat pump	£3000
(e)	Cost per tonne of CO_2 ($d \div c$)	At least £250

The issues with heat pumps

In some countries – such as Switzerland and Sweden – heat pumps are very common. In these places, insulation standards have been high and heat pumps can heat houses even in very cold weather. In countries with low-carbon electricity supplies like Switzerland, which has large amounts of hydro electricity, there is a strong reason to move to using electric power rather than gas or oil for heating. For the UK, this is not the case. In recent years, we've actually seen a slight increase in the carbon dioxide produced in electricity generation as the nuclear power stations have become increasingly unreliable and large amounts of coal have been burnt rather than cleaner gas.

So the climate argument for using heat pumps in Britain does rather depend on whether we do successfully develop new and low-carbon sources of electricity. The attractiveness of heat pumps will rise as we switch to wind energy, to biomass and other low-carbon sources of power. However, I think it probably makes sense to wait for this to happen rather than buying a heat pump now.

There are some other issues. Experience from the first ASHPs suggests that some do not heat the house effectively in winter. A gas boiler has enough power to pump huge amounts of heat into a house in a short time. You can turn it on at five o'clock in the morning and the house will be warm for when people get up. Heat pumps aren't like this. They are kept on constantly, but delivering heat at lower levels. This is fine if your house is well insulated because the heat will remain. But in a draughty older house the heat will leak away and the lack of warmth may be a problem, particularly when outdoor temperatures have fallen rapidly. One householder intending to install a heat pump responded to this point by saying to me that his home would also have electric immersion heaters to increase the temperature in the central heating system when necessary. This is an unusual configuration but it may work – although at the price of higher electricity bills and reduced carbon savings.

It should be stressed much more prominently in the literature that advertises air source heat pumps that they are not suitable for many houses that were built more than ten years ago. Before this time, insulation standards were simply too low for heat pumps to maintain reasonable temperatures in the coldest weather. As we mentioned above, in many houses the installer should also think about replacing small radiators for much larger ones with greater surface area. Ideally, householders should replace radiators entirely with underfloor piping. This would help spread the heat effectively but because it would be costly and disruptive most companies selling ASHPs don't push this option.

Another disadvantage may become evident when the heat pump is heating hot water for bathing. Heating enough water for two baths will take almost an hour with a standard 8.5kW pump. During this time, the heat flowing into the central heating system will inevitably be much colder because all the energy from the pump will be going into the bathing water. In a well-insulated house, having the central heating off for an hour shouldn't matter very much, but in older homes the impact will occasionally be unpleasantly noticeable.

A proponent of air source heat pumps responds

I rang Ice Energy, one of the largest installers of domestic heat pumps, to discuss some of these concerns. Andrew Sheldon gave me his company's response.

- **Small savings**. At current gas and electricity prices, this may be the case. But, Andrew argued, gas prices are likely to rise relative to electricity prices. I think this is possible, but it is equally likely that the reverse will be true as the government forces the development of higher-cost sources of electricity such as offshore wind. Andrew also said that the UK's Renewable Heat Incentive, to be introduced in 2011 but which will include installations in 2010 as well, will pay a subsidy for heat pumps. The return will be 7.5p per kilowatt hour. An air source heat pump generating 10,000kWh of heat a year for a flat or small house will therefore provide a payment of £750 a year. This will continue for at least 18 years under the final scheme proposed in February 2010. This does indeed substantially improve the financial attractiveness of installing heat pumps.
- **Limited carbon savings**. The UK is on track to decarbonize its electricity supply by 2030. Once this has happened, carbon savings will be very substantial.
- **Worries over heating on cold days**. A well-insulated house should not suffer from low temperatures. Newly built houses with underfloor piping should see large financial savings and high levels of comfort.
- **The high price of heat pumps**. Andrew said we should take into account the longer life of heat pumps, which will last more than 20 years. They will also need lower levels of routine yearly maintenance.

He also stressed the greater safety of heat pumps. The radiators and bathing water temperatures are never dangerously hot, minimizing the risk to the old and to young children. The constant heat in the winter also means better indoor air quality because the high temperatures and powerful convection currents close to radiators in today's homes tended to result in high levels of dust in many rooms, particularly in older houses.

When the UK has built an infrastructure of low-carbon electricity generation, we will need to find ways of reducing the carbon dioxide emitted from heating buildings. For domestic homes, heating is much more important as a source of CO_2 than electricity use so the savings could be very important. Heat pumps and domestic fuel cells (such as those in testing from Ceramic Fuel Cells) may be the most important ways of cutting emissions from houses. But at the moment, the economics of heat pumps are not overwhelmingly attractive. Householders in existing properties, particularly those living in older homes, should be very wary of installing an ASHP.

SOLAR HOT WATER

Over 100,000 homes in the UK have some form of solar hot water heater. This number is growing rapidly as the main boiler manufacturers bring out packages that include roof-top collectors. Most solar water heaters take the form of a flat metal plate or a set of vacuum tubes on the roof of the house. These devices can provide hot water for the household for most of the year, but will only supplement conventional water heating in the winter months. They don't usually replace central heating in any way.

The advertisements for these products claim that they can replace 50–70 per cent of the energy used for heating water. The truth of this statement depends upon the relationship between the size of the installation on the roof and the total hot water demand of the household (if you never wash, then the solar system will, indeed, provide most of your hot water). Later in this section, I show that the figure of 50 per cent is probably achievable, but that 70 per cent is only attainable if the daily hot water needs of the house are restricted to providing one person a shower. The underlying difficulty is that only six months of the year give us enough solar energy to get water anywhere close to a high enough temperature to avoid using the boiler. The government's Renewable Heat Incentive, probably payable from April 2011, will provide further financial inducements to install solar water heating.

The installation

How does solar water heating work? Solar energy falling on a plate or a glass tube heats up the fluid passing through it. This hot liquid, usually water with anti-freeze in it, is pumped through a coil inside the hot water tank, heating the water. Having transferred its energy to the water in the tank, the now cooler liquid is pumped back to the roof. The technology is simple and reliable, and primitive versions have been used for centuries, particularly in countries where sunshine is plentiful. Efficient solar hot water panels – sometimes just called collectors – will work well in strong sunshine, even when air temperatures are low. However, collectors in cold climates will tend to lose a greater part of the energy that they collect. More heat is conducted or radiated to the air or to the surroundings of the solar thermal panels.

Solar collectors will heat water from a mains temperature of about 10°C up to 60°C or more. Depending upon the time of year and the number of hours of sunshine, the energy transferred from the collectors will either provide all of the water heating needed or will preheat the water so that it requires less fossil fuel energy to get it to the correct temperature.

How much water will the sun heat?

The savings in gas or electricity both depend upon the amount of the sun's energy falling on the plates and the efficiency with which the energy is collected. In southern England, 1 square metre of surface receives about 1200kWh/year in solar energy. The number is lower in the north. Of course, it is also unequally distributed between the months. The total energy received in December is about one-tenth of the June level. On a typical day in June, a 4m² solar collector in England and Wales south of the Mersey will receive about 20–24kWh, compared to no more than 2kWh in December. People often ask me whether one can use solar systems for central heating. The answer, unfortunately, is that when we need heating, there is so little solar energy reaching the UK that it would require a huge collector plate to capture more than a fraction of the heat energy we would need. The typical house requires 65kWh a day of heating (see Chapter 3), and 2kWh is only a small percentage of this.

The most efficient solar collectors are evacuated tubes, which turn about 70 per cent of this energy into useful heat, provided that the installation is facing reasonably close to south at an angle of tilt of about 30 degrees. Evacuated tubes not facing approximately south, or placed horizontally or vertically, will receive less energy. Provided that it is correctly oriented, in an average year 1m² of evacuated tubes will carry about 840kWh to the hot water tank in the south of England. Typical domestic installations are 2–4m², giving 1680–3360kWh/year, or an average of up to 9kWh per day for a larger collector (for reference, this compares to a figure of about 19,000kWh for the annual gas consumption of a typical house on the mains gas network).

The average daily figure will vary by a factor of more than 30 between a long sunny day in a summer month and a short overcast period of daylight in the depth of winter. On a sunny day in late June, the figure from a 4m² installation might be as much as 30kWh. How much water will this heat (Table 12.5)?

Table 12.5 *Number of litres of water heated by the sun in late June*

Energy needed to heat 1 litre of water by 100°C	0.11kWh
Typical UK mains temperature	10°C
Typical temperature of heated water in a shower[a]	60°C
Increase needed	50°C
Energy needed to heat 1 litre of water by 50°C	0.055kWh
Number of litres of water that can be heated by 50°C by 30kWh solar energy	545 litres

Note: [a]This figure may be somewhat high. It is difficult to measure accurately without highly intrusive research.

Is 545 litres per day enough for a typical house? The rule of thumb is that hot water demand in the UK averages about 50 litres a day per person. So, a household with two people will be hugely overprovided for in June. But this also depends upon how the household does its bathing. 80 litres will provide a full bath, so a sunny day should deliver almost seven baths. On the other hand, a quick gravity-fed shower might take only 30 litres.

The real question is whether the house has pumped showers, usually called power showers. These water guzzlers use up to 16 litres or more per minute, so the June solar energy will give a maximum of about 34 minutes of hot water.

I have not been able to find a reliable statistic on the average length of time spent in a luxurious power shower. Most sources give a figure of about five minutes, meaning that the water should last for six or seven people even if they are all using a pumped shower. In a household of two adults and two children, a sunny day in June should give enough hot water for all bathing needs, whether the family uses baths, power showers or the gravity-fed variety.

Actually, it is not quite as simple as this. When solar collectors are installed, the household usually gets a new hot water tank of about 300 litres capacity. So unless family members spread their showers throughout the day and give the hot water tank a chance to reheat, there won't be enough water. Or the 300 litre tank needs to get to a hotter temperature so that it can be diluted with cold water. The summer temperature of hot water from solar collectors can rise well above 80°C, meaning that the hot water has to be diluted with at least one part cold for two parts hot. The 300 litre tank delivers hot showers of at least 450 litres (28 minutes in a powerful shower), enough for five or six people.

What percentage of the water heating bill will be saved?

These calculations are complex and somewhat tedious. This section can easily be skipped if you are only interested in the main conclusions, which are summarized at the end.

First of all, we need to estimate how much solar energy is captured and used in comparison to the energy needed to heat a household's water. In this calculation, we must guess at the amount of energy that is not productively used because residents are away, or the system produces more energy (on a sunny summer day) than the water users actually use.

From Table 12.6, we can go on to estimate the savings that this generates. The first row in Table 12.7 shows the amount of water heating that the house still requires. The next row estimates what this costs in terms of gas use (assuming the household uses gas for water heating) by multiplying up the raw energy need by a factor to reflect the inefficiency of the boiler (to get 100kWh of water heating, the typical fairly modern boiler has to burn 133kWh of gas because it is only about 75 per cent efficient).

Table 12.6 *Standard data for a small solar hot water collector of 2m²*

	Litres of hot water needed per day			
	50	100	200	400
Yearly energy required to heat water	1004	2008	4015	8030
Energy collected by 2m² (tubes)	1680	1680	1680	1680
Amount of solar energy productively used*	800	1200	1600	1680
Remaining energy required	204	808	2415	6350

Notes: Units for energy figures are kWh/year.
*The solar collectors may heat more water than is actually needed by the household. That heat therefore does not replace heat that would otherwise have been provided by gas.

Table 12.7 *Savings from use of solar hot water*

	Litres of hot water needed per day			
	50	100	200	400
Remaining energy need (kWh/year)	204	808	2415	6350
Fossil fuel use at 75% boiler efficiency (kWh/year)	272	1077	3220	8467
Fossil fuel use without solar collector, at 75% efficiency (kWh/year)	1338	2677	5353	10,707
Saving in kWh/year	1067	1600	2133	2240
Fossil fuel saving (percentage)	80	60	40	21

The likely saving in fossil fuel is given in the penultimate line, and the percentage this figure represents of the required gas expenditure is shown at the bottom. A house using 50 litres a day (two quick showers, or a very small bath, and limited use for dish or hand washing) will typically see 80 per cent of its hot water need provided by a 2m² collector. On the other hand, the percentage is no more than about 21 per cent for a house that uses 400 litres a day.

As we might expect, the percentage of hot water heating carried out by the sun depends crucially upon the relationship between the size of the solar collectors and the household demand. Table 12.8 shows – at one extreme – that a profligate five-person household with a need for 400 litres will only save 41 per cent of their gas use by installing a 4m² collector. On the other hand, a more restrained one-person household with a

Table 12.8 *Savings from a 4m² collector*

		Litres of hot water needed per day			
		50	100	200	400
Saving in fossil fuel	kWh/year	1200	2133	3533	4400
	Percentage	90	80	66	41

50-litre a day need will avoid 90 per cent of the energy bills for water heating with a large set of solar hot water panels on the roof.

What does all of this mean in terms of carbon dioxide savings (see Table 12.9)? The benefits in terms of reduced carbon dioxide emissions will be between 0.2 and over 0.8 tonnes, depending upon the size of the installation and the hot water needs of the household. What about the cost savings?

Table 12.10 shows that the savings from a 2m² evacuated tube collector will be between £32 and £67, depending upon the amount of hot water used. For the larger collector, the figure is as much as £132.

The costs of solar hot water installations are falling. Very simple installations of flat-plate collectors now cost about £2500 for 4m², including 5 per cent value added tax (VAT). The cost might be less if it was part of an integrated system supplied along with a new boiler and hot water tank. A 4m² evacuated tube system will be more – probably costing between £3600 and £3900 before a grant. A 2m² installation will be cheaper, but only by a few hundred pounds (nevertheless, most installations do seem to be less than 4m² or its equivalent for flat plates; many households may have gone for false economy). And, of course, for new houses, or for houses that need to replace roofs, the costs are much lower.

Table 12.9 *Savings in carbon dioxide from using a solar hot water collector*

		Litres hot water per day per house			
		50	100	200	400
Energy savings (kWh/year)	2m² collector	1067	1600	2133	2240
	4m² collector	1200	2133	3533	4400
CO_2 savings (tonnes/year)	2m² collector	0.20	0.30	0.41	0.43
	4m² collector	0.23	0.41	0.67	0.84

Table 12.10 *Typical savings per year from installing a solar hot water collector*

| | Litres hot water per day per house | | | |
	50	100	200	400
2 m² collector	£32	£48	£64	£67
4 m² collector	£36	£64	£106	£132

Note: These figures all assume evacuated tube installations, rather than flat plates. To give equivalent performance, the flat plate would have to be 40 per cent larger. In other words, to match the heat generation of a 2m² evacuated tube array, the flat-plate installation would have to be 2.8m².

Collectors are generally thought to have a life of over 25 years, so the cost per tonne of carbon dioxide saved for a 4m² evacuated tube system ranges from about £375 down to less than £200, depending upon the household's use of water, before grants. The grant will reduce the cost by £20–70 per tonne. The direct financial benefits would, however, be unlikely to repay the cost of installation on an existing house unless the price of gas continues to rise. However, the introduction of the Renewable Heat Incentive in 2011 will radically improve the financial returns to householders.

However, as I say elsewhere, the impact of having an energy-saving device such as a solar collector on the roof is largely felt in changed family behaviour. The actual savings from a solar collector will be much larger because of the increased awareness of the costs and consequences of fossil fuel use.

One cautionary point needs to be made. Solar hot water is becoming interesting to large numbers of householders in the UK. Inevitably, perhaps, some unscrupulous firms are using aggressive sales tactics and are hugely over-promising the benefits from installing solar collectors. They are also greatly overcharging – one household I know was charged £12,000 for solar collectors and a new condensing boiler. Typically, the salespeople will say that their system will save '50 to 70 per cent of energy costs'. Please treat this claim with huge scepticism:

- Remember that the solar collectors only heat water for your baths and showers and do not heat the house.
- Keep in mind that water heating is generally less than 30 per cent of your gas bill.
- Finally, even a large collector will probably only replace 50 per cent of your water heating needs. So you cannot expect to save more than 15 per cent of your gas bill unless your circumstances are very unusual.

Some issues with solar thermal

Most users of solar thermal systems are very happy with their systems. The apparently free supply of copious hot water during summer gives people particular satisfaction. The owners I know are all enthusiastic advocates of solar collectors. But it is worth mentioning a few quibbles:

- The water can get very hot in some systems. Of course, it can be mixed with cold water to achieve the right temperature; but the risk of scalding is ever present in high summer unless a temperature controller is installed.
- Second, the effectiveness of solar thermal hot water in the summer months means that the boiler is very rarely on. Many households use the boiler cupboard or room as a place in which to dry clothes. From April to September, clothes won't get dry as fast because the room isn't being heated by the operation of the boiler.

OUR EXPERIENCE: A SOLAR PV AND A SOLAR HOT WATER SYSTEM

We installed a solar PV and solar hot water system in December 2004. The search for an installer was not simple; prices varied widely and most companies were reluctant to come to Oxford. In the end, the installation was done by a firm almost two hours' drive away. Except in the most eco-friendly areas, such as around Machynlleth in north Wales, there is no proper infrastructure of local firms ready to do solar installations, although the position is undeniably getting better. The introduction of feed-in tariffs will probably cause a massive expansion of the industry.

Our installer provided a quote for both systems separately and offered a substantial discount if we bought both at once. The firm would only have to pay for one set of scaffolding, and a lot of the work on the roof would not need to be duplicated. After grants of 50 per cent for the PV and £400 for the solar hot water, the cost was just over £8000.

The installation itself was trouble free, but took the best part of a week. Both systems have worked perfectly since being inaugurated, except for a short period when one of the two sets of PV electronics mysteriously failed. It was replaced under guarantee without any quibble. The meters recording the electricity generated tell us every second of the day how much electricity is coming into the house. For those of us with an interest in the economics of renewable energy, this is endlessly fascinating. More conventional people in the household do not have the same tendency as me to go to look at the meters whenever the sun starts shining.

The track record of the system has been slightly better than we thought – 2005 was a sunny year and the installers are forced to be conservative in their sales promises by the conditions of the grant-making bodies. The total amount of electricity generated was about

1430kWh. (This figure would, perhaps, be 20 per cent higher if we had a roof that was south facing. One of our sets of panels faces east, the other west, so we don't get as much solar radiation as many other houses.) The output pattern is shown in Figure 12.1.

The pattern is not quite what statisticians call a normal distribution, symmetrical around a peak. The generation faded fast after the second week of September after five months at a rate of about 6kWh a day.

The solar thermal collectors worked very well indeed in their first year. For the six months when the sun was highest in the sky, the collectors reliably gave us a large tank of hot water, except on the cloudiest days. Even in early February, when the sun is strong the tank will be heated to over 45°C, and possibly reach 50°C, after being only 10°C after the morning showers. The water is scalding in summer and care needs to be taken to ensure that children don't ever use our mixer taps fully set to hot. The profligate nature of our water use means that we still use a small amount of gas in the summer to heat up part of a tank of hot water for morning washing before the sun starts really shining.

The total savings from our investment in solar energy of £8300 are about £300 a year at current prices, even before the feed-in tariff. As we say to ourselves when justifying the expense, it's better than having money in a taxed savings account. We saved about 1.5 tonnes of carbon dioxide in the first year.

This is the rational side of the analysis. Something more significant went on when we installed the solar equipment, and this goes on in most solar homes. Suddenly, energy conservation becomes more important. Wasteful appliances are turned off at the wall, the thermostat gets turned down and the microwave is used instead of the gas oven. So, for example, our gas consumption fell by about 35 per cent, even though the solar water heating was probably responsible for no more than one-third of the reduction. The visible economic benefits of using domestic renewables may be small; but the psychological impacts are noticeable and sometimes even dramatic.

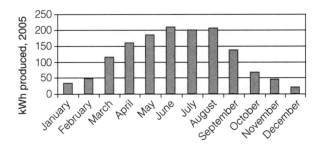

Figure 12.1 *Monthly energy output from a solar photovoltaic system in Oxford*

BIOMASS, PRIMARILY WOOD FOR STOVES

A wide variety of agricultural crops can be used for combustion and heat generation. In the next decade we may well see an enhanced role for woods, grasses and straws as a source of energy for commercial electricity and heat generation, particularly in community schemes covering all of the housing in a new development. This is certainly the case in other countries in Northern Europe, such as Sweden. At the moment, wood is the only real option for burning biomass in the home in the UK.

Is wood truly renewable? In the UK, at least, the answer is yes. Despite most people's impression to the contrary, the area under woodland is growing year on year, particularly in areas where arable agriculture is of marginal financial viability. Using wood from trees that are grown, cut down and then replaced by more saplings means no net emission of carbon dioxide to the atmosphere. As wood is burned, of course, it emits carbon; but the next generation of trees grown on the same land will naturally take up an equivalent amount from the atmosphere as they grow. In other countries in Europe, the position is broadly the same; but in some tropical countries wood should not be considered renewable, since the area under forest is tending to fall; in some places, very rapidly.

A wood-burning stove with a glass front panel sitting in a niche in the centre of a living room is an attractive thing, and a good fire has a visual value, as well as providing a replacement to fossil fuel heating. Up to 80 per cent of the energy value of the wood can be transferred to the house from a good stove – a much higher figure than will be achieved with an open fire. Well-designed stoves can provide heat for less than peak electricity costs, but almost certainly more than gas, even at today's prices. A hot stove, working efficiently, emits very low levels of non-carbon-dioxide pollution; nevertheless, it will normally be prohibited in the clean air zones of large cities. Some people, rightly noting the low emissions of their stoves, choose to ignore this rule.

Typical stoves of reasonable size (500mm wide, 600mm high and 500mm deep) might deliver 5–6kW of heat. This will typically provide enough heat to warm a large and well-insulated room of 35m^2 or so (375 square feet). The average home in the UK is little more than 80m^2, so a stove can replace a significant fraction of all gas or electricity heating. You can also buy large stoves that provide the space and water heating needs of an entire house.

How much wood is required? A full load of logs might be 800kg, but probably contains 30–40 per cent moisture. If left to dry for a year, this could fall to 20 per cent or so, and the weight of the wood would be reduced to as little as 640kg. Dry wood of this type generally provides slightly more than 4000kWh per tonne, so a load of this would offer just under 3000kWh. The cost of a load of this size will be about £100 in most parts of Britain. The cost per kilowatt hour is therefore about 3.5p, or possibly slightly more. This is almost exactly the current price of gas.

This is not quite the full story. An efficient wood-burning stove delivers a very large fraction of its energy into the room. A well-insulated house will capture about 80 per cent of the stove's output. Most older domestic boilers waste more energy and heat is also lost moving the hot water from the boiler to the radiators. At present gas prices, wood is a reasonably cost-effective substitute. Wood pellets, which are becoming increasingly popular because of the ease of handling and cleanliness, are up to 50 per cent more expensive than wood logs, although the price differentials vary across the UK. Recent prices in the south-east for wood pellets have been about 4–5p per kilowatt hour delivered to the home.

A typical 5kW room-heating stove will deliver about 7000kWh of heat it used for eight hours a day across the six months of the UK heating season. You would need several tonnes of logs to provide the fuel, but the saving could be as much as two tonnes of carbon dioxide from not using the central heating boiler as much. Even if you are using wood pellets, the higher fuel cost will only add a maximum of a hundred or so pounds a year above the cost of gas.

Of course, installing the fire is quite costly – a figure of £1500 to £2000 should be budgeted; but wood-burning stoves look so nice and last forever that I don't count this. If you did, it might add another £30 to the incremental cost per tonne.

The lazy among us would want to incorporate the cost of the labour to stack and store the wood. I resist this; it is one of the true pleasures of life, and you will find that a neat pile of well-ordered logs stacked against the house is much admired by the neighbours.

Living-room stoves like ours are all very well; but real savings can be had from installing a large boiler, fuelled by pellets with the capacity to heat hot water as well. The wood for these monsters is cheaper than from the gentleman who delivers logs to us. If you have a big house and plenty of room for a wood boiler and a pellet or wood stove, buy one. The pellets are usually fed automatically into the boiler and the ash can be easily disposed of on the garden, where it has some small value as a fertilizer. The cost of £5000 or so will be partly offset by the government's Renewable Heat Incentive which will pay about 9p for every kilowatt hour generated. (These numbers may have changed by the time this book is published.)

The cold winter of 2008/2009 produced very tight supplies of logs, chipped wood and even wood pellets. The suppliers around Oxford all ran out of fuel because demand had risen and woodland owners hadn't cut enough wood the year before to dry out before delivery to customers. This may continue to be a problem in the future as the number of wood-burning stoves and boilers increases every year. Schools and other public buildings are also enthusiastically trying to reduce their carbon emissions by installing biomass heating systems and are causing the supply/demand balance to tighten in some parts of the country. However some large companies, such as Dulas in Scotland, are investing in huge plants to dry wood and turn it into pellets. The pellets will then be taken by ship to a port in the south-east of England and transported by road to customers. At houses with large external pellet stores, the fuel is then blown into the bunker. Very quick, clean and convenient.

FUEL CELLS AND MICRO-CHP

Conventional large power stations waste a lot of the fuel they use. In an old coal-fired plant, only about a third of the energy is converted into electricity. The rest disappears up the cooling towers as heat. Although gas power stations are better, they still only manage to convert half the energy value in gas into electricity. At the same time as power stations are trying to dispose of excess heat, homes and businesses are using fuel to keep their rooms warm. The logical answer is to run tiny power stations at home, using the energy lost during the electricity production process to heat the building.

Several companies have tried to commercialize small 'combined heat and power' (CHP) units for the home. Up to this point they have generally burnt gas to drive a Stirling engine to produce electricity, with the waste energy used to produce hot water for space and water heating.[7] Early experiments have not produced impressive results either in terms of cost or carbon savings. This may be about to change as a new generation of tiny power stations comes onto the market. Or, as so often happens, what works on the test-bed fails miserably when subjected to ordinary domestic conditions.

Two innovative companies are using fuel cell technology to run their small power station. You can think of a fuel cell as a sort of continuously recharged battery. When fuelled by hydrogen or other energy sources, the battery creates a flow of electricity that is sufficient for the average house. Of course most houses don't have access to a supply of hydrogen so it has to be generated by splitting mains gas (which is largely methane) into its constituent atoms of carbon and hydrogen. Ceramic Fuel Cells, an exciting Australian company, has a fuel cell device in trial which is about the same size as a home dishwasher. This machine can generate 2kWh of electricity all the time. This is available for the house to use, or it can be exported to the grid, like the electricity from solar panels. This extraordinary machine converts about 60 per cent of the energy in gas into electricity, a percentage higher than all but the very best and most modern large power stations. The other 40 per cent is heat and can be used to provide warmth and hot water for the house. So alongside 2kWh of electricity comes enough heat to provide all the hot water a house needs and much of the heating for a new, highly insulated home. The only waste matter, by the way, is water and carbon dioxide. This is potentially a very clean technology.

A quick look at the numbers shows that fuel cells might be financially attractive – and save a lot of CO_2. Ceramic Fuel Cells is claiming to be able to produce their machines for about £2000 at large scale. Let's assume that actually their micro power plant comes onto the market at £4000, installed in the kitchen.[8] If it operates all the time, it will generate about 17,000kWh of electricity a year. If 5000kWh is used at home and 12,000kWh is sent out into the grid and sold at wholesale prices, the value of the energy is about £1250. The full numbers are in Figure 12.2 and Table 12.11. For the next few years, the feed-in tariff scheme will pay 10p per kilowatt hour generated. This is very important to the homeowner.

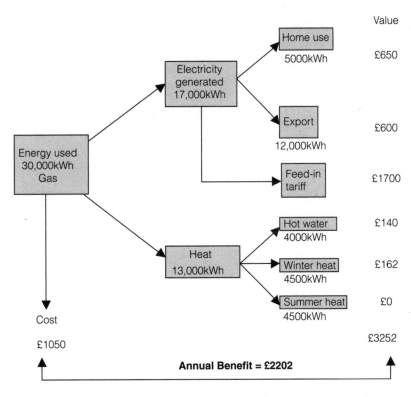

Figure 12.2 *Financial calculations for domestic use of a Ceramic Fuel Cells CHP system*

Table 12.11 *Summary of carbon savings*

Electricity replaced – 17,000kWh	8.5 tonnes saved
Heat replaced – 9500kWh	1.8 tonnes saved
Total saving	10.3 tonnes saved
Gas used – 30,000kWh	5.7 tonnes
Net saving	4.6 tonnes

The numbers in Figure 12.2 suggest a yearly saving of over £2000 for an investment that I've suggested may be about £4000. This is an attractive return compared to any other renewable technology and the UK government has indicated that these incentives will only be available for the first 30,000 installations. My advice would be to install one of these machines as soon as you can, provided that at least a thousand homes have been using one over a full year. Home fuel cells are complicated pieces of technology and I'd want to be sure that all inevitable problems had been ironed out before I put one in my house. Also note that the central ceramic components will need replacing every five years or so and this cost is not included in the figures I have provided.

13

cancelling out emissions

13

Describing our emissions

Choices about consumption levels, patterns of food purchase and where one is employed are the crucial determinants of indirect emissions. For those things we can't do anything about, the best choice is to offset our emissions. Offsetting means reducing the greenhouse gases from another source of emissions to compensate for our own actions.

Let's look at the various ways in which we might do this. This chapter covers green electricity, investing in new renewable power plants, planting trees or buying into other 'offset' schemes. It suggests that probably the best way of counterbalancing your own greenhouse gases is to buy certificates from the European trading scheme.

GREEN ELECTRICITY

We shouldn't focus too much on our personal use of electricity. Out of the total greenhouse gas emissions of about 14 tonnes per year, less than 1 tonne results from electricity use in the home. Gas for heating and cooking is far more important. Nevertheless, it is worth cancelling out the carbon dioxide from electricity. Each kilowatt hour of electricity (about as much as it takes to run a dishwasher) generates over 0.5kg of carbon dioxide.

The UK electricity system does not, of course, separate out electricity created from renewable and fossil fuel sources. The thousands of different generating plants around the country – ranging from Sizewell B nuclear power station, supplying about 2 per cent of the UK's electricity, to the 1500kWh generated on our roof each year – all put their output into the transmission system. The big plants insert it into the main network, usually called 'the grid'. Our solar panels put surplus power into the local network in our street. Both Sizewell B and our panels help to keep the whole network across the country 'pumped up' to 240V and 50 alternating current cycles per second. On a sunny day, our panels mean that a power station somewhere else in the country is having to work very slightly less hard than it otherwise would have. This will generally be a fossil fuel generating plant. So, our solar photovoltaic panels are reducing the total amount of carbon dioxide in the atmosphere.

It might therefore seem obvious that buying your electricity from a supplier that produces renewable energy would 'save' carbon dioxide. In the UK, this means electricity companies operating wind turbines, hydroelectric schemes and less important sources, such as burning biomass or solar panels. Actually, this is a very complex issue and many 'green' tariffs do not reduce the UK's carbon dioxide emissions.

Great care is needed – if I buy my electricity from a green supplier that has owned the same wind farm for ten years and is not investing in new generating capacity, my decision to switch to this supplier has no impact whatsoever on carbon dioxide emissions. On the other hand, if I buy power from a company that is currently entirely fossil fuel based but which has committed to buying renewable energy to cover the needs of all new customers, it might well be that total emissions would go down if I switched to this firm.

Ideally, I want my purchases to influence the electricity market into providing new renewable generation as a direct result of my custom. Given that renewables generation is rising already (albeit at a much slower rate than the government wants), how can I be sure that my decision results in more supply than would otherwise have come into operation? I think the honest answer is that you can't, and anybody who says anything different is probably trying to sell you something.

The best green tariffs are, I think, provided by those companies investing most heavily in new renewables. At the very worst, your decision to buy from them is helping them to grow their business and provides a signal that the market wants more renewable electricity generation. As of September 2009, probably the most effective green tariff is that provided by Ecotricity, which claims to be investing far more per customer in new renewable plants than other suppliers. It quotes a figure of over £400 investment for each account holder in 2008, greatly in excess of any other retail electricity company.[1] Ecotricity claims to have erected one in eleven of the UK's commercial-scale wind turbines, and when people ask me to recommend a green tariff, I always mention this company's name. It charges the same price for its electricity as the regional electricity companies, although it doesn't attempt to match their best online tariffs.

Don't assume, however, that all Ecotricity's electricity is from renewable sources – only about 50 per cent is, up from only 23 per cent a few years ago. Nevertheless, as one of the most important backers of new wind projects, customers do appear to get some carbon reduction in return for their patronage. On the other hand, Good Energy, a small supplier with an excellent reputation and its own wind farms and hydroelectric plants, sells only renewable energy. But it is not systematically growing the number or size of the locations at which it captures renewable electricity. (Although as at September 2009 it does offer the highest prices for electricity produced by microgenerators to sell on to its customers and proposes to expand its main wind farm at Delabole in Cornwall). Therefore, we can argue that switching to this supplier does not actually reduce emissions. This is a controversial conclusion with which many would disagree.

Many of the other so-called green tariffs have some environmental respectability but probably don't do enough to really warrant being called green. Take, for example, one of the current EDF schemes. It adds 0.40 pence to the price of the conventional tariff and uses this – matched by an equivalent amount from the company – to invest in new renewables schemes. Very approximately, 6 per cent of the customer's bill goes to small-scale carbon-neutral energy production from new sources. This is better than nothing, but doesn't compensate for EDF's very low level of investment in large-scale renewables.[2]

Increasingly, large manufacturing or office sites are putting up their own renewable capacity or getting a generator to do it for them. These companies let electricity suppliers, such as Ecotricity, construct wind turbines on their land and then buy some or all of the output at a reduced rate. The Michelin tyre factory in Dundee has two large turbines, owned and operated by Ecotricity, that provide an estimated output of 8 million kWh/year. Clearly, persuading an employer to build or sponsor a wind turbine is an exceptionally efficient means of increasing the total amount of renewable electricity capacity in the UK.

But at a household level, buying from Ecotricity, or a company with similar credentials, will 'offset' about 1.6 tonnes of carbon dioxide, or about 0.7 tonnes per head.

ZERO-EMISSIONS POWER GENERATION

A second way of definitely neutralizing carbon emissions is to invest personally in zero-carbon emissions power generation. There are already a small number of cooperative ventures in electricity production that would be perfect for offsetting emissions. The recent projections for a community-owned wind farm in the Fens showed that the investment needed from shareholders (£3.0 million plus bank loans) could be expected to generate 11.2 million kWh/year for the 25 years of the farm's operation.[3]

These figures suggest that the average individual's total carbon dioxide emissions for the whole life of the turbines would be offset by an investment of less than £7000. The cost per tonne of carbon dioxide cancelled is less than £30, and makes mutually owned wind farms an exceptionally cheap way of neutralizing emissions. Compare this, for example, to installing a solar hot water system that costs at least £170 per tonne of carbon dioxide avoided. The wind investment will, if the projections turn out to be accurate, earn a return of over 12 per cent a year over the life of the project.[4] The site at Deeping St Nicholas in the Fens is also not particularly windy. Turbines elsewhere will be even better at turning cash from individuals into substantial emissions reductions. I think that cooperatively owned wind farms are an extraordinarily good way of neutralizing the carbon dioxide for which we are all indirectly responsible. At the time of writing I'm aware of several groups trying to organize investment funds to channel investment money directly into commercial wind farms and other renewable energy projects.

Ideally, we want local communities to develop wind power projects themselves. The planning permission obstacles would be reduced or entirely eliminated. In my view, wind developers should sensibly bribe local communities by offering a share in the projected profits and thus getting their turbines up and running more quickly.

By providing a portion of the capital to build new renewable power stations such as this, individuals can be reasonably certain that their money actually diminishes global emissions. Of course, the number of such opportunities is not unlimited but the demand from investors for these opportunities is now clear. In Denmark, over 100,000 people own a share in a wind farm and in Germany the figure is almost 200,000. We can hope to see a larger and larger number of renewables ventures to tap these willing, and relatively cheap, sources of finance.

TREE PLANTING

Other than turning your neighbour's lights off or giving her low-energy light bulbs, the ways of directly cancelling out emissions are few (commercial 'offsetting' is discussed in the next section). But it is possible to buy 1 acre (0.4ha) of land currently used for agriculture and plant it with permanent trees, or a biomass crop such as willow which can be used for fuelling central heating stoves.

In this case, the idea is that a fully grown tree planted on an area of land that would otherwise be cultivated (and therefore not store carbon from the atmosphere) will offset substantial amounts of greenhouse gas emitted elsewhere in the economy. One source says that 1 acre of broadleaf trees will eventually capture up to 2.6 tonnes of carbon dioxide a year.[5] So it needs about 2.5 acres (or about 1ha) to capture half our emissions. If one bought 1ha of land and put trees on it, how much would it cost? For maximum effect, this would need about 1000 trees (see Table 13.1).

Table 13.1 *Cost of establishing 1 hectare of woodland*

Item	Cost
1000 saplings at £0.50 apiece	£500
Good tree guards at £0.65 apiece	£650
Post and tie at £1.50 each	£1500
Three applications of herbicide around the trees	£120
Total	£2770

The figures in Table 13.12 are drawn from a source that details the cost of planting woodland at lower density so that sheep may productively graze as well, and I have adjusted the numbers appropriately.[6]

Before costing the labour, or the value of the land, 1ha of woodland will save around 600 tonnes of carbon dioxide over a 100-year period. The cost per tonne is less than £5. So, even if the full cost were twice the cost of saplings and materials, the cost per tonne of carbon dioxide is below £10. Unsurprisingly, planting trees that would otherwise remain unplanted is one of the most effective and cheapest ways of cutting back carbon. There are sometimes doubts about how much benefit trees in temperate climates really provide but it seems to me that adding to the stock of UK woodland is highly beneficial. Nevertheless, it needs to be admitted that the sceptics will claim that the new woodland will reduce Britain's requirement to reduce emissions in other areas (because reforestation subtracts from the UK's total greenhouse gas output under international treaties such as the Kyoto Protocol).

'OFFSET'

Most people won't be able to buy 1ha of land for planting trees and will be thinking about handing the obligation over to a commercial firm that specializes in the neutralizing of carbon dioxide. The seductive promise of carbon offset is that by planting a tree, or some other such carbon-reducing act, one's greenhouse gas emissions can be counterbalanced, or 'offset'. The thought is that the Western consumer's lifestyle can be made carbon neutral by careful investment in reducing carbon emissions elsewhere. Other than tree planting, typical offset projects include efficient cooking stoves that reduce the need for cutting down firewood.

In theory, the idea is useful. Much of the domestic cooking in some tropical countries is done by burning wood in open fires. As population pressures increase, this causes much of the deforestation seen around the world. Properly constructed stoves reduce the need for wood two- or three-fold and so decrease forest loss. Investing in good quality stoves (and large numbers of attractive designs are now being produced around the world) means emissions from forest burning will decrease. If we can find projects that genuinely reduce emissions, we can diminish our own responsibility for climate change. One person I know takes energy-efficient light bulbs in his suitcase to offset his flights to the US, though I fear he is running out of places to install them in his friends' houses.

In some ways, these schemes are good. They increase awareness of climate change issues and bring home the point that individuals in the rich world do have a moral responsibility not to cause further climate change. Whether they actually achieve genuine reductions in greenhouse gases is much less clear. The proponents, who are usually very thoughtful people concerned about the future of the planet, think that offsetting can neutralize the impact of Western lifestyle choices, such as the desire to fly for business and pleasure. These people think that we cannot do much about the levels of emissions from advanced societies, and paying for offset projects provides a valuable example of how individuals can take some steps to recognize their own responsibilities. The critics say that offsetting is both ineffective in reducing emissions and allows modern society to avoid any consideration of how to achieve a sustained diminution in overall emission levels.

Offsetting is also suspiciously cheap. One UK offset company offers a price of about £7.50 per tonne of carbon dioxide, less than the cost we calculated for planting trees in the UK that neutralized this amount of greenhouse gas. We should also understand what this means: it implies that an individual's yearly carbon dioxide output – direct and indirect – could be abated by a payment of less than £120. Scaled up to the whole UK population, the payments would be less than £5 billion. If it is really so cheap, why doesn't the government do it?

On balance, I think the critics of offsetting are partly right. I don't think offset offers a full alternative to the systematic reduction of emissions. Let's look first at whether offsetting is effective in neutralizing greenhouse gases. If I plant a tree that eventually grows to contain 1 tonne of carbon, does that counterbalance those activities of mine that result in the release of 1 tonne of carbon to the atmosphere? This depends upon many things. First, and most importantly, the tree must be planted on land that otherwise would not be forested. In other words, planting a tree in my garden that I would have done anyway, or which simply replaces an existing dead tree, is not sequestering any new carbon. In the UK, guaranteeing that a new tree is genuinely additional is tricky. Forest cover is growing anyway as we take land out of intensive agriculture. The land now under tree cover is over twice as much as it was in 1900.[7] How can we be sure that our payment to the offset company does not go towards planting a tree in a plantation that would have been introduced anyway? Next, we have to be sure that the area we have planted with trees remains as woodland for centuries to come, otherwise the carbon that the tree has captured will be returned to the atmosphere.

These are relatively easy questions compared to those arising with other types of projects used by offsetting companies. One good example of the problem of ensuring that emissions are genuinely balanced by offset schemes was provided by offsetting company ClimateCare's project to give energy-efficient light bulbs to South Africans. The idea is that if one gives low-wattage bulbs to households, power consumption will be reduced below what it would have been. Of course, it is difficult to measure whether households increase their usage of electric light if it becomes cheaper, or whether they would simply add a new light fixture in the house.

But in this case the situation was made even more complicated by the fact that the South African power generation company Eskom has had substantial problems guaranteeing electricity availability because demand was running ahead of its capacity to generate electricity. So, it also gave out free low-energy bulbs to householders. Newspaper reports said at the time that Eskom had bought 5 million energy-efficient bulbs from China for handing out to any homeowner who wanted one.[8] It is, I suspect, totally impossible to say whether the 50,000 bulbs given out in 2005 (1 per cent of Eskom's number) by ClimateCare actually resulted in any net reduction in emissions above what was otherwise achieved by Eskom's much bigger campaign to flood the Western Cape area with free bulbs. Other extremely valuable schemes, such as the provision of energy-efficient cooking stoves, probably do reduce forest loss, but quantification of the precise benefit has proved extremely difficult.

More formal mechanisms for trading emissions, such as through the various European carbon exchanges, suggest a price per tonne of CO_2 of about €15.[9] This, very approximately, is what it costs a major polluter to reduce its emissions. (It cannot be any higher or the company would buy more emissions permits instead.) Another offsetting technique that can be used is for individuals and companies to buy permits from the European Emissions Trading Scheme (ETS) which reduces, albeit very marginally, the supply of permits and increases their price. Over the long run this encourages companies to invest in technologies and business practices to reduce their emissions.

I know of at least two companies that use the ETS as a way of allowing customers to offset their greenhouse gas output. Witney-based Ebico is a small electricity and gas retailer that encourages homeowners to buy ETS certificates to balance the emissions resulting from their use of fuel.[10] Sandbag operates a similar scheme, buying ETS permits from institutions that do not need them and then retiring them from the European market.[11] Both schemes work to reduce the total volume of permits, tightening the supply and therefore increasing the price that polluters have to pay.

As a result of Ebico and Sandbag's schemes, industrial power users or electricity generators in the EU will be obliged to produce slightly less carbon dioxide than otherwise would have been the case. In my view, this is the simplest and most effective way of ensuring that offsetting payments results in genuine net emissions reduction.

The critics of all types of offsetting launch strong attacks on the principle of letting people buy themselves out of responsibility for emissions. One writer says: 'the overall effect of the industry is to make it even harder to persuade people to actually "reduce" their emissions from source'.[12] He goes on to say that offsets 'send the wrong signals to high polluters', as well as working with projects that are sometimes 'highly contentious' in the countries that they are meant to help.

Carefully chosen and well-managed offset schemes can work to neutralize the odd emergency flight to see relatives; but they are not a long-run solution to the need to reduce greenhouse gases across the world. So, if you need to pay into offset schemes, do plenty of research. The main question is: does this project stand a good chance of genuinely reducing overall carbon dioxide emissions? A vague promise by the offset company to plant some trees or to 'work with a community to improve the techniques used to cook food so as to use less wood and reduce deforestation' is not sufficient. The best way of offsetting is probably to use Ebico or Sandbag's scheme for buying and retiring European emissions certificates.

Notes

CHAPTER 1

1   This includes an allowance for aviation – usually omitted from government figures – with air travel emissions adjusted to allow for the impact of water vapour and nitrous oxide emitted at high altitude.

2   EIA (US Energy Information Agency) (2006) *International Energy Output*, Energy Information Agency, Washington, DC, June. The EIA sees a 75 per cent rise by 2030.

3   'When carbon dioxide changed there was always an accompanying climate change': comment by Dr Eric Wolff of the British Antarctic Survey (BAS) to the BBC on 5 September 2006, explaining the significance of the BAS's examination of Antarctic ice cores dating back 800,000 years.

4   I used a slightly higher level in the first edition of this book. I got several letters from irritated cyclists who claimed that I was too generous since even ultra-fit Tour de France participants average much less over the course of the daily race.

5   The estimate that half the UK population now flies at least once a year appears in *The Future of Air Transport*, published by the UK Department for Transport, 16 December 2003.

6   This information can be found at http://corporate.easyjet.com/investors in the presentation entitled '2009 full year results'.

7   IEA (2006) Oil Market Report, International Energy Agency, Paris, France, 12 April, p4, available for download at http://omrpublic.iea.org/.

8   Information from a personal conversation with Rudolph Kalveks, the corporate development director of Rexam, one of the world's largest can manufacturers.

9   Office for National Statistics (2006), *Family Spending 2004/5*, Office for National Statistics, London.

10 UK Department for Transport (2005) *National Travel Survey 2004*, Department for Transport, London, July.

11 Estimate provided by Freescale Semiconductor, a maker of components for electric, rather than hydraulic, power steering: see www.freescale.com.

12 Commission of the European Communities (2000) *Taxation of Aviation Fuel*, Commission of the European Communities, London, 2 March.

13 A short summary of this case can be found in Can Makers (2005) UK Market Report, www.canmakers.co.uk.

14 First Group (2005) *Corporate Responsibility Report 2004*, First Group, Aberdeen, Scotland/London.

15 Estimate from British Airways in a newsletter entitled 'Environment matters' sent to its staff (no date, but available at www.ba.com).

16 UK Department for Transport (2003) *The Future of Air Transport*, Department for Transport, London, December, Chapter 2, p6.

17 Government White Paper (2003) *The Future of Air Transport*, December.

18 Assumes duty of just under 50 pence a litre, 11,000km round trip and fuel consumption of 4 litres per 100 passenger kilometres. If VAT were included as well, the cost would have to rise by a further £60 or so.

19 This figure is based on CO_2 emissions of about 1.5 tonnes from a single flight from London to New York (source www.jpmorganclimatecare.com).

20 Press release from the European Commission (2005) *Climate Change: Commission Proposes Strategy to Curb Greenhouse Gas Emissions from Air Travel*, 27 September 2005.

21 UK Department for Transport (2004) *The Future of Transport*, Department for Transport, London, 20 July.

22 Reported in *The Financial Times*, 7 June 2006.

23 See, for example, the references on www.climatedenial.org.

24 To be found on the Friends of the Earth website at www.foe.co.uk/living/poundsavers/deborah_moggach_pride_prejudice.html.

25 Wiener, M. J. (2004) *English Culture and the Decline of the Industrial Spirit: 1850–1980*, Cambridge University Press, Cambridge. This is one of the most powerful books on this subject and, although first published in 1981, it is still extensively read today.

26 *Health Statistics Quarterly* (2005) 'Live births, stillbirths and infant deaths, 1976–2004', *Health Statistics Quarterly*, vol 27, autumn.

27 See www.statistics.gov.uk/cci/nugget.asp?id=881.

28 But note that Cuba's infant mortality rate is almost as low as in the UK, even though Cuba is materially much less well off.

29 For example, Denmark now gets 25 per cent of its electricity from renewable sources.

30 Dresdner Kleinwort Wasserstein research, quoted by the analyst James Montier on the Investors Insight Publishing website (www.investorsinsight.com), indicates the average holding period for New York Stock Exchange shares is now about 11 months.

31 The UK organization WRAP works with local authorities to help build confidence among householders about the effectiveness of recycling in reducing waste.

32 John Kay, 'Thinking outside the blue box on recycling', *The Financial Times*, 25 February 2004.

33 *Wrap* (2006) 'Environmental benefits of recycling', *Wrap*, May.

34 New Economics Foundation (2005) *The Ethical Consumerism Report*, NEF, London.

35 London Renewables (2003) *Attitudes to Renewable Energy in London*, London Renewables, December (available on the Greater London Authority website, www.london.gov.uk).

36 New Economics Foundation (2005) *The Ethical Consumerism Report*, NEF, London.

37 Some of this research is analysed in 'Shaping pro-environment behaviors', published at www.pyschologymatters.org.

CHAPTER 2

1 See www.decc.gov.uk/en/content/cms/statistics/projections/projections.aspx (the numbers can be found at Table B: Greenhouse gas emissions tables). UK monitored emissions for 2008 are about 624 million tonnes and the population was approximately 61.4 million in late 2009.

2 I am very grateful to Mike Berners-Lee for giving me sight of his numbers so that I could compare them. Some of Mike's numbers are different but we are in broad agreement. His book *How Bad are Bananas*, to be published in 2010, gives detailed carbon footprint figures for a large number of day-to-day activities.

CHAPTER 3

1 AECB (2006) AECB Consultation response on 2nd Draft E.S.T. Best Practice Standards, Association for Environment Conscious Building, Llandysul, Wales, January.

2 How can a 1 degree reduction cut use by nearly 15 per cent? The arithmetic is reliant on the fact that homes are also heated by cooking, by electric appliances such as lights and by water heating, as well as by solar gain in spring and autumn. The boiler is topping up a base load of other sources of heat.

3 The average UK house is about 76 square metres in extent. A figure of 14,000kWh of gas is used to heat the typical property, meaning that the house uses about 184kWh per square metre. This assumes that gas-heated properties are typical of all UK homes. This assumption may slightly bias upward the energy consumption figures.

4 This information is from www.passivhaustagung.de/Passive_House_E/step_by_step_towards_passive_houses.html.

5 Shorrock, L. D. and Utley, J. I. (2003) *Domestic Energy Fact File 2003*, Building Research Establishment, available free on the internet at www.bre.co.uk. Figure 3.2 contains data resulting from manipulations of Figure 35 in Shorrock and Utley.

6 The latest *Digest of UK Energy Statistics* is available at www.decc.gov.uk/en/content/cms/statistics/publications/dukes/dukes.aspx.

7 Boilers that are not frequently and well serviced will have efficiencies lower than these figures.

8 See www.theyellowhouse.org.uk/themes/heatwat.html.

9 This information may seem unbearably trivial or obvious. However, some recent research has shown that many people think that the thermostat is a simple on/off switch. Many also think that turning the thermostat up high increases the speed at which a room heats up.

10 WarmWorld Ltd. www.warmworld.co.uk

11 Information from the National Energy Foundation website, www.nef.org.uk.

12 From a manufacturer (Rockwool) of the insulation materials in a personal communication. For the technically minded, Rockwool says that its product will cut the typical 'U' value, a measure of thermal conductivity, from about 1.1 to about 0.

13 Such products are available from companies such as the Green Building Store – www.thegreenbuildingsite.co.uk.

14 Office of Fair Trading (2004) *Doorstep Selling*, Office of Fair Trading, London, Annexe H, May.

15 'Good' double glazing should use low emissivity glass, such as Pilkington K, and argon filling.
16 Barnet Borough Council's energy advice pages at www.barnet.gov.uk.
17 See www.oxford.gov.uk/environment/insulation.cfm.
18 See www.theyellowhouse.org.uk/themes/ventil.html.
19 Boyle, G. (ed.) (2004) *Renewable Energy*, 2nd edn, Oxford University Press, Oxford.
20 Rudge, J. and Winder, R. (2002) *Central Heating Installation for Older, Low Income Households: What Difference Does It Make?* Network for Comfort and Energy Use in Buildings, Proceedings of Indoor Air 2002, Monterey, CA.
21 AECB (2006) AECB Consultation Response on 2nd Draft E.S.T. Best Practice Standards, Association for Environmental Conscious Building, Llandysul, Wales, January.
22 Enderdata, www.odyssee-indicators.org/publications/chapters.php, p17.
23 The numbers in this box are taken from a very interesting presentation by Enerdata, available at www.odyssee-indicators.org/publications/chapters.php, p13.

CHAPTER 4

1 The website www.dti.gov.uk/energy/consumers/fuel_poverty/hot_water_consumption.pdf gives estimates for 1998. I have increased these figures slightly to reflect the rise in general water consumption since then.
2 One Australian supplier of this type of shower can be found at www.ecoshower.com.au. The cost in the text does not allow for shipping.
3 This information can be found on the government's Market Transformation Programme website, www.mtprog.com.
4 Matilde Soregaroli of the market research firm GfK, presentation at Sabaf, May 2006, available at www.sabaf.it.
5 These figures are based on a 70kg free-standing cooker, made mostly of steel with embedded energy of 5500kWh per tonne, made using the electric arc method.
6 Paul Waide, presentation at Sabaf, March 2006, available at www.sabaf.it. I have made this calculation from raw data provided by Mr Waide in this presentation.
7 Dr Tudor Constantinescu, presentation at Sabaf, March 2006, available at www.sabaf.it.
8 Nicola King, Market Transformation Programme, presentation to Sabaf, March 2006, available at www.sabaf.it.
9 Paul Waide, presentation at Sabaf, March 2006, available at www.sabaf.it.
10 Paul Waide, presentation at Sabaf, March 2006, available at www.sabaf.it.
11 See note 8.

CHAPTER 5

1 Assuming that the home doesn't also use electricity for heating. IEA (2006) *Light's Labours Lost*, International Energy Agency, Paris, France, July, p185.

2 People worry about the mercury in CFLs. Mercury is a human and environmental poison. But here's a fact to impress your friends. Well over one-third of UK electricity is provided by burning coal. Coal contains mercury. Adding a compact fluorescent to your house reduces electricity production. This reduces mercury emissions by more than the mercury contained in your new light bulb.

3 IEA (2006) *Light's Labours Lost*, International Energy Agency, Paris, France, July, p273, reporting a study by ECODROME in 1998.

4 IEA (2006) *Light's Labours Lost*, International Energy Agency, Paris, France, July, p273, reporting a EURECO 2002 study.

5 These figures are from Table 4.1 in IEA (2006) *Light's Labours Lost*, International Energy Agency, Paris, France, July, p189.

6 Odysee (2004) *Energy Efficiency Indicators in Europe*, Enerdata, Paris.

CHAPTER 6

1 Ecofys (2004) Electricity Conservation as Alternative for Building Power Plants, Ecofys, Utrecht, the Netherlands, July. DTI (2006) *Digest of UK Energy Statistics*, annual tables, UK Department of Trade and Industry, London, updated 27 July.

2 A number of the headline figures in this chapter are derived from work carried out by the Market Transformation Programme (MTP), an agency of the UK government. MTP is usually extremely optimistic about future possible energy efficiency gains, an optimism not entirely shared by this chapter (see http://efficient-products.defra.gov.uk/cms/market-transformation-programme/). The detailed reports and commentary from this organization are excellent and deserve the highest praise. The detailed follow-up analysis is generally my own work, and I accept responsibility for errors and omissions.

3 International Energy Agency's Demand Side Management Programme (www.iea.org).

4 Stamminger, R., Barth, A. and Dörr, S. (2005) *Old Washing Machines Wash Less Efficiently and Consume More Resources*, University of Bonn, Bonn, Germany, www.landtechnik.uni-bonn.de.

5 www.johnlewis.com

6 Stamminger, R., Badura, R., Broil, G., Dörr, S. and Elschenbroich, A. (2004) *A European Comparison of Cleaning Dishes by Hand*, University of Bonn, Bonn, Germany. Because it compares in intimate detail dishwashing habits across several European countries, the paper gives us unfettered scope for reinforcing prejudices about national characteristics. I cannot recommend it highly enough as a source for anthropologists.

7 Assumes a ten-year life and a dishwasher cost of £250.

8 www.comet.co.uk

9 For the economists, this is the result of a simple ordinary least squares regression of energy consumption against size.

10 The data in this box are garnered from Enerdata, www.odyssee-indicators.org/Publication/PDF/households_eu04.pdf, p42.

11 From the Market Transformation Programme, http://efficient-products.defra.gov.uk/cms/market-transformation-programme/.

12 This is an approximate figure. I'm sure a more accurate number exists, but I have had problems finding a good source.

13 See www.smecc.org/litton_-_for_heat,_tune_to_915_or_2450_megacycles.htm.

14 See www.efficientpowersupplies.org/pages/SeptNRDCLaptopSummary_digital.pdf.

15 Data from a paper by the International Energy Agency to be found at www.iea.org/textbase/papers/2002/globe02.pdf.

16 Energy Saving Trust (2006) *The Rise of the Machines*, Energy Saving Trust, London, July.

17 Ibid.

18 www.theowl.com.

CHAPTER 7

1   For more data see 'Transport at a crossroads', EEA Report No 3/2009, European Environment Agency, May 2009, www.eea.europa.eu/publications/transport-at-a-crossroads.

2   See www.behrgroup.com/produkte/fahrzeug/klimatipps/text5.php#. But note that the Australian government says that over 50mph, having a window open has more impact on fuel consumption than having the air-conditioning on, because of the worsened aerodynamic characteristics of the car.

3   The National Travel Survey (NTS), published by the UK Department for Transport gives copious detail on all these matters. These figures are the most regularly cited in the UK; but they are inconsistent with other estimates, particularly those relating to the average number of miles that the typical car travels in a year. NTS figures suggest that the average car does less than 6000 miles (9700km) a year, whereas this chapter suggests the real figure is about 9000 miles (14,500km).

4   Data from F. Unander (2004) *Thirty years of Energy Prices and Taxes*, International Energy Agency, Paris, France.

5   See www.direct.gov.uk/en/Motoring/OwningAVehicle/HowToTaxYourVehicle/DG_10012524, accessed 4 January 2010.

6   This conclusion has been disputed. A 2007 analysis by CNW Research suggested that the energy cost of the aluminium used in a Prius outweighed the energy savings when the car was in use.

7   See note 5.

8   Dual-fuel cars use a sip of petrol to get started.

9   See, for example, www.newscientist.com/article/mg19526134.500-meat-is-murder-on-the-environment.html.

10 L. Hivert (1996) 'Dieselisation et nouveaux dieselistes: Les évolutions récentes', *Actes INRETS*, no 59.

11 On another page on its website, Streetcar says 6 cars, not 20, are removed from the road for every one of its own cars.

12 See www.esru.strath.ac.uk/EandE/Web_sites/02-03/biofuels/quant_waste_fuel.htm#summary for details of how this estimate is generated.

13 www.news.cornell.edu/stories/july05/ethanol.toocostly.ssl.html.

14 See www.eccm.uk.com/httpdocs/publications.html Technical document number 7.

15 See www.monbiot.com/archives/2005/12/06/worse-than-fossil-fuel.

16 Quotation is from Saab UK website.

17 'New Car CO_2 report' from the UK Society of Motor Manufacturers and Traders, 2009.

CHAPTER 8

1 Defra (2005, updated 2009) *Guidelines for Company Reporting on Greenhouse Gas Emissions*, UK Department for Environment, Food and Rural Affairs, London, Annexes, updated in September 2009 and available at www.defra.gov.uk/environment/business/reporting/conversion-factors.htm

2 National Express Group (2005) *Corporate Responsibility Report*, National Express Group, London.

3 First Group (2005) *Corporate Responsibility Report*, First Group, Aberdeen, Scotland/ London, data from AEAT Environment.

4 Association of Train Operating Companies (2005) *Ten Year European Growth Trends*, Association of Train Operating Companies, London, July 2005.

5 The figures on diesel consumption are from AEA Technology's report to the Rail Regulator on the Environmental Costs of Rail Transport, August 2005.

6 R. Kemp (2004) 'Environmental impact of high speed rail', Presentation to the Institution of Mechanical Engineers, London, 21 April 2004.

7 See www.defra.gov.uk/environment/business/reporting/conversion-factors.htm, updated in September 2009.

8 From AEA Technology's report to the Rail Regulator on the Environmental Costs of Rail Transport, August 2005 available at www.defra.gov.uk/environment/business/reporting/conversion-factors.htm, updated in September 2009.

9 All of these figures are from Eurostat, the European Commission's statistical agency.

10 A typical private car with two occupants would produce about 90g of carbon dioxide per person kilometre, somewhat less than a bus.

11 Data from National Express Group (2005) *Corporate Responsibility Report*, National Express Group, London.

12 National Express Group, *Corporate Responsibility Report*.

13 See www.defra.gov.uk/environment/business/reporting/conversion-factors.htm, updated in September 2009.

14 See www.defra.gov.uk/environment/business/reporting/conversion-factors.htm, updated in September 2009.

CHAPTER 9

1 See www.ipcc.ch/publications_and_data/ar4/wg3/en/ch5-ens5-5-2-1.html for IPCC figures. The lower figures comes from the EU's continuing TRADEOFF project.

2 RCEP (Royal Commission on Environmental Pollution) (2002) *Environmental Effects of Civil Aircraft in Flight*, RCEP, London, November 2002.

3 The three sites, www.climatecare.org, www.co2balance.com and www.carbonneutral.com, were accessed on 5 June 2006. On the British Airways offset site, run by www.climatecare.org, the calculator produced a figure of 1.16 tonnes.

4 These figures are from Civil Aviation Authority (2006) 'CAA figures show increased traffic at UK airports in 2005', press release, 19 April 2006. This release is a confusing document because

it double counts internal air travel, once as a departure and once as an arrival at UK airports.

5 About 11,000km to New York and back, compared to 14,500km for the average UK car.
6 British Airways (2005) *Corporate Responsibility Report*, British Airways, London, indicates that the airline's fuel efficiency had improved by 25 per cent over the previous 14 years.
7 Quoted in Tyndall Centre for Climate Change (North) (2005) 'No chance for the climate without tackling aviation', presentation; the figures are for the period of 1993–2004.
8 See www.caa.co.uk/docs/589/erg_recent_trends_final_v2.pdf.
9 See http://collections.europarchive.org/tna/20090510222507/dft.gov.uk/about/strategy/whitepapers/air/.
10 See note 7.
11 See note 7.
12 Response to a question from John Denham, MP, at a meeting of the House of Commons Liaison Committee meeting of 7 February 2006.
13 Royal Commission on Environmental Pollution (2003) 'Royal Commission disappointed by government White Paper', press release, 16 December 2003.
14 Quoted in Friends of the Earth (2004) 'Government must listen to top scientist's warning on aviation', press release, 30 March 2004.
15 See www.paulflynnmp.co.uk/newsdetail.jsp?id=444.
16 Sustainable Development Commission (2004) *Missed Opportunity: Summary Critique of the Air Transport White Paper*, Sustainable Development Commission, London, June.
17 IPPR (2003) *The Sky's the Limit*, Institute for Public Policy Research, London, May.
18 Oxford University Transport Studies Unit (2006) *Counting Your Carbon*, March 2006.
19 There may be an arithmetic problem here – mathematically, the top 10 per cent cannot have emissions ten times the average, perhaps suggesting some problems with the Oxford data. If 10 per cent of people have over ten times the average, then the net emissions from all the rest of the population must be less than zero.
20 *Financial Times* (2006) 'Letter to the Financial Times', *Financial Times*, 7 June 2006.
21 Such as the House of Lords Committee on Economics Affairs in its report *The Economics of Climate Change*, published 6 July 2005.

CHAPTER 10

1 2004 figures from the UK's Environmental Accounts suggest that the iron and steel industry had greenhouse gas emissions of about 24 million tonnes of carbon dioxide equivalent, compared to the figure presented in this book of 126 million tonnes for the food supply chain.
2 Elm Farm Research Centre (2002) 'Eating oil', January 2002. This paper provides a reference to support the figure of 8 tonnes; but documents to which reference is made do not appear to actually cover the topic.
3 These two figures are used by the European Environment Agency and most climate change bodies around the world, though not the US, which uses a higher figure for methane and a slightly lower figure for nitrous oxide.

4   The Soil Association (one of the organic certifying bodies in the UK) estimates that 4 per cent of UK farmland is in organic use: Soil Association (2005) *Stern Review of the Economics of Climate Change: Soil Association Evidence to HM Treasury*, December, available from www.hm-treasury.gov.uk/d/climate_change_azeez.pdf. The Soil Association seems to suggest in this document that sales of organic food are growing by about 10 per cent per year.

5   Soil Association (2005) *Stern Review of the Economics of Climate Change*, p3. Soil Association numbers are 1.2 million tonnes of fertilizer at 6.2kg of carbon dioxide equivalent per 1kg of fertilizer. This includes the transport of fertilizer and the energy consumption arising in the manufacture of the raw materials used to make the product.

6   See http://ftp.eia.doe.gov/pub/oiaf/1605/cdrom/pdf/ggrpt/057308.pdf, best accessed from the Environmental area of the EIA website, www.eia.doe.gov.

7   Defra (2006) *UK Climate Change Programme 2006*, UK Department for Environment, Food and Rural Affairs, London, March.

8   Defra, *The UK Climate Change Programme 2006*.

9   Available from www.statistics.gov.uk under Environmental Accounts, Greenhouse Gases.

10 British Association for the Advancement of Science (2005) 'Soil cancels out UK's efforts to reduce CO_2', press release, www.the-ba.net/the-ba/Events/FestivalofScience/FestivalNews/_Soils.htm.

11 See note 10.

12 Defra (2005) *The Validity of Food Miles as an Indicator of Sustainable Development*, UK Department for Environment, Food and Rural Affairs, London, July 2005. The average distance for each trip by heavy goods vehicles carrying food has risen by 50 per cent since 1978.

13 See note 12.

14 See note 12.

15 Defra (2005) *Agriculture in the United Kingdom*, UK Department for Environment, Food and Rural Affairs, London.

16 See note 12.

17 Some of the biggest companies in the food industry provide data to the Carbon Disclosure Project.

18 Page 9 of the Food and Drink Federation's submission to the Food Industry Sustainability Study suggests a figure of about 1 per cent per year; but as the UK is becoming less self-sufficient in food at about the same rate, this reduction is not significant.

19 Food and Drink Federation (2005) *Response to Defra's Public Consultation on Draft Food Industry Sustainability Strategy*, Food and Drink Federation, London, August.

20 An INCPEN (Industry Council for Packaging and the Environment) report said that a major grocery retailer had reported that 55 per cent of vegetables were sold loose and 45 per cent packaged. INCPEN (undated) *Consumer Attitudes to Packaging*, INCPEN, Reading, UK.

21 INCPEN (1996) *Environmental Impact of Packaging in the UK Food Supply System*, INCPEN, Reading, UK.

22 See www.tescoplc.com/plc/corporate_responsibility_09/environment/climate_change/leading_by_example/carbon_footprint/.

23 See www.tescoplc.com/plc/corporate_responsibility_09/environment/climate_change/leading_by_example/carbon_footprint/.

24 Figure quoted by Transport 2000, www.transport2000.org.uk/factsandfigures/Facts.asp.

25 Defra *The Validity of Food Miles*, note 12. This is also consistent with National Travel Survey data showing that the average car was driven about 600km per year for food shopping, with the typical car producing about 180g of carbon dioxide per kilometre, and with about 29 million cars on UK roads.

26 Figures from www.wasteonline.org.uk/resources/informationsheets/wastedisposal.htm.

27 These figures are based on calculations shown at www.climatechange.gov.au.

28 Severn Trent published a figure of 71.2 per cent for December 2004.

29 These figures are from www.wasteonline.org.uk/

30 Trade data can be found at https://statistics.defra.gov.uk/esg/reports/afq/afqbriefsup_dec.pdf.

31 1900 kilocalories equals about 2.2kWh.

32 Quoted in the European Environment Agency article on household consumption at www.epaedia.eea.europa.eu/page.php?pid=526.

33 *Time to Eat the Dog?: The Real Guide to Sustainable Living* by Robert and Brenda Vale, Thames and Hudson, London, 2009.

CHAPTER 11

1 I calculated this from figures given in Southern Water (2005) *Environment Report*, Southern Water, Worthing, West Sussex.

2 This is a small fraction of the total environmental impact of making the T-shirt. See The Carbon Footprint of a Cotton T-shirt. Available from www.continentalclothing.com.

3 See 'Well dressed?' from the Cambridge University Institute for Manufacturing, available at www.ifm.eng.cam.ac.uk/sustainability/projects/mass/UK_textiles.pdf, p12, acccessed 6 January 2010.

4 We have to estimate the CO_2 emissions from electricity generation in the countries where the fabrics are processed and the clothes made.

5 A. K. Chapagain et al, *The Water Footprint of Cotton Consumption*, UNESCO – Institute for Water Education, September 2005. Many agricultural crops require large amounts of water to grow properly – wheat in the UK gets over 100kg of water per kilogram of grain. The difference with cotton is that much of the water comes from irrigation, using up increasingly scarce supplies of fresh water.

6 This information can be found in a very useful presentation by Oakdene Hollins entitled 'Recycling and re-use of clothing', published in June 2007, see www.oakdenehollins.co.uk/.

7 See, for example, 'Sony Ericsson unveils "green" handsets that cut carbon footprint by 15%', *Guardian*, 4 June 2009 or Emmenegger et al, 'Life cycle assessment of the mobile communication system UMTS', *International Journal of Life Cycle Analysis*, 2004.

8 www.nokia.com/press/press-releases/showpressrelease?newsid=1234291, accessed 6 January 2010.

9 Quote from Mats Pellback Scharp on the Sony Ericsson GreenHeart website dated 9 June 2009.

10 Apple Computer Environmental Reports. Available at www.apple.com/environment/reports/, accessed 3 April 2010.

11 The full statement can be found at www.apple.com/environment/

12 Most estimates of the energy and emissions from making a tonne of steel from scrap metal are about this level. The Carbon Trust uses an estimate of 1.75 tonnes in a report on the manufacture of underwater tidal turbines. See www.carbontrust.co.uk/technology/technologyaccelerator/life-cycle_energy_and_emissions.htm. Other estimates range from 1.2 tonnes and upward per tonne of steel.

13 The British trade association The Society of Motor Manufacturers and Traders says in its 2008 Sustainability Report that only 10 per cent of the lifecycle emissions of a car come from its manufacture and distribution.

14 J. Hacker et al, 'Embodied and operational carbon dioxide emissions from housing: A case study on the effects of thermal mass and climate change', *Energy and Buildings*, vol 40 (2008) pp375–384.

15 'Britons lead the way in toilet paper use', *Daily Telegraph*, 5 February 2007, based on research by the European Tissue Symposium.

16 The figure for clothing and paper is given in the text. The figure for cement is the UK emissions from manufacture of cement divided by the population. The car figure assumes a mid-size car and that there is one car per two people in the UK. The computer figure is from the Apple desktop estimate, spread over four years. The gold and silver figure is largely composed of the footprint from gold manufacture. The estimate for mobile phones is based on 30 million phones sold in the UK and a population of 60 million.

CHAPTER 12

1 The electrical retailer Currys is now advertising a price of about £9000 for a simple 2kW system.
2 DECC consultation on feed-in tariffs for micro-renewables in mid 2009. At the time of copy-editing this volume, the final figures had still not been announced.
3 Data from Energy Saving Trust website, www.est.org.uk/myhome/generating/types/wind/, accessed November 2006.
4 See www.provenenergy.co.uk and www.evancewind.com.
5 You can find estimates of your local wind speed at www.bwea.com/noabl/index.html.
6 Standard tariffs from British Gas and other suppliers are higher which is why I have used different figures in the rest of this book.
7 A Stirling engine works by turning the expansion and contraction of gases as they heat and cool into rotary motion.
8 Presentation by Ceramic Fuels Cells at BlueGen product launch, 22 May 2009.

CHAPTER 13

1 Figure is from *The Ecologist* (2005) 'Green Energy – are you being conned?', *The Ecologist*, June, and repeated to me on the phone by a company sales representative on 19 June 2005.
2 The EDF tariff is detailed at www2.savetodaysavetomorrow.com/DualFuel.html.

3   Westmill Wind Farm (2005) Prospectus, Westmill Wind Farm, Barrow in Furness, UK, November.

4   I should disclose that my family owns £5000 worth of shares in this wind farm.

5   These data are from www.merseyforest.org.uk/pages/fun_carbon.asp. Figures from Australia (www.greenhouse.gov.au) are somewhat higher.

6   Information from the Macaulay Institute, Aberdeen, www.macaulay.ac.uk/agfor_toolbox/try_it.html.

7   Forestry Commission (2001) Forestry Statistics, Forestry Commission, Edinburgh.

8   Business Day (2006) 'The market and energy security', Business Day, Johannesburg, 23 May.

9   The price of a tonne of carbon traded inside the European Emissions Trading scheme was about €15.

10 www.ebico.co.uk.

11 www.sandbag.uk.com.

12 Adam Ma'anit from Carbon Trade Watch, 10 April 2006, available at www.carbontradewatch.org.

Acknowledgements

I have had substantial help in revising the first edition of this book for the current version. I'd particularly like to thank Mark Yeung, Julia Hollander and Ursula Brewer for their assistance in creating spreadsheets for the sections on electric appliances and carrying out research to help make the book up to date.

Hamish Ironside and Gudrun Freese have coped wonderfully well with the stresses of producing both editions of this book. Thank you to them both and to the other people at Earthscan: you could not hope to meet a more dedicated and helpful group of people.

I am also extremely grateful to my employer Claire Enders of Enders Analysis for her support over the years. No one could have been more generous in letting me work part-time to give me the opportunity to write books. The list of causes assisted by Claire gets longer and longer – she is a true philanthropist.

To my wife, Professor Charlotte Brewer, I express my love and deepest thanks.

Index